THE LIFE OF
GEORGE BASS

*Portrait of George Bass (1771–c.1803), c.1800, engraving from a
photograph of an original portrait that has been lost.
(ML Ref: P1/B, Mitchell Library, State Library of New South Wales)*

THE LIFE OF
GEORGE BASS

Surgeon and Sailor of the Enlightenment

Miriam Estensen

Jacket images: George Bass (1771–c. 1803), engraving, ML Ref PI/B
Mitchell Library, State Library of New South Wales; pocket compass used
by George Bass on his whaleboat voyage during his exploration of Bass
Strait (1797–1799), from the private collection of William F. Wilson,
Melbourne and 'Bass River'.
Jacket designer: Zoe Sadokierski

First published in the UK in 2005 by the National Maritime Museum,
Greenwich, London, SE10 9NF

First published in Australia in 2005 by Allen & Unwin

ISBN 0 948065 68 0

To the memory of John Iremonger

CONTENTS

Preface and Acknowledgments

George Bass stood between two of the profoundly important developments of the late eighteenth and early nineteenth centuries—the acceleration of scientific discovery and its methods and the global expansion of maritime exploration and commerce. He was a man of an age of new enlightenment, versatile, avid for knowledge, intellectually demanding, ardent and courageous in his pursuits, but in the shadow of those who voyaged and charted or traded more widely he has received scant biographical attention. This book attempts to bring forward an intriguing personality who exemplified much of the remarkable time in which he lived.

Tracing the adventurous life of George Bass was a journey through letters, journals, ships' logs, certificates and other documents, and visits to places he knew two centuries ago. There are many to whom I must express my gratitude for assistance at numerous points along this journey.

George Bass began life in England's Lincolnshire countryside, and for making possible my better understanding of his background and boyhood through their hospitality and many additions to my store of information, I thank the Reverend and Mrs Charles Robertson of Osbournby; Sonia and Nicholas Playne of Aswarby Park, Sleaford; Pamela and Tony Cook, Donington; and for his considerable time and effort in uncovering much of the Bass family background, Canon David Pink of Swarby, Sleaford. My appreciation also to the Reverend Charles Hedley, St James Church, Piccadilly, and for informative discussion on sailing the Pacific, I thank Pat and Noble Smith. The marvellous collections of Bass manuscripts, charts and images in the Mitchell Library of the State Library of New South Wales were essential, and for their assistance I owe many thanks to Warwick Hirst, Jennifer Broomhead, Helen Harrison, Arthur Easton, Rosemary Block, Margot Riley and Martin Beckett, who responded to my numerous queries and requests with inexhaustible patience. The provenance of the only known portrait of George Bass is one of the mysteries of the Bass story, and I thank Elizabeth Ellis for sharing her views on this. To Paul Brunton, Senior Curator, Mitchell Library, I am most grateful for his initial as well as ongoing encouragement in the writing of this book and for his generously shared scholarship and numerous constructive suggestions on many aspects of George Bass's story. I owe a very special debt to William Wilson, of Melbourne and 'Bass River', for a remarkable opportunity to draw from a number of Bass documents and objects and to explore some of the countryside that Bass penetrated upriver in his whaleboat. To Valda and Harry Cole, much appreciation for most kindly providing important material. And to Rebecca Kaiser, Allen & Unwin, my warmest thanks for the support and enthusiasm that did so much to make this book possible.

I express my appreciation as well of the following persons and institutions for their help in obtaining access to countless documents and, where necessary, permission to reproduce such material: the John Oxley and James Hardie Libraries, State Library of Queensland; the Fryer Library, University of Queensland; the State Library of Victoria, Melbourne, with particular thanks to Gerard Hayes then of the Australian Manuscript Collection; John Harris of the Bureau of Meteorology, Brisbane; Nigel Wace of the Australian National University, Canberra; Matthew Sheldon, Head of Research Collections, Royal Naval Museum, Portsmouth, UK; Julie Cochrane of the Museum of London; Nina Waters, Leeper Librarian, Trinity College, University of Melbourne; the Hocken Library, Dunedin, NZ; the National Topo/Hydro Authority, Wellington, NZ; the National Archives: Public Record Office, Kew, Richmond, UK; Ann Browne and Joan Teale of the United Kingdom Hydrographic Office, Taunton, UK; and the staff of the City of Westminster Archives.

The possibility that George Bass reached South America on his final voyage required further investigation, and for their assistance in this I wish to thank Claudia Betalleluz Otiura of the Embassy of Peru, Canberra; Mark Argar, Australian Consul-General and Trade Commissioner, Lima, Peru; and importantly, Jorge Ortiz-Sotelo, Asociación de Historia Marítima y Naval Iberoamericana, Lima, Peru;

Armando Donayre Medina, Director del Archivo Colonial; and Gregorio Morales Orellana, Técnico en Archivo IV, of the Archivo General de la Nación, Lima, Peru.

Finally, for patience, encouragement and help in many, many ways, my very great gratitude to my family.

CONVERSIONS

LENGTH

1 inch = 2.54 centimetres
1 foot = 30.48 centimetres
1 yard = 0.91 metres
1 mile = 1.61 kilometres
1 fathom = 1.83 metres or 6 feet
1 league = varied in different countries and periods, but usually estimated at approximately 3 miles or 5 kilometres

WEIGHT OR MASS

1 ounce = 28.3 grams
1 pound = 454 grams
1 ton = 1.02 tonnes

VOLUME

1 pint = 0.568 litre
1 quart = 1.1 litres
1 gallon = 4.55 litres

TEMPERATURE

Fahrenheit = 9/5 degrees
    Centigrade + 32

AREA

1 acre = 0.4 hectares

CURRENCY

1 shilling (s) = 12 pence (d)
1 pound (£) = 20 shillings
1 guinea, from 1771 = 21 shillings; not issued after 1813
1 dollar = term generally used by English-speaking people for the Spanish peseta or peso, international currency at the time; the peseta was issued in Spain, the peso generally in Spanish American colonies. In 1800 Governor King fixed the dollar's sterling value in NSW at five shillings.

Modern values for currency in use in the past can only be estimated.

Maps and Illustrations

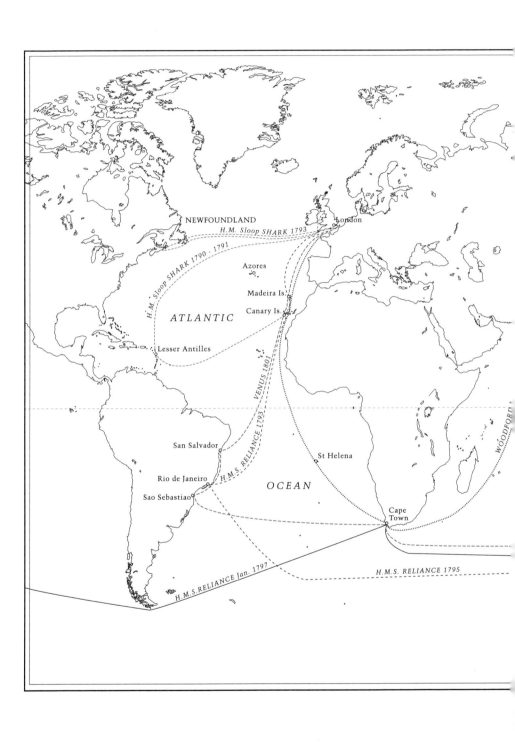

NEWFOUNDLAND
H.M. Sloop SHARK 1793

London

H.M. Sloop SHARK 1790 - 1791

Azores

Madeira Is.

Canary Is.

ATLANTIC

Lesser Antilles

VENUS 1801

H.M.S. RELIANCE 1793

San Salvador

St Helena

Rio de Janeiro

Sao Sebastiao

OCEAN

Cape Town

WOODFORD

H.M.S. RELIANCE Jan. 1797

H.M.S. RELIANCE 1795

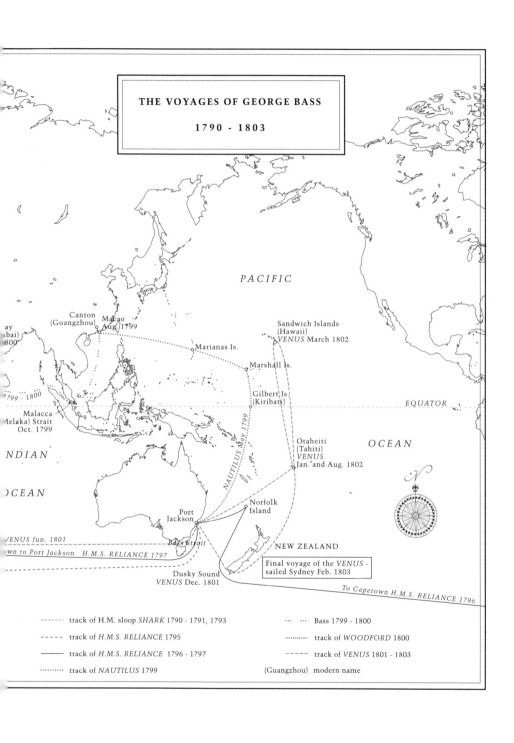

THE VOYAGES OF GEORGE BASS

1790 - 1803

PACIFIC

Canton
(Guangzhou) Macao
ay
bai)
800
Aug. 1799

Sandwich Islands
(Hawaii)
VENUS March 1802

Marianas Is.

Marshall Is.

799   1800

Malacca
Melaka) Strait
Oct. 1799

Gilbert Is.
(Kiribati)

EQUATOR

NDIAN

NAUTILUS, May 1799

Otaheiti
(Tahiti)
VENUS
Jan. and Aug. 1802

OCEAN

OCEAN

Port
Jackson

Norfolk
Island

VENUS Jun. 1801

Bass Strait

NEW ZEALAND

wn to Port Jackson   H.M.S. RELIANCE 1797

Dusky Sound
VENUS Dec. 1801

Final voyage of the VENUS -
sailed Sydney Feb. 1803

To Capetown H.M.S. RELIANCE 1796

------- track of H.M. sloop SHARK 1790 - 1791, 1793

····· Bass 1799 - 1800

----- track of H.M.S. RELIANCE 1795

············ track of WOODFORD 1800

——— track of H.M.S. RELIANCE 1796 - 1797

----- track of VENUS 1801 - 1803

·········· track of NAUTILUS 1799

(Guangzhou)   modern name

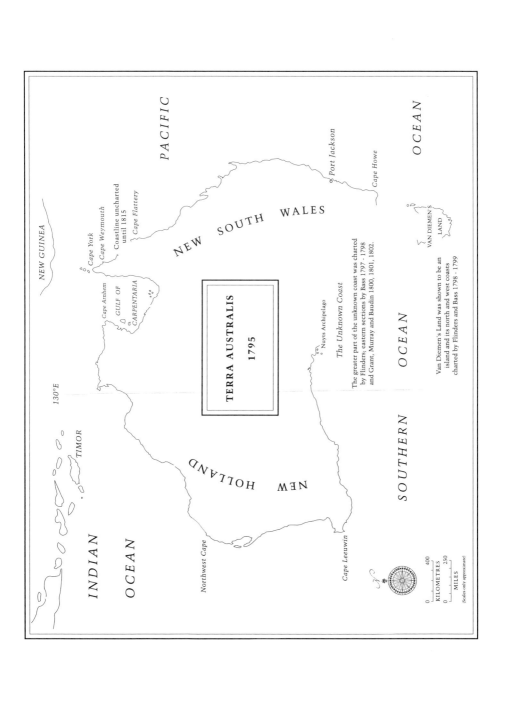

NEW GUINEA

PACIFIC

OCEAN

130°E

TIMOR

Cape York
Cape Weymouth

Coastline uncharted
until 1815

Cape Flattery

Cape Arnhem

GULF OF
CARPENTARIA

NEW SOUTH WALES

Port Jackson

Cape Howe

OCEAN

TERRA AUSTRALIS

1795

Nuyts Archipelago

The Unknown Coast

The greater part of the unknown coast was charted
by Flinders; eastern sections by Bass 1797 - 1798
and Grant, Murray and Baudin 1800, 1801, 1802.

VAN DIEMEN'S
LAND

Van Diemen's Land was shown to be an
island and its north and west coasts
charted by Flinders and Bass 1798 - 1799

INDIAN

OCEAN

NEW HOLLAND

SOUTHERN   OCEAN

Northwest Cape

Cape Leeuwin

400
0
KILOMETRES
0   250
MILES
(Scales only approximate)

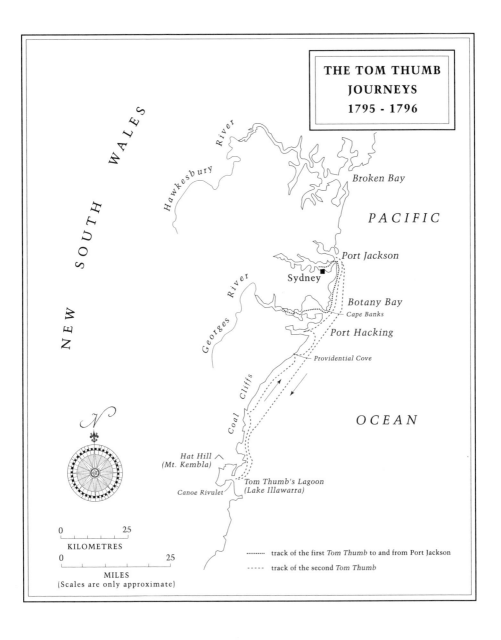

THE TOM THUMB
JOURNEYS
1795 - 1796

River Hawkesbury

Hawkesbury River

NEW SOUTH WALES

Broken Bay

PACIFIC

Port Jackson

Sydney

River Georges

Botany Bay
Cape Banks

Port Hacking

Providential Cove

Coal Cliffs

OCEAN

Hat Hill ∧
(Mt. Kembla)

Canoe Rivulet

Tom Thumb's Lagoon
(Lake Illawarra)

0   25
KILOMETRES
0   25
MILES
(Scales are only approximate)

·········· track of the first *Tom Thumb* to and from Port Jackson

----- track of the second *Tom Thumb*

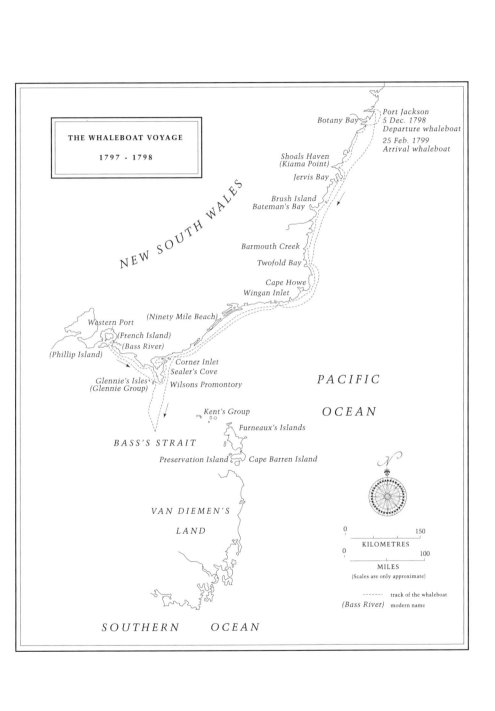

THE WHALEBOAT VOYAGE

1797 - 1798

Port Jackson
5 Dec. 1798
Departure whaleboat
25 Feb. 1799
Arrival whaleboat

Botany Bay

Shoals Haven
(Kiama Point)

Jervis Bay

Brush Island
Bateman's Bay

NEW SOUTH WALES

Barmouth Creek

Twofold Bay

Cape Howe
Wingan Inlet

(Ninety Mile Beach)

Western Port

(French Island)

(Bass River)

(Phillip Island)

Corner Inlet
Sealer's Cove

Glennie's Isles
(Glennie Group)

Wilsons Promontory

PACIFIC

OCEAN

Kent's Group

Furneaux's Islands

BASS'S STRAIT

Preservation Island   Cape Barren Island

VAN DIEMEN'S

LAND

0 _____ 150
KILOMETRES
0 _____ 100
MILES
(Scales are only approximate)

------- track of the whaleboat
(Bass River) modern name

SOUTHERN   OCEAN

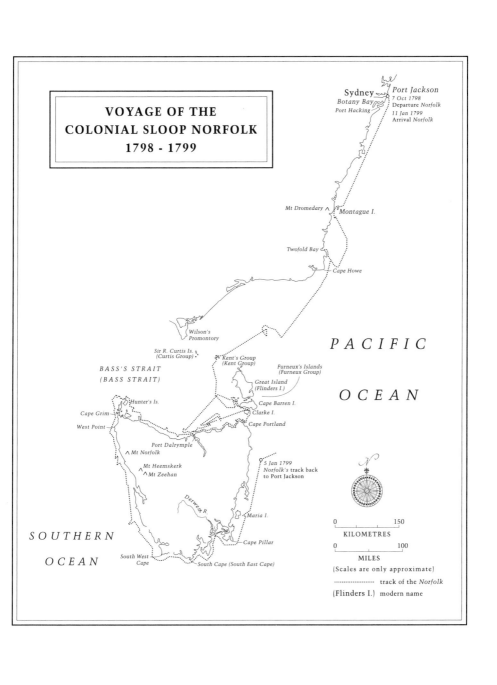

VOYAGE OF THE
COLONIAL SLOOP NORFOLK
1798 - 1799

Sydney
Botany Bay
Port Hacking

Port Jackson
7 Oct 1798
Departure *Norfolk*
11 Jan 1799
Arrival *Norfolk*

Mt Dromedary ∧   Montague I.

Twofold Bay

Cape Howe

Wilson's
Promontory

PACIFIC

Sir R. Curtis Is.
(Curtis Group)

Kent's Group
(Kent Group)

Furneux's Islands
(Furneux Group)

BASS'S STRAIT
(BASS STRAIT)

Great Island
(Flinders I.)

OCEAN

Hunter's Is.

Cape Barren I.

Cape Grim

Clarke I.

West Point

Cape Portland

Port Dalrymple
∧ Mt Norfolk

Mt Heemskerk
∧ ∧ Mt Zeehan

5 Jan 1799
Norfolk's track back
to Port Jackson

Derwent R.

Maria I.

0   150
KILOMETRES
0   100
MILES
(Scales are only approximate)

SOUTHERN

Cape Pillar

OCEAN

South West
Cape

South Cape (South East Cape)

.... track of the *Norfolk*
(Flinders I.) modern name

On 5 February 1803 the 142-ton brig *Venus* cleared the Sydney Heads and in the bright heat of the Australian summer sailed into the Pacific Ocean. The horizon was a pure, straight line of blue against blue and the world of islands and the distant continent towards which she was headed lay far below the ocean rim. In command was one of her owners, the naval surgeon, navigator and entrepreneur George Bass, aged 32. Watching his sails, alert to every sound and movement of his ship, intensely alive with the thrill of the adventure he had laid before himself, he was a man held by elements of character and circumstance that were building relentlessly into a mysterious and presumably tragic final event, for at some point beyond that day, George Bass and the *Venus* vanished into the vastness of the Pacific.

1

The Young George Bass

The road to Aswarby ran across some of Lincolnshire's gently rolling farmland, skirted the occasional coppice and, near the steepled stone church of St Denis, entered the village. Shaded by great trees, a lane branched off towards the manor house with its stables and outbuildings, the seat of the Whichcote family since 1723. A nearby spring with reputedly invigorating waters drew visitors, many of them stopping at the village hostelry, the Tally Ho.

Aswarby lay on the western edge of the great level sweep of Britain's fenlands, reclaimed over centuries from the sea, the terrain here rising gently. Tenants cultivated the fields of the Whichcote Estate, among them at least two generations of a family called Bass, a name which as far back as 1333 had been on a tax assessment list in the nearby parish of Wrangle. In 1731, however, the name appeared in Aswarby records when a George Bass signed the Bishop's Transcripts as churchwarden, an office he held intermittently for the next 25 years. By 1744 the family was established on the Whichcote Estate. Modestly prosperous, George Bass and a surviving son, also George, rented and farmed in addition to their Whichcote fields a part of the church's glebe land.

On 25 January 1770 the younger George Bass married Sarah Newman from the village of Frampton. Both parties signed the record of their marriage, which indicated a degree of education on the part of Sarah as well as her husband. Then in her mid-thirties, she was by reputation a strikingly beautiful woman. People who knew her in her youth maintained that she had been assiduously courted by the son of an eminent local family, declining his proposal because of the difference in their social positions. Nevertheless, he remained a loyal friend into their old age.

George and Sarah Bass prospered on their farm at Aswarby. Bass was evidently a respected individual. He probably served as church-warden, like his father, once or twice, and his election six times to the office of overseer of the poor required good standing within the community. The particular land allotted to him by the Whichcotes also indicated the approbation in which he was held. George Bass's rates assessment was the second or third highest in the parish.

Land reclamation projects were still underway in this part of Lincolnshire, for the region bordered the great shallow bight of the Wash, a melding of land and water, of shoals and channels, a deep inroad of the North Sea that in winter created serious flooding of the Witham and other rivers flowing into it. Possibly as a result of an arrangement whereby parcels of reclaimed land were allocated to ratepayers who had financed the work, Bass evidently acquired an allotment of two roods of land in Skirbeck Quarter on the south side of the Witham River in the town of Boston.

Probably in early 1771, the couple's son was born near Grange Farm in the northern Aswarby area, for on 3 February the child was baptised at the stone-carved Norman font, the bowl resting on shafts with leafy capitals, in Aswarby's centuries-old church, receiving the family's traditional name of George. Thus the boy's earliest memories would have been of a farm cottage, furrowed earth, green meadows and tawny fields of grain.

In September 1777 his father, George Bass, died at the age of 38.[1] Two weeks earlier the dying man had made his will in the presence of the rector of Aswarby and two other men of some distinction. That he was already *in extremis* is suggested by his inability to sign the document with anything other than a shaky cross. On 15 September he was buried in the graveyard below the walls and spire of St Denis. His table tomb was placed outside the south wall of the chancel, a mark of distinction enhanced by Whichcote burials close by. He had willed his estate to his 'dear wife Sarah Bass', who was appointed sole executrix.[2]

Sarah Bass evidently made an attempt to run the farm, possibly with the help of her ageing father-in-law, but in the following year she moved with her seven-year-old son to the town of Boston. Here her brother Joseph Newman was an active citizen, involved in a commission for land drainage and at one point evidently a warden of Boston's great church of St Botolph. Sarah Bass was apparently financially secure, continuing to pay rates on her properties for a number of years. Of her father-in-law there is scant record. His will, drawn up in 1780, provided for his personal estate to be placed in trust for his grandson, to be used for his maintenance and education or to be paid to him on attaining the age of 21. The elder Bass died in 1784, the value of his goods, chattels and effects amounting to less than £600. Young George was thirteen. There is no record of the actual disposition of the inheritance.

Boston stood on the banks of the Witham River, grey-roofed buildings clustered about the market square and the mediaeval stone church of St Botolph with its pinnacles, arched windows and great lantern tower rising monumentally 272½ feet above the town and the surrounding fields. Boston's founding went back to Saxon and Danish times, with possible Roman origins before that, and some of the principal buildings lining its streets were centuries old.

Sarah Bass and her son took up residence in Skirbeck Quarter, on the south side of the Witham River. A two-storey house in London Road, fronting the river, appears to have been her home and the site of the later Crown and Anchor Tavern, possibly known at the time as the Rope and Anchor Tavern.

Thus George grew up in Boston, from a young age watching from his home the boat traffic on the river. He probably attended the Established Boston Grammar School, a brick building with stained glass windows, where the headmaster, the Reverend Obadiah Bell, was also vicar of Frampton, which makes George's enrolment there all the more likely. The boy would have studied mathematics, reading, grammar and Latin, no doubt taking part in games on the adjacent playing fields near the square, red brick ruins of the 15th century Hussey Tower, a remnant of the home of a favourite of Henry VIII. George would have known Boston's port area. Here laden fishing boats came in from the ponds and channels of the fens and from the offshore Boston Deeps. He would have walked among the quays, the custom house and the warehouses that lined the river, stacked with the crates and bales of cargoes from the world beyond Lincolnshire, and watched as ships and boats moved in and out on the tide and with the wind. He would have seen the high tides driven by winter gales that in 1779 and again in 1782 flooded the lower parts of Boston. He would have known the sea mists that crept across fields and villages, turning windmills and church spires into insubstantial shadows. Did he learn to sail some small craft on the river, among the reed-grown islands of the fens, perhaps steering it on the outgoing tide into the Wash? At some point he learned to swim and to swim strongly. There is no record of all this, but somehow he became fascinated by the sea and the far, tantalising line of its horizon.

He was very bright, curious, fond of reading, and given to copying verses that he liked and to writing notes and comments in his books. These were lined up on a small mahogany table provided by his mother—Cook's *Voyage Round the World*, *Don Quixote*, *Sinbad the Sailor* and an old book on storms and catastrophes at sea, each with his name written inside. The accounts of danger at sea intrigued the boy. Seated at his table with his book on marine disasters, he filled several pages in it with his own thoughts on such dangers and a promise to confront the ocean's perils himself but not, he added, 'while my dear mother lives'.[3] Something of the strong tie of respect and affection between mother and son can be seen in later documents as well, but this was a promise George failed to keep.

Fascination with the sea continued to hold George Bass as he entered his teens. This was not surprising. The prosperity of Britain depended upon commerce. Throughout the 18th century its government had quite consistently maintained a policy of promoting, maintaining and extending British commerce, which for an island nation meant a vitally important merchant marine protected by an equally important navy. Behind this lay England's long tradition of seagoing activity, of exploration, discovery, warfare, even government-sanctioned piracy, illumined by such names as Drake and Cavendish, Dampier and Anson, and more recently the celebrated name of Cook. Ocean adventures would have been in the thoughts of many boys at a time when the great 1768 to 1779 voyages of James Cook were current news.

There seem to have been few things that did not capture the interest of young George Bass. He had an intellectual curiosity that was quick and perceptive, an avid interest in distant places and, apparently, even then the compelling ambitions that would shape his adult life and eventually his fate. It is evident that his mother knew her son and that she was apprehensive of her loss to the wider world of this only child, the clever, handsome boy who would have been central to her life.[4] She was clearly determined to guide him into a stable profession.

George was sixteen when his mother apprenticed him to Patrick Francis, a surgeon and apothecary of Boston; the apprenticeship was recorded in the minute book of the Boston Corporation for 22 March 1787.[5] Francis's practice was in effect that of a general practitioner, and he was also active in community affairs, serving as an alderman of Boston, and in 1784 elected chamberlain for the borough. George would have crossed the Witham River bridge into Boston's market place and on to Francis's shop in Strait Bargate, then one of the several cobbled streets dominated by St Botolph's massive, ornate tower, popularly known as the Stump. From Francis George learned the basics of the medical profession: the recognition of diseases; the procedures of surgery—blood-letting, administering clysters, applying poultices, setting bones; the preparation and uses of the common drugs of the time, among them rhubarb root, cinchona bark, calomel, laudanum and other forms of opium, which were pounded, ground and mixed with other supposedly helpful ingredients.

Perhaps contrary to his mother's expectations, work at Francis's apothecary probably stirred further the curiosity of an intelligent, inquisitive boy in the outside world. No doubt he asked questions about Peru, where the bark he worked with came from, and about China, the source, he was told, of the best rhubarb root. Francis's practice and his civic activities made him a well-known figure in Boston, and his shop was very likely something of an informal meeting place for local citizens. There were a number of Lincolnshire men in young George's time who had played a part in Britain's ocean explorations, some of whom were at least acquaintances of Patrick Francis. Richard (or Robert) Rollett, at whose wedding Patrick Francis was a witness, had sailed on James Cook's second voyage (1772–75) as 'Master Sail Maker' on board the *Resolution*.[6] Peter Briscoe and the then sixteen-year-old James Roberts, both from the nearby Revesby estate of Joseph Banks and each listed as 'footman', had accompanied their employer on HMS *Endeavour*'s 1769–71 voyage around the world. A John England, later buried at Hibaldstow, northwest of

Boston, was at Kealakekua Bay in Hawaii when James Cook was killed.[7] Joseph Gilbert, whose family lived near Wrangle, had been master of the *Resolution*, and was responsible for an early map and profile drawing of Norfolk Island, first seen in 1774. Gilbert had once unsuccessfully urged the father of a young nephew to allow the boy to go to sea. Did Gilbert now fire the imagination of young Bass? We do not know, but undoubtedly there were reminiscences of sea life exchanged by these men in the hearing of the boy.

Above all, everyone knew of Sir Joseph Banks of Revesby, whose fame as friend and shipmate of Cook had been followed by years of participation in Lincolnshire affairs, including such endeavours as draining the fens and drilling for fresh water for Boston. His fishing parties too, social gatherings on a large tented barge drawn by horses along the waterways, sometimes into Boston, caught much attention.

At the end of his two-year apprenticeship, Bass evidently decided that his main interest in medicine was surgery. Certification from the Corporation of Surgeons of London was evidently the highest surgical accreditation available, and Bass travelled to the city, where he seems to have spent a short time as a student in one of the hospitals, which mainly required simply observing treatments. The great hospital, the jostling crowds of people and carriages outside, the shops and stalls and streets lighted at night, would have been something of a wonder to the Lincolnshire youth. He then underwent an examination at the Court of Examiners of the Corporation of Surgeons in the impressive column-fronted Surgeons' Hall. On 2 April 1789 George Bass was recorded as having received his diploma as a Member of the Corporation of Surgeons, by tradition to be addressed as 'Mister'. On a list issued in July, the name of 'George Bass, Boston, Lincolnshire' appeared among those entitled 'to the several Privileges, Franchises, and Immunities' of Examined and Approved Surgeons.[8] He was eighteen years old.

Bass entered the field of 18th century surgery at a time when, like many other sciences, it was moving rapidly forward on the great intellectual tide of the Enlightenment, on the momentum generated by the great thinkers of the 17th and 18th centuries, men like Francis Bacon, René Descartes, Isaac Newton and others. Facts and reason were considered the dominant elements of knowledge. Knowledge was to be

founded upon concrete experience, upon the observation and recording of facts, and collecting such knowledge, including, in Denis
Diderot's words, the essential details 'of each science and every
mechanical and liberal art', and its presentation in a rational, orderly
and useful form, were characteristics of the mid-1700s. This was an
age of encyclopaedias, dictionaries and major works on human and
natural history. Rational patterns and social relevance were seen to link
the disciplines.

Thus advances forged in physics, chemistry and the biological
sciences were applicable to many aspects of clinical medicine. With
Bacon's emphasis on information drawn from experience rather than
from past authority, William Harvey had used meticulous observation
and precise reasoning to develop his theory of blood circulation. The
chemist Richard Boyle had physically demonstrated the necessity of
oxygen to life. Galileo worked on the development of the microscope,
and with it Antonie van Leeuwenhoek was probably the first to see and
describe bacteria.

Unsubstantiated theories and elements of superstition remained, but
medical schools were being guided increasingly by the sound scientific
thinking of such men as the anatomist and pathologist Giovanni
Battista Morgagni (1682–1771), the anatomists William and John
Hunter (1718–83 and 1728–93), and the Alexander Monros, three
generations (1720–1846) of outstanding clinical teachers. Inoculation
against smallpox became popular in the later 1700s. Public health and
hygiene, hospitals, and care for naval and military personnel received
increasing attention.

Nevertheless, a sheer lack of knowledge limited the efforts of even
the most dedicated. While a number of illnesses were recognised and
received reasonable care, their causes remained unknown or misunder-
stood. There was no awareness of micro-organisms, and contagion and
infection often received inadequate or mistaken handling. Attempted
cures were frequently based on practices that did little to help and
could, in fact, be harmful. Patients received infusions of calcined
magnesia or drops of citric and muriatic acid, onion water, leek water,
other liquids, and mercury in various forms. Bleeding, blistering,
clysters and vomiting were thought to relieve the body of its impurities,
as had been believed for centuries. And there were no anaesthetics,

other than alcohol, although 'a sirup of poppies', or laudanum, was administered in various forms for a number of illnesses.

Within the ranks of medical men there remained differences that also dated back to mediaeval times, when physicians were ecclesiastics and therefore not permitted to shed blood, and an operation was consequently placed in the hands of the barber-surgeon. While 18th century surgeons had effectively become general practitioners, there remained the academic distinction between surgeons, trained through apprenticeships, and the more esteemed physicians, who had medical degrees and were addressed as 'Doctor'.

Young Mr Bass was qualified to practise surgery anywhere in England except 'in or within Seven Miles of the City of London'.[9] But his overwhelming desire to go to sea remained. He had fulfilled his mother's wishes. He could now think again about confronting the great oceans. It was the navy that had sent out James Cook and his predecessors and, filled with intriguing prospects of exploration and discovery, determined and optimistic, George Bass made the necessary applications at the Navy Office. On 4 June 1789, two months after qualifying as a surgeon, he appeared again before a Court of Examiners, now for the examination for naval surgeons. From behind a semi-circular table the examiners questioned the candidates as to their age and background, their knowledge of physiology, anatomy and surgery, and how they would handle specific surgical cases or diseases. Bass passed easily and was certified as a surgeon's first mate on a naval ship of any rate. No doubt he jubilantly paid the necessary fee, evidently one guinea, and probably on the following day had the pride and delight of receiving his certificate. The young man of intellect and science could now turn to the pursuit of adventure.

From the 1750s the ships of the Royal Navy had been classified or rated on the basis of the number of guns they carried. A first rate was a towering floating fortress with three decks mounting a hundred or more cannon and a complement of close to 1000 men. A second rate carried 90 to 98 guns, a third rate 64 to 80 on two gun decks, a fourth rate between 50 and 60 guns, and fifth and sixth rates, or frigates, some 44 to 20 guns on a single deck, with 200 to 300 crewmen.[10] In addition there were countless smaller unrated vessels—sloops, cutters, schooners, bombs, and others with varying armament. Of these, the sloop, a small but purpose-built warship, might carry between eight and 24 guns. Her purpose was mainly to perform escort and patrol duties and to protect commercial vessels.

Bass was entered briefly on the muster book of HMS *Barfleur*, but before actually taking up duty on that vessel was reassigned as surgeon's mate to HMS *Flirt*, a 14-gun brig-sloop with a complement of 73 men, under the command of James Norman and part of the Channel Fleet. Despite being qualified to serve on a ship of any rate, including the largest man-of-war, Bass's assignment was to an unrated craft, not an unusual occurrence. Surgeons were needed on small as well as large warships. George travelled to Portsmouth and on a breezy day in early July 1789, tall and handsome in a new dark blue coat and white breeches and stockings, boarded the vessel at Spithead, the great naval anchorage in the strait between the Isle of Wight and Portsmouth harbour. Three days later the *Flirt* weighed, anchored briefly at St Helens and on 8 July headed into the Channel with all sails set in a light breeze, and for the first time George Bass saw the open sea, an endless expanse stretching toward the sky. Here was an entrancement that clearly never left him. And he had achieved his priorities. He had combined his mother's wishes with his own desires: he was a qualified surgeon who went to sea.

2

The Royal Navy

Naval medicine had its own challenges. A seaman's working environment was fraught with danger. Decks were always in motion, often wet and icy, sometimes washed over by heavy seas. Yet they had to be crossed, ropes hauled and gear secured. In a darkened hold with only the feeble light of a candle burning inside a lantern, a sailor manhandled heavy, awkward loads that could fall or roll back upon him. Aloft, his insubstantial perch swung and plunged, his hold restricted to rope and timber, in daylight or darkness, in high wind, rain, sleet and snow. The worse the weather, the more urgent it often was that the sailor perform quickly with scant regard for risk. Injury was never far away, the danger sometimes heightened by the effect of a man's daily ration of beer or grog. Sustained hard labour—heavy lifting, heaving on ropes, turning capstans, operating the pumps— brought a high incidence of abdominal hernias. Ulcers from various causes were common.

Injury was also the result of punishment. Men were flogged for offences ranging from the petty to the serious. Twelve lashes was a basic sentence, which could be multiplied almost any number of times. It was then up to the surgeon to do what he could for the lacerated back. Infection, for which there was little help other than the body's own resistance, threatened every wound.

The sea also took its toll through illness. In 1754 the naval physician James Lind demonstrated the efficacy of fresh fruit and lemon juice in the prevention of the age-old scourge of scurvy, which stemmed from a lack of vitamin C in the seaman's usual diet of salted meat and hard-baked biscuit. In 1795 the physician to the Channel Fleet, Thomas Trotter, wrote to the group's commander, Admiral Lord

Richard Howe, on the rapid cure of scurvy aboard the ships after they were supplied with lemons and oranges. He recommended daily servings in all the messes of 'a few bunches of radishes, young onions, lettuces, etc.' and fresh beef broth to which onions, leeks or greens were added. Such a diet would in fourteen to sixteen days overcome 'the scorbutic taint'.[1] Yet it was more than 40 years before the naval physician Gilbert Blane, a Fellow of the Royal Society and a commissioner of the Admiralty's Sick and Hurt Board, ordered a standard issue of citrus fruits to all ships. It was not, however, that simple. In northern Europe such fruit was not always available. There was also a strong belief in the superior effects of extract of malt, recommended by Cook and the Royal Society. In fact, malt contains only traces of vitamin C.

Inevitably, fresh foods were short-lived and not always available in the regions visited by the ships. Food and water loaded at some ports could themselves be contaminated. In the course of his circumnavigation of the Australian continent in 1802–03, Matthew Flinders took on water and fresh food at Kupang in Timor, which became suspect when dysentery developed on board. Individual captains, surgeons and pursers could be negligent, and the normal provision allowance on British naval ships simply did not include fresh greens. Thus outbreaks of scurvy continued to occur in many ships, especially those on long voyages.

Fevers contracted by the men ashore could sweep through a ship or an entire fleet with horrifying thoroughness. Yellow fever, contracted by British soldiers and seamen mainly in tropical regions, particularly the West Indies, was the most feared. That it was caused by a virus transmitted by several species of mosquito was not understood and, thus, thought to be contagious, it bred terror among ships' companies. Some anecdotes suggest that fear itself precipitated death, but the reality was grim enough. One survivor related that of 1100 military and naval men who left Spithead for the West Indies in November 1793, only 500 lived to see England again.[2] Smallpox, however, was on a decline. Trotter introduced Dr Edward Jenner's new vaccination, and by 1798 naval surgeons were regularly employing the practice.

Malaria, also mosquito-borne, was yet another disease picked up on land by sailors, and its periodic attacks of chills and fever, although long associated with swampy or marshy regions, remained unexplained until the 20th century. There was, however, a useful medication if not a cure. Jesuit missionaries in Peru had noted native use of the bark of the cinchona tree in the treatment of fevers, and brought back to Europe Peruvian or 'Jesuit' bark or simply 'bark', the basis of modern quinine, which became widely employed in treating a range of fevers. Less helpful were treatments based on the belief that sickness stemmed from an imbalance of 'humors' or fluids in the body, including blood, phlegm and choler. Balance had to be restored by expelling the bad humours through purgatives and bleeding.

Typhus went by many names, among them gaol fever and putrid fever. Caused by bacteria transmitted to humans by insect carriers, notably body lice, it raged in filthy, overcrowded conditions, as in 17th and 18th century jails, military camps, even hospitals, and was apparently particularly prevalent in the 1790s.[3] In ships epidemics flared when infected, unwashed individuals were brought on board from prisons or dredged from the slums of the cities by press-gangs. The incidence of typhus was, however, gradually reduced by the introduction of one important innovation recommended by Lind. Pressed men were sent first to 'receiving' ships, where their clothes were burned and the men washed and issued with regulation attire or 'slops' before being distributed to the various ships.[4]

Venereal diseases were common, frequently following long periods in port. Treated in various ways, usually with mercury, which apparently could relieve the symptoms, they were an accepted problem, sometimes even regarded with humour.

Enlightened naval physicians such as Blane, Lind and Trotter recognised the importance of cleanliness, fresh air and dry living conditions in maintaining shipboard health, and conscientious captains did their best to implement their recommendations. Sand and holystones were provided for scrubbing decks in order to reduce the amount of sea water used. Windsails were rigged to bring fresh air into the lower levels of the ship and portable fires introduced to combat the unrelenting humidity. The between decks were fumigated with hot tar, sulphur, tobacco or a mixture of nitre, that is, gunpowder, and vinegar. Washing of any kind could be done only with salt water—unless in a convenient rainstorm—and soap was not issued until 1810, the cost then deducted from a man's wages. Nevertheless, crewmen were mustered and inspected for at least relative cleanliness once or twice a week.

Individual surgeons exerted their own efforts. George Hamilton, surgeon of the ill-fated frigate *Pandora*, noted, 'Soft bread was found extremely beneficial to the sick and convalescent, and we availed ourselves of every opportunity of baking for half the complement at a time.'[5] Hugh Bell, surgeon on Matthew Flinders's exploration ship *Investigator*, suggested between deck rearrangements that provided the sick with more space and comfort. Admiralty regulations required ships of war to be furnished with fishing tackle, and captains were to 'employ some of the company in fishing', the catch to be distributed primarily to the sick.[6] Yet the basic problem remained. While there were serious efforts at prevention and at ameliorating the suffering of victims, the cause of an illness was rarely understood. Not unusual was a belief in the effects of weather, that changes or persistent winds from a certain direction exacerbated a sickness. Too often well-meant treatments were ineffective, mistaken, even damaging.

Inducements for a career as a naval surgeon were not high. There were the intense discomforts of crowded shipboard life, poor pay and limited prospects for advancement, with no possibility of building up a rewarding private practice. Men with ambition and promise were not often drawn to it, although in wartime patriotism was no doubt a motivation. In a fleet desperately needing personnel, the gap was all too frequently filled by those whose incompetence in some way had led to failure ashore. Nevertheless, by 1793 there were over 550 surgeons in the fleet, with surgeons' mates and other assistants adding to their number.[7] Of naval physicians, there were in the early 1790s only four.[8]

Bass, however, wanted to be at sea. His youthful interest in his work was high, learning came easily, and he had the ability to do well in almost anything he undertook. Over the years he acquired books on medicine and surgery which he studied, at times no doubt by candle-light, in his small cabin or in the crowded and noisy gunroom, where he messed with the midshipmen. Among the books he later possessed and may have acquired at this time were William Saunders's *Elements of the Practice of Physic, etc.* (1780, 1794), Samuel Sharp's *A Treatise on the Operations of Surgery* (1751), parts of the *London Medical*

Journal, and William Foredyce's *A Review of Venereal Disease and Its Remedies* (1785). Years later Bass's reputation as a surgeon was enthusiastically remarked upon by Gilbert Blane in comments to George's wife's family.[9]

The outbreak of the French Revolution in 1789 had been initially received by many in Britain with considerable enthusiasm, as a spark that would not only create an enlightened French republic, but also ignite important social, political and religious reform in Britain. By 1793, however, the nations of Europe had been thoroughly shaken by the revolution's escalating violence, French military aggression into neighbouring territories, and the spread of radical propaganda promising to sweep aside established social and political systems. Alarmed, the British government reacted with the promulgation of numerous repressive acts, and there were repeated economic and social crises. Revolutionary rhetoric together with the hard, uncompromising demands of increasing Britain's wartime readiness at sea created tensions and problems within the navy as well. Island Britain depended for economic survival on worldwide sea-borne commerce, and of necessity maintained war fleets across two-thirds of the face of the world, from the American West Indies to the East Indies of Asia.

Britain's Channel Fleet was the fulcrum of British home defence, charged with the protection of the nation's south coast and maritime trade and, with the later outbreak of war with France, sharing in the blockade of French ports and the extirpation of French commerce. In 1789 the *Flirt* joined in patrolling the roughly 100-mile width of the Channel off England's south coast, sometimes approaching the cliff-faced island of Alderney in the Channel Group, once coming within a few leagues of France's Cap de la Hague. The rolling hills of the Isle of Wight, the 500-foot white chalk cliffs of Beachy Head, and the Dungeness lighthouse off Kent became for Bass familiar landmarks, as fresh gales and squalls, light breezes under cloudy skies and the occasional clear day came and went. There were brief moorings at Weymouth or Portland Roads, when water, firewood and food supplies came on board. He listened to the reading of the Articles of War and watched his first punishment, as James Connel, seaman, received twelve lashes for theft, and then by lanternlight in the below deck sick bay tried to ease the pain and promote the healing of the man's riven flesh.

Repeatedly the *Flirt* pursued her task of chasing and bringing-to small vessels to be inspected for contraband. Watching for French privateers that hovered off the crags of Lizard Point or the Eddystone Rock, in wait for unsuspecting merchantmen, was another duty. To Bass a ship was surely becoming an inalienable part of his life. He came to know intimately the unceasing motion, the hum of the wind in the rigging, the steady, heavy creaking of timbers, and the shrilling of the bosun's pipe, the rattle of drums and the slapping of bare running feet as the sloop prepared for action. He learned his way about the dark lower decks, keeping his head down under low overhead beams and slipping past ponderous protruding timbers. He watched the work around him, asked questions and, when he was allowed, no doubt eagerly took part. Almost certainly the young surgeon was applying himself to learning seamanship.

As the days of summer shortened and chill autumn fogs gathered over a steel grey sea, the ship returned to Spithead, and on a dark November day Bass was transferred to HMS *Gorgon*, a fifth rate, 44 guns, Captain William Harvey. Storms enveloped the anchorage in mid-December. Bass watched as in the screaming wind struggling seamen brought down the topgallant mast and, the gale mounting, struck the topmast as well. The ship signalled for help with the firing of guns, and in icy winds and heavy seas the *Gorgon* was moved into the greater shelter of Portsmouth Harbour to take on stores and provisions. The immediate plan for the vessel was intriguing. She was to carry the men of a newly formed military unit, the New South Wales Corps, to Britain's distant Australian colony and from there, joined in Hawaii by HMS *Discovery* and Captain George Vancouver, take a group for settlement in North America. She was then to sail to the South Pacific in search of HMS *Bounty*'s mutineers. It was an exciting prospect. There were, however, long delays at Portsmouth, and Bass used the interval to journey to London to take an examination for promotion. On 4 July 1790 he received from the Court of Examiners the rank of naval surgeon, second rate, that is, qualification to serve as a full surgeon on a warship, second rate, with 90 to 98 guns and about 800 men.

On board the *Gorgon* Bass made an interesting friend. This was Captain William Paterson of the New South Wales Corps, in Bass's words 'a well known naturalist and traveller'.[10] Paterson was, in fact, a botanist who at the age of 22 had visited South Africa and made several excursions into the interior, in 1789 publishing *A Narrative of Four Journeys into the Country of the Hottentots and Caffraria.* Joining the military in 1781, he combined active service in India with studying the subcontinent's remarkable plant life, about which he maintained a steady correspondence with Lincolnshire's wealthy landowner, Sir Joseph Banks, now renowned as a dedicated patron of the natural sciences, and patron as well of the New South Wales settlement in distant Terra Australis. In 1789, through the influence of Banks, Paterson received a captaincy in the just-raised New South Wales Corps, with the attractive prospect of pursuing natural history explorations in largely unknown Australia. Paterson was an impressively handsome, gentle and gracious man and, in the words of the naval officer Henry Waterhouse, 'a sensible, pleasant gentleman',[11] whose abilities as a military leader in years to come would be severely tested in New South Wales. In 1789, however, he appears to have aroused a significant new interest in the eighteen-year-old Bass. Botany and natural history in general do not seem to have been among the interests of the young George, but combined with Paterson's descriptions of adventurous travels in far places they now appeared fascinating. The link between plants and medicine goes back to ancient times, and in the generation before Bass's own, such botanists as Carl Linnaeus and Sir Hans Sloane had applied their medical training to scientific plant study and classification. On ships the surgeon was generally the only member of the company who had a scientific education, and at times was instructed by the Admiralty to report on natural history matters. William Anderson, surgeon on Cook's second and third voyages, accumulated valuable collections of specimens from the Pacific islands. Robert Brown, naturalist on Matthew Flinders's *Investigator*, was an army surgeon prior to the voyage. Now Bass linked his scientific training to botanical investigations, and work and studies in this and other aspects of natural history, probably from this point on, became one of his favourite pursuits.

The long delays at Portsmouth ended his hopes for an especially interesting voyage. The plans for the *Gorgon* were shelved and some 92 men of the New South Wales Corps eventually sailed with other ships in a loose assemblage of vessels known as the Second Fleet. Paterson remained in England to organise additional recruits for the unit. Meantime, Bass's promotion resulted in his transfer in July 1790 to HM Sloop *Fairy*, fourteen guns, as acting surgeon. Here his service was brief. On 17 July he was evidently at the town of Deal in Kent, to be taken off the shingle beach by boat to board HMS *Pomona*, Captain Henry Savage, which was moored at the busy east coast anchorage of the Downs, headquarters of the North Sea Fleet. Here warships, some of them the huge first rates, arrived and departed almost continuously, amid flurries of ensigns, pennants and signal flags and the frequent booming across the water of gun salutes, while merchant ships by the hundred waited at anchor for favourable winds. The *Pomona* itself was preparing for sea, with officers and men arriving and boats and lighters jockeying for position alongside with bundles of firewood, crates of naval stores and casks of foodstuffs and water to be hoisted aboard. A shortage of crew and the practice of impressment is reflected in the captain's log, with men arriving from the 'rendezvous' house of the Dover press-gangs, and signals requesting ticket men or 'men in lieu'. These were seamen prepared to board incoming merchant vessels as temporary replacements for crew being taken off by a warship, as the law required that in cases of impressment sufficient men were left on board any targeted ship to work the vessel to its destination. Examining the new men was Bass's responsibility. His stay on *Pomona* was also short. On 26 August 1790 he reported aboard HM Fire Ship *Vulcan*.

By the late 18th century the use of fire ships by the British navy was rare, but apparently remained an option. Fire, which a change of wind could turn against one's own fleet, was a tactic to be used only in exceptional circumstances, generally against enemy ships in a harbour that could not be approached in any other way. Hence these little vessels, usually sloops, were regularly employed on other tasks. The *Vulcan* was undergoing repairs, with much activity centred about her rigging. Again Bass's assignment was short, but this time was accompanied by promotion. Within a fortnight he had boarded HM Sloop *Shark* at Spithead, as her surgeon.

The *Shark* was a sloop of 304 tons, sixteen guns, with a complement of 125 men. Bass now had the assistance of a surgeon's mate,

Thomas Thompson, and for nursing and general maintenance of the hospital area crewmen who were usually through age or some impediment unfit for normal shipboard work. There were variations, but typically the ship's sick bay was located on the orlop, the lowest deck, in candle-lit darkness well below the waterline, the area sometimes screened off by canvas dropped from the overhead beams. Here an ailing man was brought with his hammock, blankets and wool- or flock-filled mattress. Regulations required that the ship's cooper 'make, out of any old staves and hoops, buckets with covers for the necessary occasions of the sick men; and if any of them have fractured bones' the carpenter was to make 'cradles' as needed.[12] Serious cases were sent when possible to land-based naval hospitals, as at Chatham, Plymouth or Haslar near Portsmouth.

Nearby was the surgeon's very small cabin, partitioned off with canvas walls. There was the sound of the sea against the wooden hull and the stenches of mould and bilgewater in the gravel or shingle ballast below. Suspended from the beams was his cot. Here by smoky yellow lanternlight Bass arranged his gear, fitting in his trunk and the medicine chest with the drugs he had provided, and his instruments, among them a lancet, forceps and nippers, an amputating saw and knife, tourniquet clamps, a catling and a double-edged scalpel.[13] Here also he kept his journals recording treatment and his patients' progress, one for disease and another for surgery.

Bass would have ordered what comforts he could for the sick. A fire was kept burning in a stove to dry and warm the air. The deck was regularly swept and sprinkled with vinegar. Hammocks and bedding were turned out on deck to be washed and aired as weather permitted. Usually he visited his patients twice a day, prescribed treatments which Thompson carried out, and when new men were brought on board, examined them. Depending on the shortage of crew on board, it was his task to reject or accept a man on the basis of his physical condition. When a surgeon's efforts failed and a man died at sea, he was sewn into his hammock, weighted at the foot with cannon balls, and in the formally drawn up presence of the ship's company slid into the depths.

At one o'clock in the afternoon of 8 November 1790 the *Shark* weighed anchor and under a cloudy sky steered out of Spithead with a cold fresh easterly filling her sails. Undoubtedly Bass was on deck when in the chilly six o'clock darkness of the following morning a point of light to the west was tentatively identified as that of the Eddystone lighthouse.[14] Early the next afternoon, passing the rocky protuberances of the Lizard, the men on board had their final view of England. The *Shark* headed for Portugal's Madeira Islands off the north African coast.

Bass would have been enchanted by the voyage southward through the Atlantic. He saw the immensity of a great ocean, the unbroken circle of a horizon beyond which there was no land for hundreds, even thousands of miles. He would have felt the aloneness of a little ship making its slow way between sky and water. Bass was a man whose restless disposition and heuristic intelligence sought experience in many directions, but it is obvious that here was a special bewitchment that fastened itself upon his mind and would carry him again and again to sea. Probably more seriously than ever, he applied himself to learning the skills essential to bringing a vessel safely across a vast and indifferent ocean.

Latitude had for centuries been measured by a series of simple instruments, among them cross-staffs and astrolabes, culminating in the 1700s with the sextant, which with relative accuracy measured the angle between the horizon and a celestial body—the sun, the moon or a star. From this angle and the exact time of day, together with certain mathematical calculations, a specific latitude could be determined. At some point, cradling a sextant in his hands and through the lens carefully bringing the bright image of the sun or a star down to the horizon, Bass learned to do this.

Obtaining longitude, which required not only local time, but also time at a prime meridian such as at Greenwich, was a more difficult affair. A ship's position was commonly obtained by a method of lunar distances based on measurements relating to the moon, as it moved across a starry sky or in company with the sun. The angular distance between the moon and the sun or one of several selected stars was observed by the navigator, the time of the observation was recorded and several mathematical procedures were applied. The navigator then consulted tables in the *Nautical Almanac*, which provided the time in Greenwich when the same measurements would have occurred. Other calculations followed, which finally gave the difference between that time and local time, which was converted into degrees of longitude and the ship's position. The method was lengthy and subject to error. By the 1790s, however, the marine chronometer had become quite readily available. This provided a clock reading of Greenwich time which, compared to the time at sea at the same instant, gave the navigator a much simpler means of converting the difference in time into degrees of longitude east or west of Greenwich. Whether or not smaller navy craft were equipped at this time with chronometers other than perhaps a captain's privately owned instrument is not clear, but in the course of his service Bass would have become adept at both methods. The ship's position at noon each day was marked on the chart and lines joining these marks showed the ship's track across the sea. The naval day began with this noonday reading.

In the evening of 20 November the *Shark* entered the busy road-stead of the port of Funchal on the main island of the Madeira group, volcanic peaks rising many hundreds of feet from bases on the ocean floor. The great stern lantern was lit and other lights hoisted, a pilot boarded and at two o'clock in the morning the *Shark* was taken to anchor. By daylight Bass saw whitewashed houses lining the curve of the shore and amphitheatre-like hills rising into 4000-foot mountains. Along the steep, narrow cobblestone streets there were gardens with shrubs and colourful flowers he had never seen before. In the two days the *Shark* spent at anchor to take on water, fresh beef and 598 gallons of wine, Bass would undoubtedly have made every effort to go ashore. Unfortunately, he left no surviving account of his stay.

By the 23rd the *Shark* was again at sea, in rain and heavy winds steering southwest on what would become a great circular sweep through the North Atlantic Ocean. For two months on a wide-ranging patrol she rode the equatorial current and the trade winds westward into the tropics, and then the Gulf Stream and the westerlies northward and homeward to the east. Bass's love of the sea had full scope here — the brilliance of the sun's rim rising out of the water, the sense of utter freedom at the masthead, the golden threads of starlight reflected on a dark and quiet ocean. Was there in his mind a challenge to reason or to a man's abilities in all of this? Or was there simply a profound appreciation of such vivid manifestations of nature, a streak of the romantic in a man trained to think scientifically? To our knowledge

Bass recorded neither descriptions or answers, but the enchantment was clearly there. It would hold him in thrall for the rest of his life.

British naval squadrons on the West Indian stations were at this time numerically weak. This was a dangerous situation in view of the importance to the British economy of Caribbean trade—products such as sugar, tobacco and rum, and the sale of British manufactures and African slaves. Local Caribbean sea traffic as well as the hundreds of West Indiamen crossing the Atlantic each year required protection, if not from French naval forces, certainly from French privateers. The *Shark*'s assignment in 1790 is not clear, but probably it was a combination of reconnaissance, patrol and the protection of commerce.

It seems likely that on this long cruise, in the relatively informal conditions of a small vessel, Bass had further opportunities to learn the basics of seamanship—the handling and combining of sails, the intricacies of ropework, the raising and lowering of yards, and at the side of the helmsman the techniques of steering.

With a silky blue sky and light winds the men's hammocks were unrolled in the fresh air while the decks below were washed, or the crew was exercised with the 'great guns and small arms'. But just as often the day gave way to tumid cloud masses rent by flickering tongues of lightning, as the sea grew steeper and seething whiteness burst over the decks. Bass would have watched as men surged up the shrouds and rope ladders, to lean across the yards, feet on swaying footropes, as sails were reefed or furled, topgallant masts were struck, and a sail that split with a sound like a gunshot above the wail of the storm was unbent and another bent in its place, the men high above the deck, drenched, clinging, buffeted.

In early January some of the West Indies' Lesser Antilles islands came into view. Grenada, Guadaloupe, Montserrat, Antigua, Barbuda and others were sighted at a few leagues' distance. These were among the islands being contested by Britain and France. Again cannon and small arms were exercised. A brig and a schooner were sighted. In a calm sea the cutter was hoisted out to test the current, which was found to be moving west-southwest at three fathoms per hour.

On 7 January 1791 five sail were sighted, which on the next day were identified as English transports bound for home. The result was an enthusiastic mid-ocean meeting, the ships heaving to, and with the cutter plying back and forth the *Shark* received several welcome casks of salt beef and pork, half a barrel of peas and twelve bags of bread. Loud cheers would have rung out across the water as the vessels parted.

The *Shark* was now steering east in the mid-Atlantic, and on 13 January in heavy weather was some 400 leagues north of Corvo, the northernmost of the Portuguese Azores islands. Fifteen days later the gleam of the Eddystone light was sighted, and on 29 January 1791 the *Shark* was secured to her moorings among the many vessels at the Spithead anchorage.

Now the *Shark* patrolled England's southwest coast out of Plymouth, following the rocky, sea-misted and often rain-swept shores of Devon and Cornwall. In rough and windy seas she skirted the reefs and islets of the Scillies, and made her way up the passage to Bristol. On the return voyage she headed south to the familiar Channel Islands and then north again into Plymouth. Small vessels carrying contraband goods, mainly spirits, were chased, sometimes stopped with the firing of a six-pounder, brought-to and boarded, often to find that the illicit cargo had been thrown overboard. At times, despite their desperate and sometimes violent resistance, some of the smugglers were impressed. The ships of the navy had to be manned, and a smuggler was considered an excellent recruit. He was almost invariably a fit and active man, thoroughly familiar with small craft and the sea, and unlike some categories of sailors had little opportunity for redress. Confiscated boat and cargo were then conveyed to the nearest British custom house.

The outbreak of the French Revolution in 1789 had little immediate impact upon the west coast patrols. For Bass it soon became an uneventful existence. He messed with the other officers and, without critical illnesses on board, was free to be on the quarterdeck. Seamanship and navigation continued to absorb him, and at some point he acquired John Robertson's well-known *The Elements of Navigation*, as well as David Steel's two-volume *The Elements and Practice of Rigging and Seamanship*. This was not, however, enough for Bass's active mind. Somehow in the damp, crowded confines of the ship he managed to apply himself to other studies. In a letter to his mother, he later referred to the Spanish language, 'which I learnt some years since for my amusement'.[15] He acquired and presumably read an *Historia del Famoso Don Quixote de la Mancha*, together with a critical discussion of the book by G. M. Baretti. He evidently kept up the Latin he had learned in school and in the course of his medical training. He possessed Latin dictionaries, at least one grammar and a few texts. He had Portuguese dictionaries as well. Languages came easily.

In late August 1791 the monotony was briefly broken when, cruising in the Solent off Cowes in heavy fog, the *Shark* ran aground. Guns were fired in a signal of distress, spare topmasts were flung overboard to lighten the ship and top and topgallant masts struck. Efforts to lighten the ship continued the next morning as the men poured the supplies of fresh water over the side; with the arrival of two other sloops, everything portable—guns, anchors and provisions—was shifted onto them. Finally, with the help of the brig *Scout*, the *Shark* was refloated and after repairs at Plymouth resumed her patrols.

On 1 February 1793 France's revolutionary government declared war on Britain and the Netherlands. Ten days later Britain issued her declaration of hostilities against France. The British naval presence in transatlantic stations was increased and the convoy system improved by parliamentary Act. By May the *Shark* was sailing for Newfoundland with other warships guarding a convoy across the Atlantic. The island of Newfoundland, today a Canadian province, was claimed for England in 1497 by John Cabot and again in 1583 by Sir Humphrey Gilbert. Valuable for the rich Grand Banks fishing grounds off its southern coast, its ownership was disputed by France until 1713 when by the Treaty of Utrecht Britain secured Newfoundland, with France receiving certain fishing rights and in 1783 possession of the little cliff-edged, peat bog islands of Saint-Pierre and Miquelon, fifteen miles off Newfoundland's south coast. On the outbreak of war, a British military and naval detachment from Halifax, Nova Scotia, seized their fishing establishments.

Again Bass was in the blue—and often grey—world of sky and sea. He would have climbed to the masthead to watch the ships of the convoy that were in sight, the faster-sailing *Shark* sometimes shortening sail to remain with the merchantmen. There was much breaking out of signal flags, occasional shouting back and forth from deck to deck across a cable or so of water. The log records the sea-borne activity: 'at 1 P. M. spoke a Spanish Ship from Havannah bound to

Cadiz . . . made signals to the convoy . . . at 5 A.M. spoke an American brig from Salem . . . saw a Sail to the Eastward, made sundry signals, at ½ past 7 Made sail & gave chase, at ½ past 8 hauld our Wind, & stood after the Convoy'.[16] Bass saw his first iceberg, a white mountain of breathtaking size, scored with crevices of an unbelievable crystalline blue. A few leagues from the Canadian shore, a thick fog swept about the sloop and she hove-to repeatedly to take soundings.

At seven o'clock on 27 May 1793, in the twilight of a cloudy northern summer evening, the *Shark* dropped her best bower anchor into the five-fathom depth of the harbour at St John's, Newfoundland, a little settlement at the foot of the steep western slope of an almost landlocked inlet. The formalities of arrival would have taken place, but the captain's log shows chiefly that the lacks resulting from a long ocean crossing had to be met promptly. A party was immediately ordered ashore for fresh water. The next day, as the other ships of the convoy began to come into the harbour, the log notes that a group went 'on shore to brew Beer'.[17] This was spruce beer, the principal ingredient provided by the nearby forest. Watering continued and fresh beef was obtained. Men were landed to work in the Admiralty's garden, a frequent effort in various ports to provide the ships with fresh produce. The *Shark*'s men also prepared buoys and transported them to moorings in the harbour. Bass, meantime, was dealing with either an illness or a severe injury, for on 1 June the log notes that 'Died on shore John Henley (Marine)'. On 5 June at one o'clock in the afternoon, 21-gun salutes roared across St John's harbour in honour of King George III's birthday.

Seven days later the *Shark* was again ready for sea, and through the summer, frequently in fog and rain and occasionally amid ice floes, she patrolled the shoreline from St John's southward to Cape Race, and westward, guarding the British fishing fleet that worked the rich waters early and late. The transatlantic voyage, however, had taken its toll, and from time to time the sloop sought the shelter of an inlet on the Burin Peninsula, with its small British station, for repairs. In July the log noted, 'found the Maintopsl decayed, got it down & sent up a new one, sailmakers repairing the Sails—lifted the Rudder, to overhaul the Pintles'.[18] There were frequent mentions too of parties 'on shore brewing'. Undoubtedly Bass accompanied some of these groups, examining the seaweed-hung rock pools and exploring the edge of the deep northern forest, a vast timberland of fir and spruce, birch trees and hardwood shrubs, something very different for a young man raised in the English fenlands.

With Burin Inlet as her base, the *Shark* took up a position off the Canadian coast at approximately 44° to 45° north latitude and 53° to 54° east longitude, straddling a sea lane regularly used by ships catching the northeastward-flowing currents on the way to Europe. On the sighting of a strange sail, excitement rose. Here was the prospect of capturing a French prize. The sloop laid on all possible sail and gave chase amid the sharp rattle of drums as the marines beat to quarters, and a cacophony of shouts and shrilling whistles erupted as seamen pounded across the decks and scurried into the rigging. Bass would have watched, but as the sloop approached her quarry, he went below to lay out his instruments and clear the top of a large chest for casualties. The *Shark*, however, met only a series of neutral ships, mostly American, fishing schooners headed for the Grand Banks or merchantmen on their way to British ports, and occasionally a king's ship, with all of whom greetings and news were exchanged across the water. At other times fog turned Burin Inlet and the sea outside into featureless grey and any attempt to leave the harbour had to be postponed.

The *Shark* sailed for England in August and on 3 September 1793 in strong winds made her way past the familiar landmarks of Britain's south coast and through the Needles, the three 100-foot pinnacle rocks off the Isle of Wight's westernmost point, to splash down her anchor at eleven o'clock in the morning at Spithead.

Apparently on the discharge for illness of the surgeon of HMS *Druid*, Bass was posted to that ship, and on 5 November assumed his new duties at Plymouth's Cawsand Bay anchorage. The following day, by naval time, the ship boomed a salute of 17 guns to commemorate the Gunpowder Plot of 1605. Three days later she was shifted to the adjacent Hamoaze anchorage for work 'as needful'.

The *Druid* was the largest ship on which Bass had yet served, a fifth rate 718-ton frigate, 32 guns, a vessel with the clean sleek lines and speed capability of one of the most useful types of ship in the navy. One of about 150 frigates in the Royal Navy in 1793, with numbers rising to over 220 by the early 1800s,[19] she operated equally well in consort with the battle fleet's great ships-of-the-line, as part of a smaller squadron or alone, scouting, patrolling and convoying. Her gun deck of 129 feet carried 26 twelve-pounders, with additional guns on poop and forecastle. With her guns set well above the waterline, she could heel to a considerable degree without danger, and thus carry ample sail even in heavy winds and rough seas. Prepared for action, her lightweight partitions and few furnishings would be flung into the hold, leaving her decks clear.

There were 250 men on board under the command of Captain Joseph Ellison. Here Bass had two surgeon's mates to assist him, William Halfpenny and from Dublin James Fry, a ship's dispensary, and considerable sick bay deck space to keep as clean and dry as possible. His tenure on board was without incident. The *Druid* cruised the familiar coastal waters—the English Channel to the Channel Islands, across the Celtic Sea to Cork's large landlocked harbour, and northward through St George's Channel and the Irish Sea to Dublin.

3
Voyage to Australia

L ate in 1793 the Navy Board purchased two ships, the *Reliance*, a merchant vessel of 394 tons burden, built at South Shields on Northumberland's Tyne River estuary, and the *New Brunswick*, renamed the *Supply*, 382 tons and American built of black birch. Both were intended for a voyage to Britain's colony of New South Wales on the antipodean continent then generally known as Terra Australis. On the maps of the time this immense land mass carried two names. The large eastern section was New South Wales, claimed for Britain by James Cook in 1770, with a settlement established in 1788. Early Dutch explorations along the west coast had given the great western segment the name of New Holland, but here no particular claims by any European nation had been followed up.

On 6 February 1794 a new governor was commissioned for the British colony. Captain John Hunter had commanded HMS *Sirius* in the fleet led by Captain Arthur Phillip that founded the distant colony six years earlier. Now he was returning to replace the officers of the New South Wales Corps who had been acting governors since the departure of Phillip in December 1792. The *Reliance* and the *Supply*, which were to remain on colonial service, had for some months been undergoing surveys and refitting at the Deptford and Woolwich ship-yards on the Thames, and in March 1794 were finally commissioned. Lieutenant William Kent received command of the *Supply*. Command of the *Reliance* went to Nathaniel Portlock, who as captain of the brig *Assistant* had accompanied William Bligh in the *Providence* on his second—and successful—voyage to bring young breadfruit plants from Tahiti to the West Indies.

News of the projected journey ran through naval circles, and at some point in late 1793 George Bass learned of it. Immediately he saw before him a chance to leave the tedium of routine patrols, to join a service that offered the exciting likelihood of exploration, even discovery, in a land so distant and so little known to the outside world. Bass may also have been aware of John Hunter's narrative, *An Historical Journal of the Transactions at Port Jackson and Norfolk Island*, published in 1793. Hunter was a good writer, a skilled cartographer and an accomplished artist, and his book was handsomely illustrated with engravings from his own drawings, largely of exotic Australian plants, animals and native people, as well as maps. The thought of serving under a governor versed in zoogical and botanical science, interests Bass had had little opportunity to pursue during the years of his patrols, would have been extremely attractive. And thoughts of James Cook, of voyages to virtually unknown parts of the world, and hopes for exploration long held in abeyance, would have risen in Bass's mind. Some years later he wrote from New South Wales to Sir Joseph Banks:

> I arrived here with the professed intention of exploring more of the country than any of my predecessors in the colony; so that it may be expected I have not been altogether idle. Besides enlarging its geography, I was anxious to procure new or rare specimens of subjects in natural history—a pursuit well agreeing with the bent of my inclination, but badly adapted to the little extra professional knowledge I possessed.[1]

There was no mention of his medical profession.

Bass promptly made the required submission and in March 1794 received word of his transfer. In April he was discharged from the *Druid* into HMS *Reliance*.

This exciting turn of events had to be shared with his mother, and apparently without waiting to obtain leave formally Bass headed north to Lincoln, where Sarah Bass now lived. Stopping at Boston, he learned that his mentor Patrick Francis, apothecary and surgeon and long an alderman, had died on 2 April 1794, after being elected that very morning as mayor of Boston.

Bass's visit to his mother was necessarily brief. Later, hoping for his return, she wrote:

I have yet a little reserve and will give you my favorit dishes (when I have the happiness of seeing you) Roast Beef and Plumb Puding but hope next time you come you will have leave for that was unpleasant to me, that you came for so short a time and not having proper leave . . .[2]

Further comments in this letter raise the possibility that Bass may also have visited a young woman named Sally Aked, daughter of an acquaintance of his mother, but the degree of their friendship is not clear.

Stepping onto the deck of the *Reliance* would have been like the first step into a new and exciting world. Bass was now 23, tall and physically strong, with a handsome face and, in his portrait, a calm, firm, observant expression. Underlying this, however, was the dynamism of a young man of compelling initiative and determination and exceptional intelligence, with a sharp and ironic sense of humour. He had behind him five years of experience at sea and saw himself, as he would later write to his mother, as a man of two professions: he was a surgeon and a sailor. George Bass was very much a son of the Enlightenment, a man possessed of great intellectual curiosity, keenly interested in science, but also a man of restless physical energy, an adventurer and a risk-taker. From his boyhood fascination with ships, from entering the navy as soon as his medical training was completed, to joining the *Reliance,* he seems to have been intent on making the sea a world of adventure and achievement for himself.

The *Reliance* was much like other vessels on which Bass had served. At 394 tons, she was a three-masted, square-rigged sloop 90 feet in length, and Bass, ducking the overhead beams, would have easily found his way down through the twilight of the lower decks into the fetid air and darkness of the orlop to the space allotted to the vessel's sick bay, and the small nearby cabin and the cot, canvas stretched on a wooden frame suspended from the beams, that was his. This was an accepted part of his seagoing life, and here he once again arranged his belongings. In his mind, however, there would have been an overwhelming difference between this voyage and those he had made over the past years—its destination was the great, mysterious continent of Terra Australis where, on the maps he had seen, there was a shoreline with long blank spaces and an empty interior, regions unmapped, unseen by any European explorer. Here lay a thrilling promise of discovery.

At some point George Bass and some others, never named, brought on board a little boat, later described by his friend Matthew Flinders as 'of about eight feet keel and five feet beam', which 'from its size had obtained the name of Tom Thumb'.[3] An 18th century encyclopaedia of ship design suggests that with an eight-foot keel and five-foot beam, the little craft was about nine or ten feet in overall length, probably one of many that Bass had seen moving about on the Thames.[4]

Preparations for sea were in progress on board the *Reliance*. Shipwrights and other dockyard workers came and went as cabin spaces were altered, lower deck scuppers were modified, the original sixteen guns were reduced to ten, and a new windlass was installed. Lists and requests for equipment went to the Admiralty from Portlock at Deptford and from Governor Hunter, still at his residence in Berkeley Square. For each of the two ships, *Reliance* and *Supply*, Hunter asked for a box timekeeper, that is, a chronometer, a 10-inch brass sextant, a surveying compass and an azimuth compass, a thermometer, an artificial horizon of quicksilver, various charts, the *Nautical Almanac* to the year 1800 and some quires of large drawing paper for surveying purposes. He added, 'If Captain Cook's *Voyages* cou'd be allow'd, it would be a great advantage, as they contain much information in those seas.'[5] The navigation instruments arrived, as did, in the words of the Admiralty's secretary Phillip Stephens, 'a small quantity of stationary for the sole purpose and use of such maritime surveys as you may occasionally see it necessary to employ the ships' boats upon'.[6] Gradually, most requests were met.

Nathaniel Portlock's experience with the transport of breadfruit plants under William Bligh had been noted by the eminent Sir Joseph Banks, who promptly contacted him as commander of the *Reliance* concerning a shipment of useful English plants for the colony. He then wrote to the Home Secretary, Henry Dundas, at the time in charge of colonial matters, urging that a plant cabin be erected on the *Reliance*'s quarterdeck. Hunter, apprised of the proposal, replied with much courtesy that armaments on a wartime quarterdeck would allow only a very small cabin, although an additional little structure might be built on the *Supply*.

The matter went no further, but Banks's contact with Portlock was no doubt a matter of comment in the gunroom. Perhaps encouraged by this, Bass decided to pursue his earlier desire to meet the famous naturalist. From Christopher Nevile, a friend of Banks's and a naval captain with estates in Cambridgeshire near the Lincolnshire border, he obtained a letter, dated 27 May 1794, introducing, as Nevile wrote, 'a young man of the name of Bass who is very desirous of being made known to you'. Nevile cited Bass's relationship to the Newman family who, through Joseph Newman's involvement with Boston's Witham River drainage operations, were known to Banks. Bass, he said, had served with credit as surgeon on several vessels, and was now going in that capacity to Port Jackson. 'What his motives are for such a voyage at this time I know not. I should have thought he would have stood a better chance of advancing himself during the war by remaining nearer home.'[7] Nevertheless he believed the young man might be of some service to Sir Joseph and was instructing him to call at Banks's London residence. The letter reached Bass by post, and from Deptford he travelled to London and presented himself at the imposing house at 32 Soho Square. Unfortunately, Banks had departed on his annual visit to his country estates, and Bass could only leave the letter for him. Banks would have understood much better than Nevile 'the young man's motives for such a voyage'.

At higher levels discussions centred upon the selection of officers and crew, and gradually through the summer and autumn of 1794 the men who were to make the long journey joined the *Reliance*. John Shortland, whose father had served as naval agent for the convict transports of the 1788 First Fleet, was named first lieutenant. He had been part of that earlier expedition, serving under Captain Hunter on the *Sirius*, and had spent nearly five years in the colony before returning to England in 1792.

For ship's master Hunter chose Henry Moore, an experienced and capable officer who at the time did not 'belong to any Ship' but had indicated his wish to serve on the Australian coast. He was, Hunter wrote, a young man 'perfectly adapted to that kind of Service', although he 'affected to be a great Democrat'.[8] Such a political view was not welcome in a Britain at war with a stridently revolutionary republican France, and evidently was something considered best kept at as great a distance from home as possible. Bass found no difficulty in dealing with Moore. In November the two men applied through Governor Hunter for a personal servant each, with wages to be paid by the Navy. The request was granted, and Bass hired, probably in London, a thirteen-year-old lad named William Martin. Little is known of young Martin except that he was baptised at Dartford, Kent, on 4 March 1781. His task now was to attend Bass personally and to assist in the ship's surgery. In the naval terminology of the time, he was a 'loblolly boy'. Bass had chosen well. The boy was quick and eager and would loyally share his master's fortunes for years to come. In addition Bass was assisted by a surgeon's mate, William Bayley.

In June, for reasons that remain unclear, Nathaniel Portlock decided not to continue with the voyage to New South Wales. In his place as second commander of the *Reliance*, Governor Hunter being the first, Lieutenant Henry Waterhouse came on board on 29 July. Like Shortland, Waterhouse had sailed under Hunter in 1788 and had served in New South Wales until 1791. Hunter had, in fact, initially recommended him for command of the *Reliance*. Waterhouse had also taken part, as had Hunter, in Britain's great naval victory on the Glorious First of June 1794, serving then as fifth lieutenant on HMS *Bellerophon*. He was a skilled and experienced officer, an affable and good-natured man with a ready sense of humour. He was not impressed by his new ship. He later wrote to his friend Arthur Phillip, '. . . I never sailed in such a tub'.[9]

Berths at the Woolwich and Deptford yards were in constant demand, and the *Reliance*, having completed most of her refit, sailed downstream to a mooring at Long Reach on the Thames just below Purfleet. On Sunday 18 July 1794, a clear, breezy day, the ship's company was mustered on deck for a reading of the Articles of War. On the 26th John Hunter came on board and in a brief ceremony read his commission as commander. Despite frequent showers, lighters from Woolwich were now arriving alongside with *Reliance*'s guns.[10] 'Emp'd hoisting them in', states the captain's log.[11] Barrels of beer and beef and bags of bread were lifted onto the ship, as were a town clock and the interior mechanism of a windmill for Sydney. Decks were scraped, sails loosened to dry after the rains and along the sides of the ship nettings were secured to hold the tightly rolled up hammocks of the crew by day, added protection in case of enemy gunfire. In mid-August the *Reliance* moved farther downriver to the Nore in the Thames estuary and subsequently to the offshore anchorage of the Downs. Near Gravesend a collision with a merchant ship smashed the jollyboat and caused some minor damage to the ship, but within a week the *Reliance* was steering west through the Channel for Spithead, where on 24 August she joined her consort, the *Supply*, which had sailed earlier from the Thames.

Water, wood, food and other necessities now came on board in a steady stream—thousands of hard biscuits, dimpled and impressed with the broad arrow of government ownership, from the bakeries attached to the dockyard; salt beef and pork, also prepared mainly at facilities near the dockyard, a pound per man for several days in the week; beer at a gallon a day per man; oatmeal, and 1200 pounds of portable soup, a dried concentrate of meat broth with the appearance of a 'slab of glue', for the *Reliance* and a proportionate amount for the *Supply*.[12]

Bass received two bottles of 'fever powders', two pints of 'rob of lemons', which was lemon juice and sugar boiled down to a syrup, ten pounds of cinchona bark, fifty pots of essence of spruce for brewing spruce beer, considered an antiscorbutic, and two hogsheads of molasses.

Officers and crew continued to arrive. The day after Waterhouse took charge of the *Reliance*, a young midshipman named Matthew Flinders, who had served with him on the *Bellerophon*, wrote to him formally requesting a place aboard the ship. He had, he said, 'an inclination' to go on a long journey and hoped to be rated mate. Waterhouse had evidently shared the news of his new command with his former shipmate, a short, slender, dark-haired 20 year old. Flinders, son of a Lincolnshire country surgeon and apothecary, had already voyaged to Tahiti and the West Indies with Bligh in 1791–92, and in the battle of the First of June 1794 had acquitted himself well. Profoundly influenced by the heroic achievements of James Cook, and having seen something of a strange, exotic world beyond Britain, Flinders, as he later wrote, was 'led by his passion for exploring new countries, to embrace the opportunity of going out upon a station which, of all others, presented the most ample field for his favourite pursuit'.[13] To Flinders's immense pleasure, Waterhouse accepted him as master's mate, and shortly afterwards his younger brother Samuel, not yet twelve years old, joined the ship as a 'volunteer', a position in which a boy would serve, earning £6 a year, for two years before becoming a midshipman.

The arrival of Matthew Flinders was a happy circumstance for Bass, for the two young men quickly discovered they had much in common. Flinders came from the Lincolnshire village of Donington, some eleven miles from Boston, a town he knew well. Although he had rejected his father's intention that he study medicine, Flinders would have had a fair undertanding of Bass's work. And Bass's great interest in maritime exploration would have been sparked further by Flinders's experience on distant seas. Matthew Flinders was profoundly impressed by Bass, three years his senior, well read, educated to a level considerably above most of their peers, a gregarious, charismatic man, mentally and physically striking, someone, in Flinders's words, 'that one knows to be so superior'.[14] Above all, as Flinders later wrote, he had discovered in Bass 'a man whose ardour for discovery was not to be repressed by any obstacles, nor deterred by danger'.[15] It was an ardour that matched his own, a shared love of the sea and what it could reveal. They soon developed an exciting and ambitious goal: to complete, as far as their shipboard duties would permit, the exploration of the coast of New South Wales. They would undoubtedly have studied every available map and questioned at length anyone who had been in the colony.

The eastern littoral of Terra Australis had been generally charted in 1770 by Cook and Botany Bay explored. In 1788 and 1789 the large inlets of Port Jackson and Broken Bay had also been surveyed, mainly by John Hunter, but of the coast between these points and beyond them to the north and south little detail existed. Sections Cook had passed by night and openings in the coast that he had not entered remained blank spaces or just tentative lines on the map.

In addition to officers and crew the *Reliance* was taking to New South Wales three supernumeraries: the Governor's secretary, James Williamson, Daniel Paine (or Payne), a boatbuilder for the settlement, and Bennelong, an Australian Aborigine who, together with a youthful compatriot, Yemmerrawannie, had been brought to England by Arthur

Phillip in 1792. Yemmerrawannie had died and Bennelong was now on his way home.

Bass immediately found both Paine and Bennelong interesting. The boatbuilder was, in Hunter's words, 'a Clever young man from Deptford Yard ... well recommended to me both for his Theoretical and practical knowledge',[16] and Paine himself wrote that his application for the job in New South Wales was 'Instigated by motives of Curiosity and a desire to see Foreign Climes'.[17] However, serious doubts as to the wisdom of this decision kept him ashore in Portsmouth virtually until sailing time. Paine was a non-conformist, attending Congregational and Baptist churches. This he combined with some radical political beliefs, a conviction that serious political action was needed for the betterment of English society, views which he soon found were shared by the ship's master, Henry Moore. Other people's ideas interested Bass, and in the weeks of waiting and preparation he would have listened with curiosity to opinions so divergent from the usual bland acceptance of existing conditions in Britain, which he himself probably shared.

Bass's attention to Bennelong was initially that of a surgeon. The Aborigine was a man probably in his early thirties, described as 'of good stature and stoutly made, with a bold intrepid countenance'.[18] In 1794, however, he was ill and deeply depressed by the long delays in returning to his homeland. 'Disappointment', Hunter wrote anxiously,

> has much broken his spirit, and the coldness of the weather here has so frequently laid him up that I am apprehensive his lungs are affected— that was the cause of the other's death. I do all I can to keep him up, but still am doubtful of his living.[19]

Bass applied his professional skills, but he also found the man from the antipodean land to which he himself was going of keen interest.

By 19 December 1794 the *Reliance* and the *Supply* were at Plymouth Sound, in the midst of a great confluence of vessels waiting, as was required by parliamentary act, to be convoyed by Admiral Lord Howe's battle fleet clear of the Channel and beyond the range of French naval attack. The winter was bitterly cold. The Thames froze. Icy winds swept rain and falling snow in among the ships as they rolled and pitched in the chill, grey, choppy waters of the anchorage. An initial order to make sail took the convoy out of the Sound, but off Dodman Point this move was reversed. French ships had been sighted. Ten days later a second signal for departure was made and on 15 February 1795 some 500 ships began emerging from the Sound. Under a cold, clear sky and in a chilly northeast wind, a tide of tautly expanded sails bore westward, guard ships among them and Lord Howe's great fleet in sight to the southeast. For several hours the *Reliance* lay to, her head to the wind, waiting for her place in the unending procession of ships. At noon on the 16th she received the signal to proceed and made her way into the midst of the convoy, tacking from time to time to maintain her position. At five o'clock in the afternoon the men of the *Reliance* had their last sighting of England, as the rugged cliffs of Lizard Point sank into darkness and distance. Two days later the war fleet turned back towards the French coast and, in a heavy sea with strong gales and thick rain, the great assemblage of sail began breaking up, the ships steering for their separate destinations.

Fine clear weather set in as the *Reliance* and the *Supply*, accompanied by HMS *Providence*, moved south towards the Canary Islands. The snowy peak of Tenerife's highest mountain, unusually clear of cloud, gleamed in the morning sun as in a near calm the boats were lowered and the two ships laboriously towed into Santa Cruz harbour. Bass would surely have gone ashore, viewing with interest the people and the white, limewashed houses crowding the hillsides, dazzling in the sun and fairy-like in moonlight.

On 9 April the ships crossed the Equator and, as Daniel Paine wrote, 'the accustomed Ceremony of ducking those Persons who had not crossed the Equinoctial line was performed to the no small diversion of both Officers and Men the whole of whom in the end got a compleat wetting'.[20] No doubt this included the *Reliance*'s surgeon.

Hunter now laid a course across the Atlantic to Rio de Janeiro. Almost certainly on deck as daylight swept out of the east on 4 May, Bass would have seen the memorable outline of Sugar Loaf Mountain, as the *Reliance*, with the *Providence* and the *Supply* astern, entered the extensive Bay of Guanabara and came to anchor off the northwest side of the city. It was a busy harbour, with ships arriving from Europe, others preparing for departure and ships' boats plying back and forth laden with cargoes and provisions, while water was brought by launch from an aqueduct conveniently near the landing area. Brazil was a colony of Britain's traditional ally, Portugal, but her wartime loyalties were ambiguous. Governor Hunter was received with scant courtesy and members of the ships' companies were permitted ashore only if accompanied by an officer or a soldier, depending on the visitor's rank. Fresh food, however, was plentiful, as were red wine and spirits, and the ships spent three weeks taking on supplies. In clear, breezy weather sails were unfurled to dry, and the sailmaker kept busy with repairs to the huge masses of canvas, while in anticipation of the long journey yet to come topmasts and topgallant masts were struck and the rigging completely overhauled. Hot weather had caused considerable leaking in the *Reliance*'s upper works, and three caulkers, with their mallets, caulking irons and piles of fresh oakum, were borrowed from the *Supply* and the *Providence*, all receiving additional pay, as noted by Hunter. Meantime, Bass and his assistant were tending to the wounds of Seaman Robert Taylor, who had received twelve lashes for drunkenness and striking a superior officer.

On 15 May a brief entry was made in the *Reliance*'s log: 'Held a Medical Survey upon Lieut. Nicholas Johnson [by] the surgeon, where of Opinion [was that] his State of health rendered him incapable of proceeding the voyage.'[21] Neither Bass nor Hunter provided any further details. Johnson, the ship's second lieutenant, left the ship, and Waterhouse recorded that 'A Mr. Flinders' was appointed second lieutenant in his place. Flinders had not yet passed the examination for lieutenancy, and he was therefore in a temporary acting position; six months later, having completed the necessary period of six years at sea, his rank as acting lieutenant was confirmed. Now, however, Flinders was promoted ahead of the master, Henry Moore, who presumably was also short of the necessary examination. Flinders remained Moore's senior master's mate, and while there is no record of open dissension Moore's resentment can be seen in later incidents. Except that he examined Johnson and found him unfit for the voyage, nothing is known of Bass's position in this matter.

On Sunday 24 May by naval time, the *Providence* departed. The *Reliance* and the *Supply* sailed at the beginning of June, exchanging 13-gun salutes with the Fort of Santa Cruz as they quitted the bay. Now they steered across the South Atlantic Ocean, around the Cape of Good Hope and through the Indian Ocean into the cold, squall-ridden waters south of the Australian continent. Hunter had decided against the usual stop at Cape Town. Occupation of the Netherlands by the French was expected—and had, in fact, just taken place—which could mean French seizure of the Dutch-held Cape as well.

The remainder of the voyage took fourteen weeks, in rough but generally good sailing conditions. Officers and crew settled into the steady routine of a naval ship, the work enhanced by a sense of adventure, as they sailed towards what for many was a somewhat mysterious destination. Something of this enthusiasm emanated from the presence of John Hunter, at 57 a man with a reputation for integrity and a sincere concern for the remote colony. Bluff, accessible, direct in his manner and an experienced and very capable sailor, more familiar than most with the southern land, he would have encouraged the younger men's enthusiasm for the task ahead with his own considerable interest.

During the voyage Matthew Flinders took every opportunity to improve his ability as a navigator, making observations with sextant and timekeeper and carrying out lunar altitudes. No doubt Bass applied himself to perfecting his own skills, very likely together with Flinders and perhaps at times with the captain, Henry Waterhouse, who was becoming a particular friend.

Bass's care of Bennelong opened an unexpected opportunity. The Aborigine was improving steadily as the weather warmed and the ship drew closer to his homeland. On a vessel whose company was mainly young and healthy, Bass had days with little to do, and he set about learning the native language of Port Jackson from his patient. In this he was somewhat surprisingly joined by Daniel Paine, who as a passenger had no duties on board. The threesome would have passed many entertaining hours as the Englishmen struggled with the intricacies of a very different language, and gradually Bennelong regained his natural exuberance and considerable energy.

On 6 September 1795 in light winds and haze, the Australian land mass was sighted. Under a clear evening sky on the 8th the two ships sailed between Port Jackson's steep-sided headlands to enter the magnificent bay and, as the log records, 'bore up the Harbour of Port Jackson at 8 came too in 8 fathoms in Sydney Cove'.[22] In the darkness Bass saw the bare outlines of the settlement, a few small gleams of light, the wooded ridges on either side against a starry southern sky, and the shadowy shapes and lantern lights of a few other ships in the harbour.

At daybreak the settlement came into view—rows of cottages on slopes along the curve of the cove, dirt tracks leading past some low brick buildings, and on a rise the governor's residence, a two-storey, six-room stone and brick house. There were patches of cleared land scattered with tree stumps, small gardens, a few stands of tall, spare-looking trees. A short pier extended into the water below the governor's house and another from the rocky western shore. Behind a large mud flat a shallow stream crossed by a log bridge emptied into the cove. At seven o'clock the storeship *Endeavour* boomed a salute, which was returned from the *Reliance*.

At one o'clock on 11 September, 12 September by naval time, as heavy rain clouds lifted, the Governor formally took office. The population gathered behind a semicircle of troops, the king's commission was read by the judge-advocate, David Collins, and Hunter spoke on his expectations of everyone's good conduct and loyal support of the government. He was then sworn into office, the *Providence* and the *Reliance* thundered 15-gun salutes, and the crowd dispersed. Some, having been kept at a distance, did not hear what was said.

John Hunter's commission from George III created him Captain-General and Governor-in-Chief

> over our territory called New South Wales, extending from the northern cape or extremity of the coast called Cape York, in the latitude of ten degrees thirty-seven minutes south, to the southern extremity of the said territory of New South Wales, or south cape, in the latitude of forty-three degrees thirty-nine minutes south, and all of the country inland to the westward as far as the one hundred and thirty-fifth degree of east longitude ... including all the islands adjacent in the Pacific Ocean.[23]

It was an immense area, incorporating nearly half of the entire continent together with unspecified islands to the east. In reality, Hunter's effective authority extended only some thirteen miles west along a rough dirt road to the smaller communities of Parramatta and Toongabbie, and on the coast some sixteen miles northward to Broken

Bay and about five miles southward to Botany Bay. The British population of New South Wales was 3211,[24] with an additional 887 (in 1796) on Norfolk Island.[25]

It was a population that suffered from disease, rampant crime, near-starvation and a desperate lack of almost every kind of practical equipment. Inevitably the rate of crime reflected the dominant element of the population, condemned criminals. Yet theft, not violent crime, constituted the highest proportion of offences in the colony, as it had the misdeeds for which the convicted had been transported, and records of the colony's criminal court from 1800 to 1806 show that one-third of those brought before it were acquitted.[26] Crime received due attention in the records of the time, yet there were also the beginnings of some solid social and economic progress, of agrarian and mercantile activity overlapping the strictures of an administrative structure designed half a world away for the control of a penal population.

Distance from Europe meant months of sailing subject to the vagaries of the sea before a governor's requests for advice or assistance reached the Home Office, and several months again for a response to arrive, often from men in comfortable London offices who had only a very partial comprehension of conditions and circumstances in a small, faraway and very unusual community. Distance often meant periods of outright want before supplies of any kind could arrive. While the colony's fields of wheat, maize and barley gradually increased, its population, augmented by a steady influx of convicts and a few free settlers, grew much more quickly. As well, the extremes of weather conditions in a climatic pattern that was not fully understood could wipe out an entire harvest. There were young herds of cattle and sheep, but slaughtering these animals meant beginning again, with expensively imported livestock. Salt meat, brought by provision ships from England, was the colony's dietary mainstay.

Hunter was immediately alarmed by the shortages. On the day that he assumed governorship, he wrote to the Secretary of State for the Home Office, William Henry Cavendish Bentinck, Duke of Portland. There was 'scarsely a pound of salt provision in store . . . We are also destitute of every kind of tool used in agriculture, as well as such as are necessary for carpenters and other artisans'.[27] On 21 December, three months after his arrival and in the middle of the wheat harvest, Hunter wrote again: 'our difficulties, for want of the necessary implements for this kind of labour, are considerable . . . we have not now an article of slops in the colony'. He was besieged by 'continual petitions from a people nearly naked, expressive of wants which it is not in my power to relieve'.[28] There was also a serious lack of labour, both skilled and unskilled. In August 1796 Hunter would write to Portland that he was hiring soldiers and other free people to help in constructing badly needed public buildings. The colony needed a granary, a church, a courthouse and a better and larger hospital—the existing one was 'decaying fast'.[29]

Hunter was confronted by another difficulty. With the departure four years earlier of Governor Arthur Phillip, the officers of the colony's military contingent, the New South Wales Corps, had taken over the colonial administration, and in so doing had allocated numerous privileges and advantages to themselves. They had access to land and convict labour that in many instances clashed with the government control now required of Hunter. Their position as the military unit in a convict colony gave them unique access to sterling, in effect a monopoly, which provided an almost uncontested opportunity for trade, in which spirits was one important commodity. Control of the sale of spirits and of what he saw as profiteering were additional tasks facing Hunter. A conscientious man, striving to do what he saw as his duty and under pressure from London to enforce conditions that ran counter to the well-established interests of the Corps, he saw increasingly and with mounting bitterness the military as a group of men determined to undermine his authority and destroy his government.

A week after Hunter's assumption of governorship, the 800-ton storeship *Endeavour* completed her debarkation of cattle, rice and dholl from India, and under her owner-captain William Wright Bampton sailed again for the subcontinent by way of Norfolk Island and New Zealand. She had as passengers about 50 expirees, and it was discovered after she sailed that some 20 to 35 runaways, according to Captain Bampton, had also managed to 'secrete' themselves aboard her. The *Endeavour* had undergone some repairs at Sydney, but that she would never finish this journey and one day would become an attraction for George Bass no one could foresee.

4
The First Explorations

For George Bass and Matthew Flinders, arrival in Australia meant the opportunity to begin the explorations that they had planned with such enthusiasm during the long voyage from England. Cook's charts covered the general features of Australia's eastern coastline. Subsequently Botany Bay, Port Jackson and Broken Bay had been surveyed, Jervis Bay entered and Port Stephen examined but, as Flinders later wrote, 'the intermediate portions of the coast, both to the north and south, were little further known than from captain Cook's general chart; and none of the more distant openings, marked but not explored by that celebrated navigator, had been seen'.[1]

Questioning the settlement's game hunters, Bass and Flinders learned that a large navigable river had been encountered inland, which possibly debouched into Botany Bay. If this was correct, it could perhaps be the upper reaches of the George's River (now the Georges River), an estuary charted by Hunter in 1788.

The young men's excitement ran high. 'The furor of discovery', Flinders wrote, '. . . is perhaps as strong . . . as most other kinds of mania'.[2] They went to the Governor and laid before him a plan to take a boat up the Georges River. Just a few days' journey could solve an important geographical question. Hunter hesitated. As Flinders later commented, such projects as this, conceived by young men, were often looked upon as romantic notions, to be discouraged, even opposed, by more prudent friends. Further, the *Reliance* was undergoing extensive repairs to the ravages of the long journey, and there was work to be done by her second lieutenant. Nor, as Hunter pointed out, was there a boat in Sydney that could be spared. Here Bass probably stepped in. There was his little craft, the *Tom Thumb*, brought all the way from England.

Hunter and Waterhouse gave their permissions. The little boat was immediately loaded with a few essentials and the next morning, 26 October 1795, with Bass, Flinders and Bass's young servant William Martin, the *Tom Thumb* made its way through the Sydney Heads into the Pacific. There is no record of a sail, but almost certainly the boat had been fitted with oars, a mast and probably a lug sail. Very likely too, her eager company had tested her on the waters of Sydney Cove.

The *Tom Thumb* headed south, following the coast with its wooded headlands and white beaches, rounded the bluffs of Cape Banks and crossed Botany Bay to its southwest corner where shoals and indentations rimmed the outlet of the Georges River. They followed the stream's winding course some 20 miles beyond the limit of John Hunter's survey, sketching out a rough map and scribbling notes on soil and vegetation along the riverbank. Nine days after their departure from Port Jackson they were back, and presented the Governor with their report. Their journey was a useful reconnaissance for Banks Town, the riverside community Hunter established two years later. In 1795, however, the exploration of the river had raised the Governor's confidence in his two young explorers, and Bass and Flinders's own thrilling conviction that exploration was indeed their purpose. Organising their next voyage was foremost in their minds.

Their plans, however, had to wait. Flinders resumed his duties aboard the *Reliance* as her company unloaded cargo and unused provisions, worked on repairs and assisted the community with the use of her boats. Bass, with little to do, was restless. Unexpectedly, however, he found a new direction for his energies.

When cattle were landed from the ships of the First Fleet in 1788, two bulls and five cows had strayed into the bush and were not recovered. In 1795 a gathering of Aborigines in Sydney brought people from a considerable distance inland. Some of the convicts picked up from them rumours of cattle seen in the forests, and two of the prisoners, usually employed in shooting game, undertook to search for the animals. They returned to report that they had seen them. Hunter despatched the colony's principal game hunter, Henry Hacking, to verify the claim. His report was positive, and on 18 November the Governor set off from Parramatta to see for himself. With him went a small party which included Hacking, John Collins, Henry Waterhouse and George Bass. In the heat of summer, made more intense by a bush-fire, the men travelled two days on horseback in a south-southwesterly direction, crossed the Nepean River and to everyone's delight came upon a herd of over 40 cattle, grazing in pleasant and apparently fertile country. By the next day additional animals had appeared, increasing the herd to more than 60, and Hacking and two convicts approached them in an attempt to kill a calf. A furious bull turned on them and charged, and the men shot and killed it. At some 38 miles from Parramatta it was impossible to carry back more than a minor portion of the meat, and to everyone's regret the rest had to be left to the crows and the dingoes. By Hunter's subsequent order the cattle were to be left undisturbed in what was soon named Cowpastures, today's Camden, hopefully to increase to yet more substantial numbers.

Bass, apparently, had been intrigued by his surroundings—the luxuriant grass, scattered trees with little undergrowth, large ponds fringed with strange, colourful plants and crowded with ducks and black swans. His imagination was captured by this glimpse of the land beyond the settlement, and he made a number of several-day camping trips into the hills, exploring the terrain and collecting natural history specimens. These he might well have shown to his friend William Paterson, whom he evidently visited in the colonel's little house near the bridge over Sydney's rivulet, Tank Stream. Doubtless, the two men discussed Paterson's tentative explorations into lower ranges of the misty blue mountains to the west that virtually barred the Port Jackson colony from landward expansion. Quite possibly, the idea that he should penetrate, even cross those mountains now came to Bass.

For the moment, however, any such plans had to be set aside. In January 1796 the *Reliance* was ordered to Norfolk Island. She carried stores from England, relieving soldiers and Captain George Johnston of the New South Wales Corps, who was to replace the island's ailing commandant, Philip Gidley King. From the deck of the *Reliance* Bass saw for the first time the cliffs that drop down to the sea, the luxuriant rainforests beyond and the tall, symmetrical Norfolk pines that Cook had visualised as a source of naval masts and spars. The island, with two outlying islets, rises out of the Pacific Ocean 1041 miles and many days' sailing from the Australian east coast, the exposed mountaintops of an extensive submarine ridge running north from New Zealand. Perhaps Bass remembered the remarks of Joseph Gilbert, who had seen the island from Cook's *Resolution*, as the old sailor reminisced in Patrick Francis's apothecary shop.

In 1788 Governor Arthur Phillip had ordered that a subsidiary penal colony be established on the uninhabited island and Lieutenant Philip Gidley King landed on the south coast with 23 settlers. The community endured periods of serious deprivation, but by 1796 had become a reasonably successful agricultural settlement of 887 government officials and military men and their families, free settlers, convicts and expirees.[3] The village of Sydney expanded, buildings of stone gradually replacing the earlier timber shelters that fronted the island's south coast Sydney Bay. King, now Lieutenant Governor of New South Wales, was on his second tour as commandant on Norfolk Island.

Unloading and taking on fresh water and the island's limited exports occupied the *Reliance*'s company until March. In addition Governor Hunter had ordered the retrieval of as many guns as possible from the wreck of the *Sirius*, which had been his command when it ran onto the reef outside the Norfolk settlement in 1790.

Bass, meanwhile, met Thomas Jamison, an assistant surgeon and the island's only medical officer. Jamison had come to New South Wales with the First Fleet as surgeon's mate in the *Sirius*, and with the settlement of Norfolk had been assigned to duty there. Now 51, he was a conscientious medical man who had efficiently reduced the number of deaths from dysentery on the island and later, with two other surgeons, would carry out the colony's first successful vaccination of children against smallpox.[4] From Norfolk Island he wrote letters of bitter complaint regarding the lack of adequate medicines, medical equipment and assistance. He was also angered by bureaucratic confusion that at the time had deprived him of a step in seniority and commensurate pay. Jamison, however, was actively and successfully involved in trade, dealing in wheat, pork and later sandalwood, eventually becoming part owner of a ship. That he dominated the economy of Norfolk Island and had notable dealings in Port Jackson can be seen in the amounts of money he later entrusted to George Bass.

Bass and Jamison had lengthy conversations, and George found Jamison's business ventures of considerable interest. That a convict colony would allow the building of a fortune was an unexpected revelation. Clearly there were means of acquiring substantial wealth even while pursuing one's duty. In a community loosened to a large extent by distance and circumstance from the rooted traditions of Europe, economic success had begun to blur the lines of division between the colony's social groups, the military, the administration and former convicts. To Bass's quick, enquiring mind this was indeed a matter to be investigated further. The *Reliance*, however, was ready for departure and sailed again, with Captain Johnston, who had fallen sick, still on board. Late in the evening of 5 March 1796 the ship passed the gleam of the signal fire burning in its iron basket on Sydney's South Head, and sailed into Port Jackson.

George Bass and Matthew Flinders immediately took up their plans for further exploration, for which they duly received official permission. Their concern now was apparently for a boat slightly larger than the *Tom Thumb*, and it seems that they spoke to Daniel Paine, the colony's shipbuilder. Paine, with whom Bass had spent time on board the *Reliance*, had moved into town after a short stay on a farm, and now occupied a small brick house of two rooms and a kitchen with two additional rooms of wattle and thatch for the pair of servants allotted to him.

Perhaps it was Paine who suggested a suitable boat, probably one constructed at Sydney's boatyard on the eastern side of the cove and apparently under his immediate supervision. This attention would have been due, as he remarked in his journal, to the 'incapacity of the Workmen to proceed in most Works except they were closely attended to'.[5] The size of the boat has been much disputed, some maintaining that it must have been considerably larger than the *Tom Thumb*, for during the subsequent journey there were at one time seven people in it. This did not, however, occur at sea, but on a shallow river. More definitively, Paine's journal noted, 'Two gentlemen of the Reliance Lieutenant Flinders and Mr Bass Surgeon coasted about ninety miles and in returning were very near being lost the Boat not being above twelve feet long . . .'[6] It was fitted with mast and sail and a stone for an anchor, and in appreciation of their first little craft—of which there is no further word—Flinders and Bass named her the *Tom Thumb*. Governor Hunter was much opposed to the private ownership of boats, in which convicts had been known to escape, and the second *Tom Thumb* was probably government owned, perhaps intended for the *Reliance*. Whatever the circumstances, the little craft was made available to Bass and Flinders.

At dusk on 24 March 1796 the second *Tom Thumb* was eased away from the dark hull of the *Reliance* and with Bass, Flinders and young Martin on board, headed down the harbour. She carried food for ten days, two muskets with ammunition, two pocket compasses, a watch and, evidently, a pair of scissors. The expedition's goal was to locate the mouth of a river seen inland by Henry Hacking and believed to exit somewhere a little south of Botany Bay.

The three young explorers slept that night on a rock at Shark's Bay, two miles from the entrance to Port Jackson, and at three in the morning, with the stars still bright overhead and the wind from the west-southwest, they pulled out from between the heads and steered south. The wind died at daybreak and for some hours they rowed in the hot sun, watching for coastal landmarks mapped by Cook or observed from the *Reliance*. They found that their water supply, mistakenly put into a wine barica, was undrinkable, and for moisture consumed one of their five watermelons. By mid-afternoon they realised that a rise to the west was Cook's Hat Hill, today's Mount Kembla, and that a strong current had carried them eighteen or twenty miles beyond their destination. They attempted to haul to the north, but a freshening wind and breaking seas threatened to swamp the boat. At sunset the wind stilled. In gathering darkness they pulled for shore, only to find the booming, moonlit surf too high to risk. They dropped their stone anchor, shared a 'miserable supper', and for the night crowded at best they could into the bottom of the *Tom Thumb*.

The day broke clear and still. Lower land to the south seemed to offer a better opportunity for landing, and in dire need of fresh water but also curious, they continued southward. Seeing quieter water and a sand beach inside a reef, they let go their stone anchor and veered in to the edge of the breakers. Bass threw the barica into the water, dived in after it, and swam to shore. Flinders began hauling on the anchor rope to draw the boat away from the surf, but the stone lifted and a rising wall of water hurled the little craft onto the beach. Frantic to save the boat, the three rushed her farther up on the sand. The *Tom*

Thumb was almost full of water. As swiftly as they could, they scooped up the soaking muskets, ammunition, provisions and clothes, and baled the boat dry. Rumour had it that the natives south of Botany Bay were cannibals, and columns of smoke could be seen not three miles away. With their most perishable gear thrown in, they launched the boat and, picking their moment, Flinders and Martin rowed her outside the breakers, while Bass stripped and began swimming back and forth between beach and boat, rafting their remaining possessions on the oars and mast. By mid-afternoon they were again under sail.

Their position, however, was unenviable. The muskets were full of sand, powder, watch and compasses were wet, their food supplies down to some pieces of salt meat, a little rice and sago and a few potatoes. They were some 40 miles south of Port Jackson—three miles north of modern Wollongong—in a north-northeasterly breeze. Bass, who had spent nearly five hours naked in the sun and water, was painfully sunburned.

Towards sunset they reached today's Five Islands, searching among the small rocky outcrops for a place to land. Breaking surf on every side made this impossible, and they returned to a position nearer the mainland, anchored, made what meal they could and spent another wet, cramped and chilly night in the boat.

As dawnlight streamed across the sea, they were roused by a voice calling out in the native language of Port Jackson. Two Aborigines, unarmed except for fishing spears, stood on the beach, offering fish and fresh water. Warily the young explorers rowed in closer and received a little water and two fish in exchange for a few potatoes and two handkerchiefs. The two men were natives of the Broken Bay and Botany Bay areas, they said, but had acquired the Port Jackson language. Very quickly, however, several other men appeared and, with their muskets useless, the *Tom Thumb*'s company retreated and pulled around a point to land at a shallow cove, where the surf had flattened. They built a fire, cooked a meal, and started drying their clothes.

Their two Aboriginal acquaintances reappeared. Neither Bass nor Flinders describes how it came about, but in an evidently friendly encounter the two natives had their hair cut and their beards snipped off. And as it was hardly possible to consider returning to Port Jackson without a supply of fresh water, the Englishmen accepted the others' offer to guide them to a river. With the two additional people in the boat, and a stiff northerly breeze behind them, they sped south, Flinders and Bass much amused by a promise that at the river two white women now living with the Aborigines would be brought to them, together with numerous black women and quantities of fish and ducks.

About noon they reached a small stream as it emerged through the beach from an inland lagoon. With much difficulty they steered the *Tom Thumb* through the surf and rowed about a mile upstream against a strong but shallow flow. Their guides, suddenly joined by eight or ten strangers, walked knee-deep in the water abreast of the boat, which from time to time bumped on the riverbed. Whether they could get the boat out again became a serious concern.

Alarmingly, there were now almost twenty armed men around them, with more arriving. With the explorers' guns still full of sand, it seemed imperative to leave the place as quickly as they could get water, and put their boat and weapons in order. They landed. For fresh water, they were told, they would have to continue up to the lagoon, but when they refused, a source was found just yards away. 'This', as Flinders wrote later, 'made us suspect, that they had a wish, if not an intention, of detaining us . . .'.[7] He spread their powder to dry in the sun, while Bass persuaded some of the men to help him mend an oar.

In the meantime, the two men with trimmed hair and beards had become a centre of attention and were urging their fellows to have the barbering done as well. Flinders quickly obliged with this helpful distraction. The sharp-edged instrument snipping so close to their noses thoroughly alarmed the more timid, but despite some desperate looks, eleven or twelve heads and the chins of those old enough to be bearded were eventually trimmed, while Bass rapidly gathered the dried powder, filled and stowed the water cask and prepared the boat for departure. Now, pointing towards the lagoon, the Aborigines were insisting that they continue inland. Their two original guides were the most vehement, and their promise of women and food now suggested that they had even then meant to hold their visitors. Saying that they would simply move the boat for the night to a green bank closer to the river mouth, the Englishmen shoved off, whereupon four of the

Aborigines jumped into the boat while the others ran through the water alongside, dragging the boat, shouting and singing. Diplomatically, the *Tom Thumb*'s company joined in the clamour. It was, however, 'far from being pleasant', as Flinders wrote.[8]

On reaching the green bank the Aborigines in the boat got out, but others held on to the little craft until with a show of anger Bass and Flinders managed to pull away and, while the natives hesitated, set off downstream as swiftly as possible. At the river entrance both wind and surf were high, and they realised they could not possibly get out. They anchored just inside the breakers in fairly deep water, not fifteen yards from the shore. The Aborigines watched them, one of their original guides calling that they should land and go up to the lagoon. At sunset a second group arrived, and Flinders, with a gun now cleaned, fired a shot. The group stopped, then walked away, presently followed by the rest. Only one of the Botany Bay men remained, but finally he too left.

By ten o'clock the moon had risen, and wind and water had stilled. The shadowy shore was deserted. Bass and Flinders got upon their oars and quietly slipped out of the river entrance. About one in the morning they reached the offshore islets of the day before, where they anchored and again spent the night. On his charts Flinders later named the stream they had visited Canoe Rivulet and the inland lagoon, now Lake Illawarra, Tom Thumb's Lagoon. The group of islets became Martin's Isles. Discussing their escape, they speculated that Bass's old red waistcoat had been taken for a soldier's uniform, which had intimidated somewhat their would-be captors.

The morning was fine with a light breeze coming off the land. They steered north, rowing laboriously when the breeze freshened against them, and in the early afternoon reached a small beach under some cliffs, where they hauled up the boat, eventually found water and cooked their food. That night they slept on the soft sand, stretching out as if on down, as Flinders wrote, a relief even to Bass with his severely blistered back.

Breakfast was a substantial meal and they happily prepared to leave. They noticed but did not give much attention to what seemed to be a number of black, slate-like lumps of stone scattered under the cliff. By seven o'clock they were pulling northward on a calm sea. By noon, however, a strong wind was sweeping down from the north.

Unable to make headway, they anchored near a high, projecting headland, where Martin swam ashore and found a small stream. Towards evening a light southerly breeze arose. The *Tom Thumb* headed north, moving along the line of cliffs.

As darkness fell, ponderous black clouds filled the sky, with lightning ripping through on every side and thunder crashing above the sound of the sea. They pulled the *Tom Thumb* into a curve in the cliff. At ten o'clock the wind exploded into gale force, and it was obvious that they could not remain where they were. The moon had not yet risen, and in utter darkness they put the boat before the wind, black seas and ghostly white crests rising and tumbling about them, and the pounding of the surf against the cliffs terrifyingly near. Flinders steered with an oar. Bass 'kept the sheet of the sail in his hand, drawing in a few inches occasionally when he saw a particularly heavy sea following . . . a single wrong movement, or a moment's inattention would have sent us to the bottom. The task of the boy was to bale . . .'.[9]

For almost an hour they fought the sea, soon realising that they could not survive in the mounting turbulence. Then a pale, moving line of surf appeared without the looming shadow of cliffs behind it. 'It was necessary to determine, on the instant, what was to be done, for our bark could not live ten minutes longer.'[10]

They neared the edge of the breakers, 'brought the boats head to the sea,—had the mast and sail down in a trice, and got upon our oars'.[11] Pulling hard as each wave lifted and burst, they were catapulted into the lee of the reef and within minutes found themselves rocking in smooth water. A white blur ahead alarmed them but materialised into a sandy beach; 'we thought Providential Cove a well-adapted name for this place', Flinders wrote.[12] They were about 22 miles south of Port Jackson at today's Wattamolla.

At daybreak they landed, found water and investigated the sandy, barren shore. They saw no one, despite many signs of people having been there. By nine o'clock a light southerly wind was carrying the *Tom Thumb* north, and before noon they entered the sprawling waterways of Port Hacking, their original destination.

The explorers camped on the north shore, dried out their possessions, cooked a solid meal, and in the evening amused themselves by fishing from the boat. They caught no fish, which they attributed to the numerous sharks that swam around them, bold enough even to come to the surface, eyeing them voraciously, as Flinders remarked.

The next day they explored Port Hacking further, concluding that except in a few places, shoals made the waters unsuitable for shipping. Two Aborigines came onto the beach. They were friendly and although their language differed from that of Port Jackson, the two parties managed a brief exchange.

The next day Bass and Flinders sounded the entrance to Port Hacking and on a fine breeze headed north, arriving alongside the *Reliance* that evening.

Governor Hunter was pleased with their report and the sketch survey they presented. Bass and Flinders had their own feelings of satisfaction. Beyond the excitement of danger and discovery, they knew they had performed well in handling critical situations at sea and ashore, and for Flinders it had been an opportunity to test his ability in cartography. Despite the errors almost inevitable with the use of a pocket compass and observations scribbled out during their brief times ashore, he produced helpful maps of an area never before charted. To Bass the voyage would have been an exhilarating adventure in which he had proven his seamanship in perilously heavy weather and his ability, too, to deal with native people in their own circumstances. These accomplishments would have given him additional reasons for confidence as he contemplated new endeavours.

In August 1796 Hunter wrote to Evan Nepean, Principal Secretary for Marine Affairs, on the condition of the *Reliance* and the *Supply*:

> We have given both of them very considerable repairs since they have been here ... The Reliance wanted strength, which we have endeavoured to give her as well as is in our power, but she is so extremely weak in her whole frame, that it is, in our situation, a difficult matter to do what may be necessary.[13]

Flinders resumed duty on board the *Reliance*. Bass, however, found a new challenge. West of Sydney rose the ranges, now known as the Blue Mountains, that effectively blocked the spread of settlement. Despite several attempted penetrations since 1789, no one knew what lay on the other side. Speculations ran from desert to an inland sea or a great water channel that divided the continent in two. Most hopefully there would be fertile, well-watered land, capable of producing food for a growing population so far confined to the relatively poor soil of the coastal strip. The mystery of what lay under that inland sky fired George Bass's imagination. Once again his enthusiasm for change and adventure overran the bounds of his medical profession.

In mid-1796 Bass found time and opportunity for an assault on the distant blue ridges. He designed and had made scaling irons for his feet and hooks for his hands and assembled great lengths of rope. In June, with provisions for about a fortnight, he set off with two companions to attempt a crossing.

Bass's route is not easily determined, for the recorded evidence is brief and early sketch maps of the hinterland locate differently some of the places mentioned. One writer plotted his route into the ranges through Parramatta and Prospect Hill to the Hawkesbury and Grose Rivers.[14] This was possibly suggested by a remark in Matthew Flinders's *A Voyage to Terra Australis*, which implied that Bass discovered the Grose River on 'one' of his excursions—an error, as the Grose had been known to the colonists for some years and was explored and named in 1793 by Paterson.[15]

Other scholars have based their tracing of Bass's route on Grimes and Flinders's 1799 map, 'A Topographical Plan of the Settlements of New South Wales', and plot a more likely route running some 28 miles westward from a hill recorded as Mount Hunter, west of the Cowpastures and south of modern Camden. There is uncertainty here too, however, as only a few years later Mount Hunter was shown as a hill two and a half miles to the northwest, its present location.[16]

Wherever the first part of his trek, Bass was soon among the tangled crags and gorges of the mountain range. Ravines twisted and turned and ended in sheer faces of rock. Rough and stony ridges suddenly plummeted into chasms. Some years later the French naturalist François Péron met Bass and recorded what he heard in Sydney of this adventure. Bass, he wrote,

> scaled the sheer cliff faces of terrifying mountains. His path being blocked numerous times by a precipice, he would have himself lowered with ropes to the very bottom of the abyss. Such dedication was in vain; and after a fortnight of toil and unprecedented peril Mr Bass

returned to Sydney to confirm, by his own failure, what everyone already knew about the impossibility of crossing those extraordinary ramparts. Bass discovered before him, at a distance of between 40 and 50 miles, a second chain of mountains whose elevation was greater than all those he had crossed . . .

Péron continued:

> . . . they soon found themselves suffering the torment of the most horrendous thirst. This intrepid traveller [Bass] said to me: 'If sometimes we encountered some moist earth, or even some residue of mud in the spaces between rocks, then we would place a handkerchief on the surface of the material and we would suck it vigorously to extract the little moisture that was in it'.[17]

Evidently the men had forced their way up rugged sandstone heights from where they looked west to another spine of peaks. After fifteen days, hungry and desperate with thirst, they turned back. Bass brought with him some specimens of an unusual wood and reports on the location of good agricultural soil. George Caley, the contemporary explorer and botanical collector, said later that the ranges could be breached, although at 'great hazard'. Subsequent attempts to cross the mountains also failed, and on 31 December 1802 Governor Philip Gidley King wrote, 'this formidable barrier is impassable for man'.[18] Flinders agreed: 'the mountains were impassable'.[19] In 1804 Caley's own attempt also failed.

In 1813, however, a severe drought forced a search for fresh pastures for the colony's livestock, and well-organised, properly supported expeditions led by Gregory Blaxland and Lieutenant William Lawson, and subsequently George Evans, finally crossed the mountains into the plains below.

At various times Bass apparently made lesser trips into the hill country west of the settlements. A cairn of stones attributed to Bass was reported in 1805 by a group travelling west from the junction of the Grose and Hawkesbury Rivers, and a later reference by Bass to the appearance of the Grose River suggests that he saw some part of it. Another cairn was found in 1813 near present-day Linden, between Katoomba and Penrith, by Blaxland, supposedly erected by Bass to mark the extent of his exploration.[20] Energetic, enterprising and inquisitive, he very likely filled in some of the weeks while the *Reliance* was refitted with excursions of his own, but left no sure record of where he went. Perhaps the adventure itself was sufficient—a written account was unimportant.

5

Medical Practice and Political Views—Sydney 1795–1797

On 16 October 1795, just over a month after the governor's arrival, Sydney's acting principal surgeon, William Balmain, wrote to Hunter with yet another of the colony's problems. He described the 'distressed state of these settlements for the want of a due proportion of medical assistance'. Medically, he wrote, Sydney was served by an assistant surgeon and himself. There was one assistant surgeon at Norfolk Island and one at Parramatta; at the Hawkesbury settlement, 'the business is entrusted to a convict who has not much professional skill', John Francis Molloy, who had come out on the transport *Pitt* in 1792. Balmain asked that if any medical officers could be temporarily spared from either of His Majesty's ships, they 'be sent on shore for the purpose of doing duty at the hospital'.[1]

The health of the colony was adversely affected by numerous factors. Poor nutrition, exacerbated in many instances by heavy alcohol consumption, was prevalent, lowering the resistance of the population to illness. A recurring tide of sick and similarly undernourished arrivals from Britain spread further disease and taxed the colony's limited medical capacity. The inability of the ill to work placed an increased burden upon those who could, adding to the difficulties that frequently created shortfalls in food production, resulting again in malnutrition.

Obviously Hunter issued the necessary orders, and George Bass responded. The *Reliance* was at anchor and her complement, apparently in reasonable health, could be left in the evidently capable hands of her surgeon's mate, William Bayley. Work at the hospital may have been a welcome change after many months with patients in the mal-odorous, ill-lit confines of the ship's sick bay. Landing at the town's commercial wharf on the cove's western shore, Bass would have found himself before the long, low buildings that housed Sydney's medical facilities.

Sydney's hospital had been erected by Governor Phillip, in part from a portable frame building brought out with the Second Fleet in 1790. Never meant to be other than temporary, it was now 'decaying fast'. Together with some small medical storehouses and the assistant surgeon's cottage, it stood on the narrow foreshore of the cove's rocky western promontory, with an adjacent vegetable garden and a track leading to the Tank Stream, from which fresh water for the hospital was carried in pails or in casks hauled on sledges.

In the hospital Bass would have found the expected sick—male and female convicts and free settlers, soldiers, the seriously ill off the ships, and the usual range of illness, scurvy, dysentery, fevers, consumption, venereal disease, broken bones and other injuries, including the flayed backs that were the result of flagellation (one of a surgeon's duties was to be present at public floggings) and ailments which Bass could only tentatively identify. In the course of the following year his friend Matthew Flinders suffered an attack of what later appeared to be a recurring kidney problem. Presumably Bass administered what medi-cation he could and, virtually unidentified, the ailment passed. It was the first appearance of the affliction that some eighteen years later would take Flinders's life.

Despite his other interests, Bass maintained his medical skills and sought to broaden his knowledge. He acquired Thomas Beddoes's newly published *Observations on the Nature and Cure of Calculus, Sea Scurvy, Consumption, Catarrh, and Fever* (1793), and later managed to secure at least parts of *Medica Nautica: An Essay on the Diseases of Seamen* by Thomas Trotter, as well as his *Observations on Scurvy* (1792). Bass's ability as a surgeon was evidently respected. In 1801, although at the time officially on sick leave from the navy, he was asked to consult with John Harris, surgeon of the New South Wales Corps, and James Thomson, then acting principal surgeon of the colony, on the treatment of the bullet wound in the shoulder suffered by William Paterson in his duel with John MacArthur.

Bass also called at the cottage of a very sick man recently arrived as a political prisoner from England. He was Joseph Gerrald (or Gerald), a 32-year-old lawyer, the author of a radical pamphlet, *A Convention the Only Means of Saving Us from Ruin*, and in 1793 a member of a conference advocating a number of drastic political reforms. Gerrald was arrested and in March 1794 tried for sedition. Condemned to fourteen years' transportation, he arrived at Port Jackson in early November 1795.

Gerrald's trial had been one of a series of trials for sedition held in Scotland in 1793–94 which had attracted widespead interest and concern. Five men, celebrated by their adherents as political reformers and viewed by the Crown as revolutionaries, were found guilty. All were sentenced to transportation to New South Wales, four for a period of fourteen years, one for seven years. In October 1794 four of the five had arrived at Port Jackson on the provision ship *Surprize*. Joseph Gerrald followed a year later.

The 1790s were a time of serious social unrest in Britain, largely generated by the great shifts in population brought about by an industrial revolution that was turning an agrarian society into a world of factory-driven cities. Farmers dispossessed of their holdings to make way for sheep pastures and the wool industry, and cities without due parliamentary representation, were among the results. War brought additional pressures—inflation, escalating taxes, food shortages, the depredations of press-gangs. There were riots. Organised groups pressed variously for political change, relating in many cases to long-standing grievances, but heightened now by the clamour of French revolutionary concepts.

Reform societies sprang up in England and Scotland, among them the Scottish Societies of the Friends of the People, which called for a general convention at Edinburgh in December 1792. One hundred and sixty delegates attended. Thomas Muir, a 27-year-old lawyer and a passionate and eloquent speaker, was elected vice-president, and William Skirving, a prosperous farmer, was chosen secretary. Present also were two representatives of London societies, Joseph Gerrald, who had spent some years practising law in America and returned to England fired by the ideals of the French Revolution, and Maurice Margarot, who had studied on the Continent and lived in France during the French insurgency. In addition there was Thomas Fyshe Palmer, a middle-aged Unitarian minister who, although English, lived in Dundee. All of these men spoke and wrote publicly, calling for such reforms as reduced taxation, universal manhood suffrage and more frequent parliamentary elections. Some individuals overtly affirmed their enthusiasm for revolutionary France; a few might have wanted the creation of an English republic. Mainly, however, they sought what today would be termed very reasonable political reforms, reforms which to a large extent came about in the several years following.

At the time, however, such concepts were considered radical and dangerous. In January 1793 Louis XVI of France was guillotined, which sent a shock of horror through the established governments of Europe. French revolutionary armies were seizing territory beyond their borders and inflammatory expansionist propaganda was spreading. By early February 1793 France and Britain were at war. In August and September Muir and Palmer were brought to trial under several counts of sedition. Following a second convention in October and November, Skirving, Margarot and Gerrald were arrested. Amid the heightened concerns of wartime and in the face of the alarming popularity of the reformers, a notoriously harsh and biased judge imposed heavy sentences on the five men who soon became known as the Scottish Martyrs. Despite parliamentary debate and several delays involving various legalities, Muir, Palmer, Skirving and Margarot sailed aboard the transport *Surprize* in May 1794. Margarot's wife accompanied him, her passage paid by the government and sleeping accommodation found for her with the emigrating family of John Boston, reputedly a revolutionary, his wife and three children. Palmer was joined by a friend and protégé, James Ellis, who travelled as a free settler. Margarot was allowed to join his wife; the others, kept apart from other convicts, shared a cabin for which they paid £40 each.

From Rio de Janeiro on 2 August the ship's captain, Patrick Campbell, sent an extraordinary letter to the Commissioners of the Navy in London. He wrote that he had learned from two convicts of a plot to seize the ship and kill the officers, the perpetrators then to flee to France, 'a most diabolical scheme laid, and very near attempted to be put in execution, and Messrs. Palmer and Skirving apparently the advisers and ringleaders of it'.[2] On arriving in Sydney, Campbell laid his case before Lieutenant-Governor Francis Grose, as did Palmer and Skirving. The extent of any investigation is not clear, and the truth or falsehood of the matter was never established. As a result, however, Margarot, who according to Campbell behaved throughout 'in a manner honourable to himself, and not only pleasing but serviceable to us [Campbell and his officers]', became anathema to the others, a bitterness never overcome.[3]

Grose had received, evidently from the Home Office, a letter to the effect that the exiles were not likely to prove troublesome, but nevertheless should be watched. Given the privileged status of political prisoners, they were each allotted a cottage and garden, government provisions and virtual freedom of movement. Skirving, Muir and Palmer became neighbours, Palmer sharing a house with James Ellis and the Boston family; Margarot and his wife lived somewhat apart. Generally quiet and law-abiding, the exiles engaged in fishing, in buying and farming additional land, in petitioning for a review of their case and, in Palmer's instance, sending home a continuous barrage of letters filled with complaint: under a different government New South Wales would be a 'wonderful country'. A John Black, living in Sydney, described him as 'litiginous and troublesome'.[4] Following his arrival in the colony as governor, Hunter was sufficiently impressed by the orderly and industrious behaviour of the prisoners to forward their petition and his own arguments for their release to the Duke of Portland. However, the reply that reached him in August 1797 stated that the colonial lawyers declined to reconsider the matter.

In November 1795 the fifth of their group, Joseph Gerrald, arrived aboard the storeship *Sovereign*. Although gravely ill, he settled into his cottage and garden. 'Here', as Governor Hunter wrote, 'he saw his friends, and was visited by the surgeon, but he was soon pronounced to be in a rapid consumption'.[5] Bass visited him daily but there was little he could do for him, and despite the loyal care also of Thomas Palmer, Gerrald died in March 1796. Three days later William Skirving died of dysentery. Surgeon Balmain, it appears, had refused to treat a seditionary.[6] Thomas Muir had by then managed an escape. In January an American vessel, the *Otter*, had put into Sydney for the sale of a small speculative cargo. In February David Collins wrote, 'On the morning of the 18th the Otter sailed for the north-west coast of

America. In her went Mr. Thomas Muir . . .'.[7] Under the guise of fishing offshore in his boat, Muir waited for the *Otter* as she left Port Jackson, and despite a misunderstanding that nearly cost him his life, he was picked up. Wild rumours surrounded Muir's escape, one being that the *Otter* had been sent by George Washington to free him, and another that her captain, Ebenezer Dorr, had been instructed to take with him as many of the 'martyrs' as wished to go. No firm evidence exists for any of this.

Even in their exile, the 'martyrs' remained strongly committed to their ideals and the aspirations for social and political reform that had brought them to the colony. These were topics discussed at length during many evening visits, gatherings that drew several other like-minded persons. One was Daniel Paine, the colony's boatbuilder, a serious, deeply religious young man whose diary shows his association with the prisoners, if only in brief notations and at times with disapproval. 'Mr. Gerrald', he wrote, '[had his days] shortened by his strong propensity to Drinking and which the general manners of this colony too much favoured . . .'.[8] Another was Henry Moore, master of the *Reliance*, who jointly with Palmer became an executor of Joseph Gerrald's will. Two other members of the gatherings would have been John Boston, a trained surgeon and apothecary and a professed Jacobin, and James Ellis. Boston was an aggressive and ambitious man, whose several commercial ventures clashed with those of the New South Wales Corps and incensed the Governor as well. The extent of Maurice Margarot's involvement with his former associates is not clear. Urbane and well travelled, he appears in his portrait in a powdered wig and with a slightly condescending smile. John Black described him as quiet and rarely seen, but his diaries show an unrelenting hatred of the British government.

Daniel Paine's residence in the colony was short; he left Sydney in November 1796. In an altercation between Paine's servant, David Lloyd, and a seaman, John Smith, Lloyd had shot and killed his adversary. At Lloyd's trial for murder before Collins, the Judge-Advocate, Paine supported his servant with enough vehemence to be himself arrested for contempt of court. Lloyd was found guilty of manslaughter and condemned to receive 600 lashes, which in Paine's words 'produced so great an Emotion in me as to cause me to Stamp my Foot' and remark that 500 of the lashes were due to prejudice against himself.[9] Further recriminations led to an impasse between Collins and Paine which forced Hunter to dismiss Paine from his position. Thomas Moore, carpenter of the transport *Britannia*, took his place as shipbuilder.

It is obvious that George Bass found these men and their revolutionary convictions of considerable interest, and he evidently attended their meetings. Palmer, writing to a friend in Scotland, referred to 'My most worthy friend Mr. Bass . . .'.[10] Bass would also have appreciated Palmer's energy and versatility, so much like his own, for in 1796 Palmer, together with Boston and Ellis, formed a trading company, Boston & Co., and by August 1797, following instructions in an encyclopaedia apparently brought from Scotland, had built a boat in order to engage in the Norfolk Island trade. Men who had achieved success in previous careers were not content merely to exist, and the colony, they discovered, was obsessive in its pursuit of wealth. These were also educated men, and perhaps influenced by aspects of the philosophy of the Scottish political economist Adam Smith, which incorporated a belief in expanding economic growth, with competition the leading principle in an economic system founded upon individual self-interest. Certainly they recognised that in the colony trade alone could produce money and, like the military, they had access to sterling for investment. They were among those now infiltrating the colony's increasingly competitive commercial community, which Bass clearly watched with interest.

It is apparent that a maturing Bass was reaching out mentally beyond the pale of his medical training, narrowed as it was by the limited knowledge of the time and the very finite scope of a naval surgeon's practice. Bass's thirst for intellectual challenge is vividly reflected in a letter he wrote to Thomas Jamison: 'It is society, the friendly clash of opinions that brings truths to light and exalts the human intellect to the highest pitch possible.' He was impatient of ignorance and lesser minds. Aside from Jamison, he had found in Norfolk Island's society 'the tiresome insipidity of semi-men'. He added, 'Europe, Europe!!!'[11]

Evidently Bass found an enjoyable 'clash of opinions' in a variety of books. A list of some 90 titles, probably from about this time, survives, a remarkable number for a man living much of his life in the close, crowded environment of small warships, subject to frequent transfers. His reading yields some indication of the breadth as well as the trend of his thought. In addition to his medical books and several volumes on natural history, he possessed the *Iliad*, works of Hesiod and of Virgil, a volume of John Dryden's *Works* and, significantly, Francis Bacon's *Essays*, Montesquieu's *The Spirit of Laws*, Matthew Hales's *The History and Analysis of the Common Law of England* and John Bruce's *First Principles of Philosophy*. These were books that drew from the achievements of Europe's scientific revolution the conviction that rational enquiry could interpret and solve the problems of society. With reason as the basis for his analysis of political institutions, Montesquieu had arrived at the idea of the separation of legislative, executive and judicial powers, thereby limiting centralised authority. The exceptional work of the earlier judge and jurist Hale was similarly notable for its rationality.

Even within the limited context of these few books, Bass emerges as a man who accepted the imperative of reason in securing political and social order, which would create prosperity and progress and bring out the potential for happiness and achievement in human nature. It was in acquiring knowledge and applying rational thinking that these goals would be reached, and Bass's mindset included these concepts.

That he read and discussed along these lines is evident, but he left no written discourse on any of it. Of his views on the handling of convicts and the transportation system itself nothing is known, although his later possession of the works of William Godwin, particularly *Political Justice*, and Cesare Beccaria's *An Essay on Crime and Punishment* suggests his interest.

Economic theories that incorporated the principles of free trade and minimal governmental interference obviously tantalised Bass's thinking. In 1798 he would write to his mother of the awakening of the colony to 'foreign and extensive speculations' and of new commercial opportunities in the East and the South Pacific islands. Even the closed Spanish settlements on the South American coast were now involved in profitable although 'still contraband trade'.[12] Later he would discuss with Jamison commercial dealings with nations geographically and economically apart from England, and eventually, it seems, would plan to defy governmental restrictions in pursuit of trade.

Exploration was an extension of these thoughts. Exploration was pursued through the rational sciences of mathematics and astronomy, and their derivatives of navigation and cartography. It sought and acquired knowledge that might be applied to the enhancement of living. Bass's own search for adventure was also a search for information which he would evaluate, and in charts and journals preserve for others' use.

What were Bass's religious beliefs? There was the conventional yet obviously warmly meant closing of 'God bless you' in letters to those important to him. To Elizabeth, his wife, he would write, 'God of the World spare thee and make thee happy & keep thee. Now thats a fine prayer you'll say. I am no Parson Bess but I promised the Parson I would love thee truly & so I ever will.'[13] Sincere, ironic, a little self-deprecating and humorous, committed, this seems to be the only comment of a religious nature that remains. Perhaps like many educated men of his time Bass regarded God as creation's rational builder, and beyond that depended upon human reason, knowledge and industry—and a measure of good fortune—for happiness and success.

Bass was, however, a gregarious individual, whose associations went well beyond Sydney's radicals and traders to include the colony's conservative core, among whom his intelligence and charismatic personality won many friendships. His friend and fellow explorer, Matthew Flinders, however, stayed well away from the martyrs' circle. His ambitions rested squarely upon the success of his naval career, which excluded any dalliance with ideas that opposed the establishment. With Flinders Bass shared a passion for the sea, for exploration and adventure and a total disregard for danger, but the younger Flinders felt very much that he was his friend's intellectual inferior. Later he would write: 'There is one circumstance that will always keep you from me; your thirst after knowledge and information will not permit you to have the necessary consideration for one, who not only cannot afford you these; but has far less stock than yourself.'[14] This suggests that the impatience, even annoyance that Bass felt with the limited intellectual and educational resources of so many around him was obvious. It echoes something of his ruthlessly critical comments to Jamison on those he met on Norfolk Island.

On his arrival in Port Jackson Bass had renewed his acquaintance with William Paterson, then a major in the New South Wales Corps, who from December 1794 had administered the colony until John Hunter's arrival. The major, a naturalist and an enthusiastic explorer, had made a series of forays into the Blue Mountains, collecting plants for Joseph Banks and probing for a way through the ranges. Although he returned to England on sick leave in 1796, the association with Bass was resumed on his return to Sydney three years later. A further dimension to the friendship was undoubtedly the warm hospitality offered to all her guests by Elizabeth Paterson, described by a friend as 'of a very benevolent and kind disposition and a very beautiful and spirited woman'.[15] Bass also maintained a close friendship with *Reliance*'s captain, Henry Waterhouse. Good natured and sociable, Waterhouse developed his own interests, which at this time included establishing a successful farm in the colony, and the pursuit of a career that he hoped would 'go on for an admiral'.[16] Political involvements or conflicting opinions within the colony did not concern him. He wrote to his father: 'I am out of all partys & scrapes, & as the song says, "I am well so I will keep".'[17] Possibly it was this cheerful neutrality that attracted Bass's confidence, for over the years George readily shared his plans and ambitions with Waterhouse, whose response was always appreciative.

In August 1796 the *Marquis Cornwallis* arrived at Sydney with the news that the Dutch settlement at the Cape of Good Hope had been occupied by British troops. For some time Governor Hunter had worried that the French would seize this important station on the long route between Britain and Australia. Now, pleased and relieved, he wrote to Under Secretary Evan Nepean:

> In consequence of that information, I avail myself of the approaching season to send the King's ships, the Reliance and the Supply, to the Cape, in order to execute that part of my instructions from his Majesty which relates to the stocking this colony with live cattle.[18]

Both ships, but particularly the *Supply*, were in exceedingly poor condition, and Hunter, detailing their areas of weakness and decay, added, 'We have given both of them very considerable repairs'. Two weeks later he reported that 'His Majesty's ships were now upon sailing for the Cape of Good Hope . . .'.[19]

On 20 September 1796 the *Supply* sailed for Norfolk Island, followed by the *Reliance*, the colonial schooner *Francis* and the chartered transport *Britannia,* which was returning to England with Judge-Advocate David Collins, the invalided William Paterson, and several others including a number of military men and their families. The four ships met at Norfolk, taking on additional water, grain and livestock. The ailing Lieutenant Governor Philip Gidley King and his wife and children joined the *Britannia.* On 25 October the ships weighed, the *Francis* returning to Sydney with King's final reports to Hunter, the other three steering into the Pacific. A few days later the *Britannia,* a better sailer, parted company, but coincidentally the ships met again in the South Atlantic. With the westerlies in their sails, the *Reliance* and the *Supply* had crossed the South Pacific and doubled Cape Horn and then, in company with the *Britannia,* reached Table Bay at the Cape of Good Hope on 16 January 1797. Fierce gales were sweeping the bay, driving ships and boats from their moorings and even onto the shore. Blowing sand swept about the row of houses that huddled at the base of the huge, steep-sided mass of Table Mountain.

As the wind abated preparations began for the journey back to Port Jackson. While the New South Wales Commissary, John Palmer, bargained with native herdsmen for cattle, the ships took on water, firewood, fresh food and quantities of baled hay. Palmer bought 70 head of young Cape cattle for Port Jackson, and with profitable resales in mind, several of the ships' officers also purchased animals. A statement in Waterhouse's handwriting lists his own purchase of '3 cows, 2 mares, 1 colt, 24 sheep, 8 wethers'. In addition he wrote, 'Mr. Bass.— 1 cow, 19 sheep'.[20] Figures differ, but according to Waterhouse the *Reliance* took on board a total of 49 head of black cattle, three mares and 107 sheep. The crowding of men and animals on deck and in the cabins was unbelievable. Waterhouse wrote, 'I believe no ship ever went to sea so much lumbered . . .'.[21] The *Supply,* although in seriously unseaworthy condition, embarked about 40 cattle and something over 40 sheep.

The Dutch commander of the Cape of Good Hope garrison, Colonel Robert Jacob Gordon, had bred a small flock of Spanish merino sheep. Apparently unable to bear the shame of surrendering to the British, Gordon had shot himself. His widow, about to return to Europe, offered the sheep for sale to Commissary Palmer. Favouring cattle, he declined, and Waterhouse and William Kent of the *Supply* each bought 26 sheep at four guineas per animal. Six others were presented to King and Paterson to be taken to England, but King sent three of his back to New South Wales. Whether Bass's 19 sheep were bought from Mrs Gordon is not recorded.

Bass and Paterson continued their friendly contact at Table Bay, and the stay at the Cape became one of unexpected pleasure for Bass. Paterson, who had previously explored and botanised in South Africa, again demonstrated his regard for the young surgeon. Bass wrote to his mother of their meeting: 'He went to England when we went to the Cape and was kind enough to introduce me there to a number of Dutch families, he had lived there as a botanist several years ago.'[22] This was an enjoyable social break and meeting the Dutch was no doubt of particular interest to Bass. In addition there was the marvel of the region's extraordinary animal life and the unique and abundant plant life that covered the sandy hills, and Paterson's extensive knowledge of both.

On parting, the two men resumed their correspondence, Paterson writing from England to encourage Bass to continue his research in natural history. He was proposing Bass as a member of the Linnean Society, which since 1783 had preserved manuscripts and collections of the great Swedish botanist, Carl Linnaeus. In 1799 Bass became a member.

The *Supply* and the *Reliance* sailed from Table Bay on 11 April 1797, steering eastward into the fierce storms that can assail the southern Indian Ocean. The ships were enveloped in what seemed like a contracting world of tumult as feeble daylight emerged from the wild blackness of the night only to be swallowed again by chaotic darkness. The *Reliance* shook and staggered under the mountainous seas exploding across her bows and the fury of the wind screeching and howling in the rigging. Sails blew out. Restraints tore and objects of all kinds were washed about the deck. Drenched, shaking with cold and exhaustion, the men crawled aloft, at times pinned motionless by the wind against the web of the rigging, at others clinging with numbed hands as they were all but torn away. There were injuries, and in the plunging dark hole of the sick bay, by the erratic light of wildly swinging lanterns, Bass steadied himself to deal with ripped flesh and broken bones. Waterhouse wrote to his father, 'We met one gale of wind, the most terrible I ever saw or heard of, expecting to go to the bottom every moment', and the animals, thrown against bulkheads and each other, 'liv'd on air part of the time—'.[23] On 26 June 1797 the *Reliance* reached Sydney. The usual 35- to 40-day voyage had taken 78 days. Incredibly, the *Supply* had struggled into Sydney Cove some five weeks earlier, the ship 'a complete mass of rotten timber',[24] condemned by an official survey as 'irreparable . . . unfit to proceed to sea'.[25] Permanently anchored, she became a guard ship.

The *Reliance*'s surviving livestock was disembarked, and several officers sold their animals at a profit. Waterhouse retained his, and for £140 purchased a farm and a substantial house. He would 'always retain some property' in the colony, he wrote to his father.[26] Eventually, however, he sold some of his merinos to the farmer and New South Wales Corps officer John Macarthur, who began a program of breeding these particular sheep. Bass's animals survived the voyage, but there appears to be no existing record of what he did with his little flock. He clearly had no interest in farming, and presumably sold his animals, perhaps to Macarthur or to the clergyman, magistrate and farmer Samuel Marsden, thus making his contribution to the founding of an industry that, with the later crossing of the Blue Mountains and the discovery of the great plains beyond, would bring economic stability and vast wealth to the young nation. The *Reliance* had brought another advantage to the colony, as the additional cattle made it possible for teams of six or eight animals to replace men in pulling wagons. The *Reliance* itself, leaking badly even as she lay virtually empty in, as Waterhouse put it, 'water as smooth as a mill-pond',[27] was surveyed and found to be in a 'weak and feeble state' with serious damage close to the keel.[28] She was careened and months of repair work begun, with Flinders tied to many related duties. Any prospect of further exploration with Bass had to be put on hold.

In mid-May a fishing crew in a 'small row-boat' was working 22 miles south of Botany Bay in the inlet named Providential Cove by Bass and Flinders, now Wattamolla, when to their amazement they saw three men frantically waving from the boulder-strewn shore.[29] They were three survivors from the merchant vessel *Sydney Cove* which, sailing from Calcutta to Port Jackson, had been struck by violent weather and in sinking condition was beached on one of the islands of the Furneaux Group off northeast Tasmania. Seventeen men set out in a longboat to seek help at Port Jackson. The boat was smashed by gales on the New South Wales coast and the men began a 400-mile trek northward. Starved, sick and at times attacked by Aborigines, they one by one died or dropped behind until just three men, barely alive, reached Wattamolla.

Governor Hunter immediately sent the colonial schooner *Francis* and the decked longboat *Eliza* to the island to take off the survivors. The *Francis* brought the ship's captain, Guy Hamilton, and some of his lascar crew safely to Sydney. The *Eliza*, also carrying crewmen, disappeared in gale-force winds on the voyage home.

One of the three survivors found at Wattamolla was young William Clarke, of the Calcutta trading establishment of Campbell, Clark and Co., who had been travelling aboard the *Sydney Cove* as a supernumerary. He related to Hunter that on a beach some twenty miles south of Botany Bay he had kept a fire going with lumps of coal fallen from the cliff face. Britain wanted minerals, so Hunter was anxious to pursue the discovery. With the *Reliance* under repair, George Bass offered to accompany Clarke to the site. To his letter of 25 June 1797 to the Duke of Portland, Hunter added a postscript:

> I have lately sent a boat to that part of the coast. The gentleman who went, Mr. Bass, surgeon of the Reliance, was fortunate in discovering the place, and has inform'd me that he found a strata of six feet deep in the face of a steep cliff, which was trac'd for eight miles . . . coal . . . was seen in various other places.[30]

Bass, writing to Paterson, was more precise:

> This vein of coal, or at least the northernmost end of it that we could see, commences about twenty miles to the southward of Botany Bay. The land there is nearly twice the height of the north head of Port Jackson, not steep cliff like it, but has here and there small slopes and lodgements on which trees and shrubs grow. The sea washes up so close to the foot of it that it is no more than barely passable without

some danger in blowing weather. About twenty feet above the surface of the sea, and within reach of your hand as you pass along, is a vein of coal about six or seven feet in thickness . . .[31]

The vein, he continued, sloped to the south until it met the sea. Behind the shoreline he traced an additional six miles or so of coal strata and believed they ran well inland. Reaching the veins would be difficult as there was no landing place within several miles other than a short stretch of sand suitable only for beaching small boats.

Bass went on with a description of the area's vegetation, of interest to both Paterson and himself, unusual cabbage trees and a fern he had not seen before. There was also a tree that he thought was so far unknown, with small branches 'covered most thickly with long sharp prickles. Well I remember them, for in the blindness of my eyes I seized one of the branches and was handsomely repaid for my hasty curiosity by a handfull of them.'[32] With the letter, Bass sent Paterson a specimen of the coal.

Bass searched as well for the two men, the *Sydney Cove*'s wounded mate and a sick carpenter, who had been unable to continue just days from rescue. He found only their bloodied bones, the mate's skull smashed. Bass returned to Sydney with three bags of coal specimens, which Hunter sent on to Sir Joseph Banks, while the site now appeared on the maps as Coalscliff.

The coal strata's location in cliffs above the sea was beyond the mining capabilities of the colony at the time, David Collins expressing the view that although the coal was of good quality 'no great advantage could ever be expected from it'.[33] By 1850, however, means had been devised to excavate and ship the mineral from these seams, and the site then developed rapidly into the immense industrial complex of Wollongong and Port Kembla. Earlier, from 1791, fishermen and escaping convicts had noticed coal deposits also in the Hunter River area, north of Port Jackson. Coal and timber were soon being extracted from the region, which in 1801 was examined by William Paterson and mapped by Ensign Francis Barallier. Three years later a settlement named New Castle was established.

In September 1797 Governor Hunter decided to make a second excursion to the Cowpastures. Bass, invited to join the party, no doubt accepted with alacrity. In the Mt Taurus area they found a herd of 67 cattle and shortly afterwards a second group of about 170 animals, the original herd apparently having split, probably as a result of competition among the bulls. Bent on exploring further, Bass and James Williamson, Sydney's acting commissary, set off from Mt Taurus to walk in as direct a line as possible to the coast, where a whaleboat was assigned to wait for them some five leagues south of Botany Bay. The ground was initially level, rising gently into green and grassy hills, and they believed they could reach the sea in one day. Making their way over the next fifteen or sixteen miles of rough and stony hill country, and across swiftly running and sometimes quite deep streams, proved more demanding than anticipated, but nonetheless they met the whaleboat without incident some ten miles south of Port Hacking. Bass gave his notes on the country traversed to Hunter, who incorporated the observations into his map of the region.

6
The Whaleboat

From Norfolk Island there arrived at about this time the news that the East India storeship *Endeavour*, which had sailed from Sydney in September 1795, had encountered a severe storm and, her seams opening in the pounding of wind and waves, had sought shelter in Facile Harbour, an inlet in Dusky Sound on New Zealand's far south-west coast, together with an accompanying brig, the *Fancy*.

Struck by a second storm, the *Endeavour* hit a rock and was hauled on shore. Two hundred and forty-four seamen, convicts and former convicts now made up a rough and disorderly community with little to eat. However, this cold, windswept and island-strewn bay had for some time attracted ships and men with its large seal population, and the *Endeavour*'s people knew that on one of its beaches there lay an unfinished vessel of about 65 tons, of local timber, begun by sealers two years before. Having found it, they completed this craft with fittings from the *Endeavour*, rigged it as a schooner and sailed with the *Fancy* for Norfolk Island with as many people on board as was safe. The excessive number of passengers and stowaways on the *Endeavour* meant that a large group remained on shore, but the carpenters among them quickly reconstructed the *Endeavour*'s longboat into a seagoing vessel and a group of castaways reached Sydney in March 1796. Thirty-five stowaways remained on the desolate South Island shore. When the American whaler *Mercury* stopped at Sydney for refitting in February 1797, Hunter asked the captain to rescue the remaining people. They were picked up in May, having survived on fish, birds and seals for over eighteen months, and landed at Norfolk Island. The wreck of the *Endeavour* remained at the Sound.

In the meantime work continued on refitting the *Reliance*. Sprung beams were secured, knees, riders and planking replaced, additional bolts placed where needed; with the shipwrights' work finished, the vessel had then to be completely caulked. Flinders and Waterhouse were fully occupied.

For Bass the excursion to Mt Taurus had been only a passing diversion. The refit of the *Reliance* was clearly going to take months, and at the hospital Balmain and his assistant were apparently in no immediate need of Bass's help. David Collins described Bass at this point as a man possessing 'a mind and body strong and vigorous . . . endowed with great good sense, ingenuity, and observation', who was thoroughly bored with 'the idle life'.[1] No other record or letter throws light on Bass's activities at this time. Did he pursue his study of the local Aboriginal tongue and on occasion speak with Bennelong, who spent time in and out of the settlement? We do not know.

Two years later, when he left Port Jackson, Bass entrusted his library to Thomas Fyshe Palmer, and it seems likely that while the *Reliance* was emptied and careened, he would have resorted to this friend for the care of his books. If he did, he probably spent some time at Palmer's cottage, for Palmer not only shared Bass's interest in the continent's unique plants and animals, but with his friends Boston and Ellis was operating a small trading company with connections on Norfolk Island. Bass became friendly with James Ellis, whom he later described to Thomas Jamison as a 'sensible, well-informed, modest and honest man'.[2] Seemingly, Bass found these men and their varied backgrounds and activities of interest.

Did Bass maintain a relationship with a woman during his three years at Port Jackson? At home in Lincolnshire he had had a friendship with the young Sally Aked, but no letters to or from her seem to exist. Liaisons with convict women were common among the young naval and military men of the colony. Waterhouse never married but in 1791 became the father of a daughter by Elizabeth Barnes (or Baines), a young woman transported for theft, who had arrived in Port Jackson with the *Lady Juliana* transport, part of the Second Fleet. Barnes died in April 1794, aged about 25, and it appears that Waterhouse, returning in September 1795 from England on the *Reliance*, then took responsibility for the child. His loving concern for 'little Maria' is obvious in his letters, and in August 1796 he sent his daughter in the care of the Patersons to his family in England. Land grant documentation relating to John Shortland, first lieutenant of the *Reliance*, refers to a son, and before his marriage Philip Gidley King lived for three years with Ann Inett, a convict woman, by whom he had two sons. No surviving document indicates any similar connection for Bass, but there could very well have been temporary relationships.

Whatever his actions in this respect, a letter he wrote several months later reveals a deep discontent with his life and his career at this time. A Table of Medical Officers' pay for 1793 indicates that Bass would have been earning approximately £5 per month, from which income tax and other deductions were made.[3] As a surgeon he enjoyed the status of a gentleman, but technically he was a warrant officer; nor could a surgeon look forward to a commissioned officer's promotions that would bring him higher rank and new commands, better pay and perhaps fame and a greater share of prize money. Despite his evident care in furthering his professional knowledge as much as he could through his books and perhaps in discussions with fellow surgeons, the routine of his work on board and at the colony's hospital held little intellectual stimulus. There was a superior grade of naval medical officer, known as physician, to oversee and coordinate the work of the ships' surgeons,[4] and a letter from his mother written in mid-1797 suggests that Bass was considering this possibility. But further training was necessary, and 'a fortune is wanting to accomplish it', his mother wrote.[5] Advancement in the Royal Navy also required patronage, and Bass, a farmer's son, had no useful connections, no influential patron. He would have been aware of the high quality of his own intelligence. He might once have thought it possible that through sheer ability he could attain such a goal, but evidently he came to recognise that with neither funds nor patronage this was unlikely. The idea of establishing a medical practice in England, suggested by his mother, Bass rejected at once. The first year or two were invariably years of penury and humiliation, he said. Nor could he submit to 'the fiddle faddle and necessary quackery' of such a practice.[6] How discerning he was of the sheer folly of some of the medical practices of his time is impossible to say.

George Bass turned instead to his enduring passions, his love of the sea and his aspirations for adventure, the chance for further exploration and the range of information it could bring. His journeys south with Flinders had been minor excursions. There remained huge distances along the coast that were unknown to the British, and what really held his imagination was the likelihood of a seaway separating New South Wales from Van Diemen's Land. This he was now determined to investigate. He went to Governor Hunter.

In 1773 Commander Tobias Furneaux in HMS *Adventure* rounded Van Diemen's Land from the south and sailed up the east coast, discovering the island group later named for him by Cook. He observed that at this point Van Diemen's Land trended to the west, and assumed it formed a deep bay. Others on board suspected a strait, but Furneaux quitted the coast and sailed for New Zealand. Sixteen years later John Hunter, on a passage from the Cape of Good Hope to Port Jackson in the *Sirius*, observed the same westward-trending coastline, and conjectured that this was a strait, not a bay. Now Hunter decided that an expedition led by Bass could provide further evidence of the facts, whatever they were. He wrote to the Duke of Portland:

> The tedious repairs which his Majesty's ship Reliance necessarily required before she could be put in a condition for going again to sea hav'g given an opportunity to Mr. George Bass, her surgeon, a young man of well-informed mind and an active disposition, to offer himself to be employed in any way in which he could contribute to the benefit of the public service, I enquired of him in what way he was desirous of exerting himself . . .[7]

Bass asked for the use of a good boat, a crew of six volunteers from the King's ships and permission to examine the coast southward. Hunter was much impressed by this 'young man of much ability in various ways out of the line of his profession', as he wrote to Secretary Evan Nepean, and 'accordingly furnished him with an excellent whaleboat, well fitted, victualled, and manned to his wish . . .'. Bass was to investigate the southward coast 'as far as he could with safety and convenience go'.[8]

The possibility that the strait had previously been at least approached from the west has been raised by a later reference by Governor Philip Gidley King to a Captain William Reid of the sealing schooner *Martha*, but just how far Reid sailed is not known. Years later the *Naval Chronicle* mentioned that in January 1795 the Madras

Courier reported that the ships *Duke of Clarence* and *Duchess* had passed through the strait. The description of the strait they gave was sufficiently absurd to have the *Chronicle* declare the assertions to be obviousy false.

Bass's locally built whaleboat was about 28½ feet long.[9] He received food for six weeks and a crew of six naval seamen, four of them, apparently, from the *Reliance*. The fact that they all volunteered shows their liking for Surgeon Bass, their confidence in him as a leader and a seaman. Perhaps there was also the prospect of doing something more interesting than ship maintenance at Sydney Cove. Crewing a boat into unknown waters was not an issue; they had done this before. Among the men was Able Seaman John Thistle from Lynn in Norfolk, who had joined the *Reliance* in 1794 at age 22. An adventurous and exceptionally capable sailor, he would later join Flinders's exploration voyages and perish in the course of those investigations. None of the other whaleboat crew can be identified. Bass's servant William Martin would now have been a sturdy sixteen year old, but his presence on the expedition is nowhere noted.

At six o'clock in the evening of 3 December 1797, as Bass recorded, 'we rowed out between the Heads, and finding the wind at N.E. by E. set the sails and stood to the southward'.[10] But the night sky filled with storm clouds, and with the boat's equipment not yet properly organised they sailed into the shelter of Little Bay, some fifteen miles from Port Jackson, and dropped anchor at nine o'clock. As he would throughout his journal, Bass recorded his dates by naval time.

As sunrise began tinting a grey dawn sky, they set sail in a light northerly breeze. By eight o'clock, however, the wind had veered to west-southwest and was blowing fiercely, and 'we therefore took in the sails and pulled in under the cliffs', hoping to reach Wattamolla.[11] But gaining force, the wind swung more and more to the south, and Bass steered into Port Hacking. Weather was not going to favour this voyage, and the pattern of sailing when conditions were to their advantage, regardless of the time of day or night, was set early. Rowing was resorted to in adverse winds. When shelter had to be found, it was an opportunity to rest, prepare food and explore their surroundings.

The following day, in erratic flurries of wind, they reached the protected inlet of Wattamolla. They sailed again the following afternoon, at sunset passing the five small rocky islands that the *Tom Thumb*'s adventurers had approached. The night was calm and with morning a light stir of wind from the east allowed them to maintain their course. By afternoon a freshening breeze from the south frustrated their progress, so they steered into a bight and landed.

Bass set off on foot to explore the surrounding country. Along the shore he was intrigued to find what appeared to him to be 'evident marks of volcanic fire', basaltic rock in various forms.[12] Geology at the end of the 18th century was a very young science, the study and classification of rock strata going back no more than 75 years. Volcanic activity along the New South Wales coast was of special interest to both Flinders and Bass, but their knowledge was minimal. They were entirely unaware of the great age, tens of millions of years, of such features as they examined.

On a point of land Bass found a very large, roughly circular indentation in the earth where, as he wrote, the ground

> seemed to have given way; it was now a green slope. Towards the centre was a ragged hole of about 25 or 30 feet in diameter, and on one side of it the sea washed in through a subterraneous passage with a most tremendous noise. The pieces of rock that lay scattered about had all been burnt, but some were in a state of scoria.[13]

The formation is, in fact, a blowhole, where the ocean's wave action has eroded a tunnel into the seaside cliff and a section of the roof of the passage has fallen in. With strong southeasterly swells, the sea spurts up through the hole in a cloud of spray. This blowhole at Kiama Point, although reportedly less forceful than in past years, remains a tourist attraction.

In the afternoon of the next day they entered an inlet where they sighted a rocky point that seemed to offer shelter for the night. Rowing towards it, they came upon the narrow mouth of a small river running through low, swampy ground, its course repeatedly obstructed by shoals of mud and sand. Bass named the area Shoals Haven, for 'it deserves no better name'. Farther inland, however, they found a magnificent expanse of open country, 'many thousands of acres' with scattered groves of trees. Bass assumed the ridges to the west to be an extension of the Blue Mountains behind Port Jackson; they are, however, the interlaced heights of other ranges.

The men camped in the area for three days. Bass explored the hinterland, examining the soil—'a rich vegetable mould'—and discovered a larger river, which he traced down to the sea and also followed inland. This he called Shoals Haven River, which issues from the mountains through a deep and heavily forested gorge and then, flowing eastward at the bottom of a precipitous canyon, evidently the 'high rocky banks' described by Bass, spreads into the creeks of a mangrove-covered delta.

Despite the region's good soil, Bass felt that the difficulty of shipping agricultural produce out across the swampy, sand-blocked river entrance 'must ever remain a bar to its colonization'.[14]

On Sunday 10 December the whaleboat and its men entered Jervis Bay, an extensive open bight seen and named in 1795 for Admiral John Jervis, Earl of St Vincent, by Lieutenant Richard Bowen, naval agent aboard the transport *Atlantic*. Here Bass and his party again made camp. They found two streams of fresh water 'and holes like tanks, seemingly always full'. Bass continued, 'Any launch might at half-tide fill her casks with a hose, baling it out of the tank into the mouth of the hose.'[15]

He was not impressed with the open bay as an anchorage, but acknowledged that despite a large swell rolling into it, the protection of a long promontory provided smooth water and safety in at least one place. Again he found sandy lagoons and swamps, with stony brushland to the north and grassy areas, possibly suitable for cattle, along the southern shore. Once more he believed he had found evidence of 'volcanic fire' in the rocks as well as in the large amounts of scattered pumice stone.

Four days later in a fresh northeast wind they passed an island, apparently today's Brush Island, on which they sighted a pole or tree stump on so high and conspicuous a location that they thought it must have been placed there by some shipwrecked person. The heavy following sea made it impossible to approach the island, and they left it for their return voyage.

For the next five days they tracked along the coast, taking advantage of every favourable turn of the wind, rowing when the breeze failed or pushing through the surf in order to land and explore on foot when the weather made the sea unduly hazardous. Bass refused to risk the open boat and its crew unnecessarily.

Keeping a written record of the voyage was extremely difficult in wet and windy conditions, in the crowded open boat or on exposed beaches. Bass's journal entries were brief, recording wind intensity and direction, sightings and latitude, which under the circumstances he knew to be merely approximate. Bearings taken with a small, hand-held compass from a moving platform a few feet above sea level, with the horizon sometimes obscured by waves, could not be precise. Under a generally cloudy sky and without a chronometer, he appears not to have attempted calculating longitude. The whaleboat's progress has subsequently been estimated at about three knots in favourable conditions.[16]

From time to time Bass inserted information on the countryside, notably the availability of water. One area had clearly suffered drought: 'we could not find a drop of fresh water, altho' the heat of the day made us search for it with extreme eagerness'. They came upon deserted native huts and dried-up waterholes dug deep in the largest of the swamps. A delight, however, was 'one of the prettiest little harbours as to form that was perhaps ever seen. One would take it to have been intended as the model of some large deep harbour. Every small bight has its little white sandy beach, and every turning its firm rocky point . . .' Trees and shrubs clung with a network of exposed roots to the rocks right down to the water's edge. 'I have named the place Barmouth Creek.'[17] For some time historians assumed Barmouth Creek to be at the mouth of the Bega River, but a more recent identification has it as the lower reach of the Pambula River, a short distance farther south.[18]

A day later the whaleboat and its men entered a large, hitherto uncharted bay. In a good sea breeze Bass took the boat around the inlet and made a sketch of it. Rowing past a point, the Englishmen encountered a group of Aborigines in canoes. Very much startled, the natives paddled hastily to shore, took their canoes upon their heads and ran, disappearing into the woods. The wind, holding fair, was too good to lose, and the voyagers left the bay, standing away to the south. Closer inspection of the double-lobed bight which Bass later named Two-Fold (now Twofold) Bay would have to wait for the return trip.

At eleven o'clock in the morning of 20 December the whaleboat and its company passed Cape Howe. At noon Bass's calculations put their latitude at 37° 30' south. The shore now seemed increasingly low and sandy and very dry, and Bass's concern for fresh water grew. Unless the group was again supplied, they could be forced to return northward, nullifying the purpose of the expedition. Thus the whaleboat was steered into a little bay, evidently the present Wingan Inlet, a mile north of Ram (or Rame) Head, where they landed and set up camp among the sand hills. To their surprise they found numerous rills of excellent water draining out of the sandy cliffs, then trickling over rocks or sinking through the sand into the sea.

The next day gale-force winds swept in from the southwest. The sea rose in tumbling green ridges, with surging white crests whipped into spindrift. At high water the surf rushed in over the beach to swirl and claw at the base of the dunes. Unable to beach the whaleboat safely, the men anchored her where they found that the swell rose and fell, but did not break. The strong winds and currents frequently seen on this southeastern corner of the Australian continent held the expedition in the inlet for ten days.

Bass walked several miles into the back country. There were low hills grown with gum trees that he found notably short and deformed, tea trees and shrubs and an almost impenetrable undergrowth of rich green brush, ferns and vines. Elsewhere there were areas of dense, waist-high grass. He climbed the rise named Ram Head by Cook for a height near Plymouth Sound, and studied the view of wooded hills and patches of sand. Despite the vegetation, Bass found the soil mainly a blackish sand, very poor, he thought, for agriculture.

On 30 December the wind subsided into a light breeze at east-northeast. In retrieving the whaleboat, the men found the anchor so completely buried in sand that they could not raise it from the boat. At low tide they tried again, pushing the sand away with their feet and with sticks, but the anchor, buried at least four or five feet deep, could not be moved. At the next low water they resumed the struggle, but the cable broke and after some additional ineffectual efforts they gave up. Possibly on their return the sand would have been shifted away by the tide.

On the last day of 1797 they quitted Wingan Inlet and 'steered along to the southward in anxious expectation, being now nearly come upon an hitherto unknown part of the coast'.[19] Somewhere on the long, low beach front they passed Cook's Point Hicks, named by the navigator for Lieutenant Zachary Hicks, who first sighted the Australian mainland from HMS *Endeavour*. The exact spot of the sighting remains uncertain, and Point Hicks has become Cape Everard. From the whaleboat the men could not distinguish the point from the rest of the shore. They were fully aware, however, that they had passed the southernmost extent so far reached by British exploration.

Through the first day of the new year Bass continued to follow closely the low, sandy shore, today's Ninety Mile Beach on Victoria's south coast, noting the smoke that rose from many places farther inland. At ten o'clock that night, with a bright moon in a cloudless sky, they could see distinctly the outline of the land. Towards midnight, however, a mist set in and the land became barely visible. Two hours later the motion of the water beneath the boat suggested shoals, and they hauled out seaward until a little after three in the morning, when as the darkness thinned and the stars began to dim in a paling sky they again saw the land, still low and level.

In the morning brightness of seven o'clock the men were astonished to see in the distance straight ahead a high, projecting headland. By noon they were abreast of a promontory that soared some 2000 feet above the whaleboat, while great flocks of petrels, gulls and other birds swirled about them. Mistakenly, Bass wrote that this high ridge, consisting of the peaks of several massive granite projections, could be none other than land seen by Tobias Furneaux in HMS *Adventure* in 1773. Back at Port Jackson, it was later realised that this was not Furneaux's sighting. Matthew Flinders wrote, 'At our [Bass and Flinders's] recommendation governor Hunter called it Wilson's Promontory, in compliment to my friend Thomas Wilson, Esq. of London.'[20] A friend of Hunter, Wilson had apparently recommended Matthew Flinders to the governor elect. Bass approached the promontory, hoping to land at one of the small sand beaches at its base, but a contrary wind and heavy surf made this impossible, and at six in the evening they dropped anchor in the lee of the headland. Vast numbers of birds roosted on the slopes, and on the rocks washed by the sea there were numerous seals which Bass noted as having remarkably long, tapering necks and sharp-pointed heads. Possibly they were the smaller of the two Australian fur seals, *Gypsophoca dorifera*.

Day broke with strong winds from the northeast, and Bass decided to steer south and then to coast eastward along Van Diemen's Land, hoping to reach the wreck of the *Sydney Cove* in the Furneaux Group. If he could obtain rice from the cargo of the wreck he would be able to prolong his exploration, which had suffered so many delays in difficult weather. Then the wind, still very strong, shifted capriciously to east-southeast. At noon Bass observed his latitude to be 39° 51' south. There was no land in sight. The possibility of soon reaching the Furneaux islands dimmed.

Suddenly water spurted into the boat through a split in the side towards the stern. Hours before the men had remarked on 'how much looser the boat had become by the last two or three days' working' and they now faced the frightening possibility of a plank coming loose. Bass immediately decided to return to the mainland from which they had come. He wrote, 'At 4 wore and stood to the northward, keeping the boat close to the wind.' By nine o'clock the wind had risen. The seas mounted, lifting, dropping and washing over the boat. Night fell, the men fighting their way through a demented blackness of pounding waves and flailing wind, terrified of further damage to the boat. Bass wrote simply, 'We had a bad night of it . . .'.[21] Later Flinders attributed their survival to 'the good qualities' of the little craft and Bass's 'careful steerage'.[22] According to Hunter, those mountainous seas further convinced Bass that there was an open strait to the west.

At six in the morning they again saw Wilson's Promontory and Bass steered for it. By early afternoon they were coasting it closely, looking for a place to land, when smoke rising from one of the small islands to the west caught their attention. Eager to speak to the local natives, they rowed in and to their amazement saw seven Europeans on the beach, ragged and half-starved. They were part of a group of fourteen escaped convicts who four months earlier had stolen a settler's boat at Port Jackson and made a run for it. Having heard of the wreck of the *Sydney Cove* in the Furneaux islands, they planned to reach and plunder it but, becoming lost, landed on this small island in the Glennie group. They now found themselves too many for their boat, and while these seven slept the others put to sea. The stranded men had been on the island for five weeks, subsisting on petrels and an occasional seal. Desperate, they were now more than willing to return to Sydney and, as Governor Hunter wrote, throw themselves 'upon His Majesty's mercy'.[23] To take them into the whaleboat then was not possible, but Bass promised to return on his journey back. He resumed steering for the mainland and, although finding the surf too high for landing, by eight o'clock in the evening they were anchored in a sheltering bay.

For two days they cautiously followed the shoreline westward. In the fading light of seven o'clock in the evening of 5 January 1798 they saw a pronounced opening in the land, by Bass's calculations some 60 or more miles northwest of Wilson's Promontory. A long spit and numerous shoals obstructed the entrance, but waiting for high tide at two hours or more after midnight, they crossed the spit on the flood and probably by moonlight entered an extensive bay.

The bay was roughly circular with a circumference of about 90 miles, the water edged by a generally flat, level shoreline backed by low hills. Stretching inland, the light brown earth was luxuriantly grown with grass and ferns, the country beyond lightly timbered with gum trees, casuarinas and some large areas of thick brush. Along the shore Bass found broad flats of mud so yielding that in places the land was 'not approachable except towards the top of high water, and then at the risque of having your boat left until the next tide, for the mud runs out far and flat, so soft there is no walking the boat over it'; even reefs of sand 'tail off in mud'.[24] At first the men's search for fresh water produced only something too brackish to drink, but as they rowed through the bends of a deep, winding creek they finally found fresh-tasting water. It is likely that the group camped here, on level ground beyond the reach of the tide, on the banks of what was later to be called the Bass River. Bass indicated the place by writing 'Fresh water' on his sketch map. Perhaps from here too he noted the charm of the inland hills, softly brown and 'rising as they recede . . .'.

'We stayed here until the 17th', Bass wrote of the bay. With the difficulties of weather, the necessity of repairing the boat and resting the men and the opportunity to explore an unknown bight, 'I did not find myself able to make up my mind concerning it sooner. I have named the place, from its relative situation to every other known harbour on the coast, Western Port'.[25]

With the whaleboat repaired, Bass explored the inlet. He found that an island lying at the mouth of the bay created an eastern and a western outlet to the sea. 'We went in and came out by the former, which is winding and narrow', he wrote. 'The latter, the western entrance, is, in the present imperfectly known state of them, the preferable one . . . [but] the weather would not allow us to go through it.'[26] He examined it, however, from the western side of the island, walking along the shore in a strong southwest wind with heavy surf exploding onto the beach. At its eastern end the island rose into a high point which Bass thought looked like a snapper's head. He gave its latitude as 'somewhere about 38° 25'. Its position is actually at 38° 34' south. Bass was in error some thirteen miles in latitude, an error Flinders later attributed to some damage to their quadrant. The island itself, today's Phillip Island, he found stony and barren except for some 'starved' shrubs.

Bass was not an accomplished cartographer, but despite wind and rain he managed to produce an 'eye sketch . . . which I am sorry to say, after all the vexation I have had with it, is but imperfect'.[27] This sketch has not survived and certain copies that were redrawn and published in subsequent years were captioned to the effect that they were taken 'from' Bass's original, raising the possibility that they are incomplete representations.

Western Port holds a second island, now French Island, to the north, and whether Bass knew that this projection of land was in fact an island has been much debated. Redrawn versions of Bass's original eye sketch show channels on either side of the island that, although detailed with soundings, extend only a relatively short distance. A large blank space suggests that Bass did not see any part of the north side of French Island. However, when Matthew Flinders returned from the Furneaux Group just a fortnight after Bass's return from Western Port, Governor Hunter 'directed Mr. Flinders to take into one chart the observations of Mr. Bass and his own'.[28] Bass would thus have given Flinders his eye sketch, notes and observations from his voyage, including his data from Western Port, together, no doubt, with comments and suggestions. The result was Flinders's 'A Chart of Basses Strait, 1798'. The Western Port section of this map indicates that Bass followed the channels on either side of French Island far enough to have reached Western Port's northern waters, with the island linked to the mainland by an isthmus of only moderate width. Flinders's original manuscript chart goes even further. Here the channels on either side of French Island show breaks in the shoreline, suggesting that there was water access to the north of the island, although evidently of sufficient depth only for a small boat and then possibly only at high tide. Seeing just shallow channels through mud flats, Bass probably would have felt it of little purpose to continue. This is, in fact, confirmed on Flinders's chart in his atlas of 1814. Here a sizeable blank space between the island and the mainland is labelled 'A boat communication over the flats at high Water'.[29]

While Bass's journal contains no clear reference to an attempt to circumnavigate the island, it has been argued that someone of his intrepid nature would not have stopped short of completing the investigation. The limited time and provisions left to him at this point and the greater importance to navigation of examining the entrances to the bay and areas suitable for the passage of ships must be borne in mind. He remarked in his journal that in his sketch he did not 'attempt to lay down all the shoals except in that place where any vessel would be most likely to anchor . . .'.[30]

Bass recorded the animal life he saw—a few kangaroos and wallabies, hundreds of swans in flight and thousands of ducks, 'a small but excellent kind', presumably tasty.[31] The day after the Englishmen arrived four Aborigines appeared, but they were too shy to be approached. Paths and other marks of human habitation were not recent, and Bass speculated that the extreme dryness might have driven the population elsewhere.

The 17th of January ended the seventh week of their excursion, and their stock of provisions was very low. They were forced, Bass wrote, 'to turn our heads homeward. We did it very reluctantly'.[32] Provisioned for only six weeks, Bass would finally extend his journey over eleven weeks with, as Matthew Flinders later wrote, 'the assistance of occasional supplies of petrels, fish, seal's flesh, and a few geese and black swans, and by abstinence . . .'.[33] Sufficient supplies would probably have enabled the expedition to prove the existence of a strait. It was a wonderful prospect that had to be surrendered with sharp regret.

At five o'clock in the morning of 18 January they sailed from Western Port in a fresh wind, running along the shore towards Wilson's

Promontory. By midmorning the wind had risen to a gale, with a massive swell from the southwest. With a cross-sea and the gale driving thick rain against them into the afternoon of the 19th, Bass took the boat into the shelter of a headland. Rounding Wilson's Promontory was clearly going to be difficult, and Bass's concern was heightened by the condition of the whaleboat, which had been repaired but now faced heavy battering again. In stormy winds and ponderously rolling seas, they repeatedly had to seek shelter in coves and on small beaches. When the weather moderated, they landed on one of the little islands to capture a supply of petrels, which they salted for food. They then returned to the island on which they had left the seven escaped convicts. To take them all into the whaleboat was an impossibility. Bass took on board the oldest man and one who was sick, first obtaining his crew's consent to divide their food supply equally with them. The other five he put ashore on the mainland with the best instructions he could manage on how to reach Port Jackson, almost 500 miles away. They should, he said, follow the coast, where food would be found more easily. They received their share of the whaleboat's provisions, a musket and ammunition, a pocket compass, fish hooks and lines, and items of clothing from the crewmen. The parting was painful; there were tears on both sides.

By the afternoon of 26 January the weather had calmed and the sky seemed to be clearing. Shortly before midnight, with a fresh wind blowing from the west, the whaleboat and its men finally rounded Wilson's Promontory and late in the afternoon of the following day pulled up on a beach to the east of the headland.

Bass now wanted to investigate an island, soon to be named Seal Island, which appeared to lie eight or nine miles to the east of the Promontory. They reached their goal the following afternoon, and found the island to be moderately high, sloping up to a hill in the middle, and although without trees or shrubs, thickly covered with tufted grass in which seals had made numerous paths and petrels had dug their burrows. The seals they found were mainly nearly full-grown pups, several of which they killed for meat. The island, Bass thought, could sustain a small-scale sealing operation.

Again the sky darkened, and the sailors hastily loaded their supply of meat into the boat and sailed back to a small bight on the east side of Wilson's Promontory, which Bass named Sealers' Cove. It was well shielded from the gale that was building outside, with ample fresh water. Sealers would also find sufficient wood close by for boiling any amount of blubber.

Strong winds holding the company at Sealers' Cove for three days, Bass put the time to use in exploring the promontory. He saw the low, sandy neck of land that connects the headland to the mainland and the stunted vegetation on the great rock mass itself, noting the depth and direction of the tides sweeping about it. As the skies cleared, the expedition headed north along the east side of the headland to enter Corner Inlet, a large shallow bay, most of it dry at low water. Here they met the five convicts they had previously set on the mainland whom, as Matthew Flinders later wrote, they assisted further by putting them 'across to the long beach' they had sailed past on the first day of the year. Flinders added, 'Nothing more had been heard of these five men, as late as 1803.'[34] Nor were they ever heard of again.[35]

A persistently contrary wind kept Bass and his men in Corner Inlet until 9 February, when the wind turned and came from the west. Steering east-northeast they passed the same long, featureless shoreline they had followed on the voyage out, but two days later, in a very rough sea, Bass judged it necessary to land and, driving the little craft through a heavy surf, ran her onto a beach. Several Aborigines appeared, friendly and apparently unafraid, although Bass did not think they had seen Europeans before. Through the night the surf continued to rise. Afraid that later they would not be able to get out, they waited until daylight and then rammed the boat through the breakers and bore away to the north.

The familiar landmarks of Ram Head, Cape Howe and Twofold Bay appeared over the next few days. In the bight at Ram Head they looked for the anchor they had lost in the sand, without success, and at Twofold Bay Bass spent the afternoon exploring the surrounding country until sunset filled the sky behind the mountains. Bass was no more impressed with the region than he had been on his first visit, but later commented with amusement that the bay 'may be known by a red point on the south side of the peculiar bluish hue of a drunkard's nose'.[36] A few miles north of Batemans Bay they landed on the small island where eight weeks earlier they had observed a pole like a flagstaff. It proved to be the particularly tall and straight trunk of a dead tree.

Six days later, as they neared Sydney, they eagerly 'got upon the oars and rowed up to Port Jackson by 10, when we entered the Heads'.[37] It was the evening of Sunday, 25 February, naval time.

Bass concluded his journal with a few general comments on the coast he had followed. He remarked on what he found to be a complete lack of suitable harbours, except for such sand-barred lagoons as might be entered during wet season floods. He mentioned plants not seen around Port Jackson and the exceptional sweetness of bird song heard at Wilson's Promontory. On minerals he said he could not speak with any authority, and so said little.

Bass delivered his journal and his sketch map to the governor. In a subsequent letter to the Duke of Portland Hunter summarised the journey. Where the New South Wales coast fell away in a north-westerly direction, Bass had

> found an open ocean westward, and by the mountainous sea which rolled from that quarter, and no land discoverable in that direction, we have much reason to conclude that there is an open strait through, between the latitude of 39 and 40.12S.[38]

Flinders later wrote that 'Mr. Bass, himself, entertained no doubt of the existence of a wide strait, separating Van Diemen's Land from New South Wales . . .'.[39] Bass's eye sketch of Western Port was redrawn, engraved and in 1801 published by the cartographer Aaron Arrowsmith. It was entitled *Western Port on the South Coast of Nw. South Wales from Mr. Bass's Eye-sketch, 1798*. To Matthew Flinders, Bass's 'voyage *expressly* undertaken for discovery in an open boat, and in which six hundred miles of coast, mostly in boistrous climate, was explored, has not, perhaps, its equal in the annals of maritime history'.[40] Bass wrote no such tribute to himself for this epic journey, but he would have felt a triumphant awareness of his own skill and ability as a seaman, a navigator and a leader.

On 1 January 1798 Bass had been awarded a land grant of 100 acres at Banks Town, the settlement being planned on the Georges River which he and Flinders had explored in the little *Tom Thumb* three years before. A property at that distance from Sydney was of little use to a navy man, and Bass displayed no particular interest in his landholding. He made no attempt at farming, and apparently it eventually reverted to the crown, to be claimed by possession some 80 years later by others. It was the only reward Bass received from government authorities in recognition of his explorations. Matthew Flinders and John Shortland received adjacent properties at the same time, and on 1 January 1800 Flinders acquired a grant of 300 acres in the same general location, the earlier grant evidently having been cancelled. A year later he sold the entire property to a friend in England. Eventually some 1200 acres were granted to marines, expirees and others, but the only safe access to Port Jackson was by boat, and Banks Town developed slowly.

In the meantime, six crewmen and part of the cargo of the *Sydney Cove*, wrecked in the Furneaux Group in February 1797, remained where the vessel had been run aground on what was being called Preservation Island. Three weeks before Bass returned, Governor Hunter ordered the schooner *Francis* south to complete the rescue. Flinders asked to join the *Francis* and to his extreme pleasure Hunter agreed, sending him as a passenger charged with carrying out a hydrographic survey of the area.

The *Francis* sailed from Port Jackson on 1 February 1798, heading south, and twelve days later reached the wreck site. The ruins of the *Sydney Cove* remained on the beach. Of the six men left to guard her cargo, one had died. The rest had survived in reasonable health.

In the *Francis*'s boat Flinders began his survey of the waterways, shoals and brush-grown islands. Although hampered by the lack of a chronometer and adequate compasses, Flinders produced a chart and a 22-page quarto manuscript of comments and description. Observing the strong tides and currents, he was convinced there was good evidence for a strait.

Flinders returned to Sydney with the *Francis* on 9 March, to find George Bass already back from his whaleboat voyage. With immense enthusiasm the two young men studied each other's sketches and reports, and arrived at the conviction that a strait did separate the New South Wales mainland from an island or a group of islands known as Van Diemen's Land. The final proof of this conclusion could be had by one means only: by sailing through the passage.

The refitting of the *Reliance* was, however, complete, and the ship was prepared for a return to Norfolk Island. The transport *Barwell* arrived on 18 May with 287 convicts, four families of free settlers and a welcome cargo of wheat, salt provisions and other stores, from which Hunter was sending 1200 bushels of wheat and 100 casks of salt meat to the island. The *Reliance* put to sea on 29 May for a journey that on the return to Port Jackson was beset by storms. Pounding through an angry sea, the ship arrived on 25 July, after an absence of 60 days, 27 of which had been spent battling her way home.

On Norfolk Bass had resumed his contact with Thomas Jamison, and his interest in the colony's commercial prospects sharpened. From a letter he wrote from Port Jackson to Jamison the following September, it is clear that he was acting as Jamison's representative in a business deal involving Sydney's principal surgeon, William Balmain, also very active in trade. Bass was to deliver to Balmain £200 of Jamison's money. Of his own intentions Bass wrote, 'I am quite unsettled what steps to take. I believe trade will catch me in the end.' Typically, his ideas were already wide-ranging. He continued, 'I don't mean trade in this place, only an occasional cargo here now and then.' He was not ready, however, to share his thoughts generally. 'Say not a word of this to any soul living', he cautioned Jamison. 'Remember! Silence is one of the greatest virtues in trade.'[41] Commerce was the only means of achieving wealth in New South Wales, and the competition that developed as a result was what Judge-Advocate Collins later described as a 'rage for trade . . . which prevailed so universally in the colony'.[42]

Bass's involvement deepened. On 1 October 1798 he wrote an additional letter which indicates that he transmitted £2342 13s 6d from Jamison to James Ellis in Sydney, who was to act for Jamison for a percentage. Bass then proposed that he invest and manage up to £2000 of Jamison's money in a commercial venture that evidently they had discussed at length, a proposal to which Jamison agreed in a letter of 1 November. The profits were to be divided equally between the two. Bass's part of the venture can be seen in Jamison's warning of the dangers of the seas through which Bass would be sailing and his reference to a suitable 'Cargo of Teas Nankeen Calico and China Ware'. Jamison also mentioned sealing 'amongst the Islands', an idea probably based on Bass's description of the seals seen during the whaleboat voyage.[43] Clearly Jamison accepted Bass's competence as a navigator. For his part, Bass understood the economic potential in the colony's geographic location. This scheme did not eventuate, but Bass was now thinking seriously about leaving the navy.

The proposed venture with Jamison was not a precipitating factor in this consideration. In the three years of his service in New South Wales Bass had watched the economic development of the colony and the people responsible for it. It was clear to him that Sydney was emerging from its position as simply a penal settlement to become a community in which a small but ambitious clique of free persons was taking every advantage of the colony's unique circumstances to accumulate substantial wealth. As early as September 1798 Bass had written to his mother, describing and analysing the colony's commercial prospects with remarkable insight and prescience:

> Here, where the voyages are long, the countries open to a trade distant, and the merchants in them unconnected and unknown to each other, the master of a ship must sell her cargo and do the business of a merchant as well as of a master, consequently much more is required of him and his pay and profits are in proportion. I have now upon my hands two offers of this kind, one from a brother surgeon of the colony who has scrapped together a small fortune which he wishes to increase in trade, the other from the commander of a King's ship who has done the same and wishes to increase it. You may be surprised to hear of fortunes made at Botany Bay, but it is so. This country is now come to that period when foreign and extensive speculations begin to open themselves and the inhabitants are anxious to embark in them. The war has opened by the conquests new tracks of commerce in the East and the first to take advantage of them are the fortunate. The South Sea Islands are now, also, fast approaching towards civilization and gainful barter; we are their neighbours. The Spanish settlements on the coast of Peru and Chile so long shut up from all the world are gradually attaining a profitable, though still contraband trade . . .[44]

This was much more than an impersonal summary of conditions, for in this letter Bass also made his feelings about the navy very clear. 'I have two professions, I am a sailor as well as a surgeon', and he was capable, he said, 'of navigating and conducting a ship to any part of the world and of carrying on the purchase or sale of her cargo wherever she may happen to be ordered'. And all this he prefaced by a seemingly implacable remark: 'I have told you that I hate the Navy and that I despise the pay and the prospects held out in it.' It was the unadorned statement of a man completely frustrated with the limitations of his work and who understood with keen discernment the promising conditions and opportunities unfolding around him. It reflected too his now absolute confidence in himself as a businessman and a navigator. It was a forecast of the events and the further decisions he would make, leading, as they would, to a mysterious fate.

Nevertheless, he was cautious. 'You may see by this that although I have some idea of dropping my profession for a few years yet I don't intend to relinquish the pursuit of it altogether and lose the knowledge I already have.' He continued, 'I have let you into my views because I wish to prepare you for a change in my way of life before it takes place, if it ever should, for as I have told you, my mind is not by any means yet made up.'45

And whatever his decision, to Bass knowledge remained important.

7

'And Should A Strait Be Found...'

M ore immediate events did for the moment capture Bass's interest. By the beginning of September 1798 Governor Hunter had decided to explore further the possibility of a strait between Van Diemen's Land and New South Wales. On the 3rd he wrote to Secretary Evan Nepean that Bass's sketch map, combined with Flinders's chart of the Furneaux region, seemed to indicate that 'a safe and navigable passage' existed, and 'to ascertain this is of some importance'. He added, 'I am endeavouring to fit out a deck'd boat of about fifteen tons burthen for that purpose, in which I propose to send the two officers above mentioned.'[1] Hunter must have shared his decision with the two young men, and their conviction that a sea passage existed was certainly strong, for in writing to Jamison on 7 September, Bass wrote unhesitatingly of going 'to the Strait'.

Unexpectedly, a decked boat became available. Communication between Port Jackson and Norfolk Island was always uncertain, and Captain John Townson of the New South Wales Corps, King's successor as commandant on the island, had decided to improve matters by having convict labour build a 25-ton sloop of local pine, evidently Norfolk Island pine (*Araucaria heterophylla*). This was contrary to orders from Hunter, in view of convict escapes by boat, and on the little vessel's arrival in Sydney in mid-June the Governor immediately took her into colonial service. He named her the *Norfolk* and ordered her fitting-out for a voyage to prove the existence of a strait between Van Diemen's Land and the continental mainland. He offered command of the expedition to Matthew Flinders, whose notice of promotion to lieutenant had been received in Sydney, qualifying him for the position. Flinders was delighted. The *Norfolk* was a sloop of about 35 feet in length and eleven feet in beam, small for an extended voyage and known to leak, but there were no objections from her young commander.

Hunter's particular interest in discovering a shorter route to and from England can be seen in his ordering a voyage at this time, for aside from its other lacks Port Jackson was in dire need of naval stores. David Collins noted that the bottoms of the boats were being destroyed by shipworms (*Teredo navalis*) for lack of tar, pitch, oil and paint. The sails of one vessel were reduced to provide for another. If it existed, a shorter, quicker route from England needed to be found.

Flinders's orders were to sail to the west of the Furneaux islands and 'should a strait be found, to pass through it' and return by rounding the south end of Van Diemen's Land 'making', as Flinders wrote,

> such examinations and surveys on the way as circumstances might permit. Twelve weeks were allowed for the performance of this service, and provisions for that time were put on board; the rest of the equipment was completed by the friendly care of captain Waterhouse of the Reliance.

He continued, 'I had the happiness to associate my friend Bass in this new expedition, and to form an excellent crew of eight volunteers from the king's ships . . .'[2] His equipment included a brass sextant, a theodolite, an azimuth compass and an artificial horizon. To his considerable disappointment, however, he was denied the use of a chronometer. Evidently it was considered too valuable an instrument to risk on a small craft going into unknown waters. Bass's particular task was to examine the natural features of the region, and two dogs were put on board to be used in flushing out wild animals. This was an unexpected opportunity to indulge in one of his principal interests, and Bass took on the role of the expedition's naturalist with enthusiasm.

The previous May a storm-battered merchant vessel, the small three-masted brig *Nautilus*, had struggled into Port Jackson. The ship had sailed from Guangzhou, then Canton, in June of the previous year for North America, but driven by fierce and unrelenting typhoons first to Taiwan, then to Kamchatka and Hawaii, she finally reached Tahiti. Here members of the London Missionary Society, besieged by hostile natives, contracted to be carried to New South Wales. Damaged, overcrowded, assailed by storms and with pumps going constantly, the *Nautilus* laboured through the Pacific to arrive in Sydney on 18 May 1798.

The *Nautilus*'s captain was Charles Bishop, a man in his early thirties, once a midshipman in the British Navy and now in the employ of a Bristol merchant, Sidenham Teast. With the expansion of European involvement in eastern trade, Teast's interest had gravitated to the Pacific rim, and he had despatched the 101-ton *Ruby* under Bishop to the American northwest to engage in the fur trade, in which British entrepreneurs had begun to participate in 1785. Bishop's two years with the *Ruby* were filled with problems of every kind, perhaps owing at least in part to his own lack of acumen and toughness in handling both men and business. At Amboyna in November 1796 Bishop, as Teast's agent, sold the *Ruby* and purchased the *Nautilus*. The brig was no more fortunate a ship than the *Ruby* had been. Joined by Roger Simpson as a 'trader and factor', Bishop sailed to Guangzhou to arrange another sally into the American fur trade with merchandise largely financed by a new partner, Conseequa, a Chinese merchant. Three days after its departure from Macao the *Nautilus* met with the first of the devastating storms that finally brought her to Port Jackson. Here, however, Bishop and Simpson were able to sell their cargo, while the *Nautilus* was extensively repaired through the generous cooperation of Governor Hunter.

Bishop and Simpson met Flinders and Bass, and an opportunity to recover their fortunes seemed to open. Flinders wrote, 'My report of seals at Furneaux's Islands had induced Mssrs. Bishop and Simpson . . . to prepare their vessel for a sealing speculation to that quarter; and on Oct. 7, we sailed out of Port Jackson together.'[3] The experience of Flinders and Bass on the New South Wales coast was an advantage to Bishop, and for the little *Norfolk* there was the added security of sailing in company.

For two days fair winds carried the two vessels southward, but on 9 October, as they approached Cape Howe, the wind swung to the southwest and an oncoming squall filled the horizon. The ships doubled back to shelter in Twofold Bay, discovered by Bass the previous year and where the navigators now observed as a marker the red point on which Bass had humorously commented at the time. The *Norfolk* dropped her anchor just off the beach of what came to be Snug Cove in the inlet's northeast corner, with the *Nautilus* a little farther out. Early the next morning Flinders and Simpson began a survey of the bay while Bass, accompanied by the dogs, landed to explore the surrounding country. Bass's journal describes the area in considerable detail. Behind the bay's rim of bluffs and beaches he found salt lagoons and brackish ponds inhabited by ducks, herons, cranes, redbills and small flights of curlews and plovers 'of a beautiful feather'. Low hills lay to the west and washed-down topsoil filled narrow valleys, which were thickly grown with trees, mainly gums, which he described with care, and shrubs 'bound together by creeping vines, of every size between small twine and a seven inch hawser'.[4] There were patches of what Bass considered to be tolerably good, even very good soil, and one grassy and lightly wooded place which, perhaps a little nostalgically, he thought similar to the 'most beautiful parts of Mount Edgecumbe, near Plymouth'.[5] The excited dogs found 'a porcupine ant-eater', an echidna, which Bass watched with fascination as it 'proved impregnable to them. He escapes by burrowing in the loose sand, not head foremost, but by sinking himself directly downwards and keeping his prickly back opposed to his adversaries'.[6]

Flinders and Simpson, making their way to a beach where they planned to measure a base line for their survey, ran into three Aboriginal women, who seized their children and fled. Soon afterwards a middle-aged man appeared. He seemed entirely unafraid, and in a courteous gesture he and Flinders exchanged bits of food, a piece of gristly fat for a ship's biscuit, which each surreptitiously spat out when he thought the other was not looking. The following afternoon, resuming his survey, Flinders was met by seven or eight young Aboriginal men, who although a little apprehensive were intensely curious about the strangers' dress and persons. For a short time they sat together, attempting to communicate, but when Flinders began his observations for latitude the Aborigines lost interest and disappeared into the woods. Bass noted that the natives were not as shy as those he had seen fleetingly on his earlier visit to the bay, but while they were in appearance very like those around Port Jackson, he found their language entirely unintelligible. Bass had seen no grass trees and, noting the solid wooden spears carried by the young men, conjectured that the light grass-reed spear and the throwing stick used at Port Jackson were unknown here. The association with the people of Twofold Bay was such that Bass later wrote, 'it is hardly to be doubted that a very friendly intercourse might be established among them'.[7]

In the morning of 14 October the two vessels left the bay on a northwesterly breeze. At about noon on the 19th the ships anchored at the east end of Preservation Island, on which the *Sydney Cove* had been run aground. Scattered and collapsing timbers remained, as did the little house constructed by Captain Hamilton at the time.

Bass observed the Furneaux islands carefully from the deck of the *Norfolk*, noting the interesting dissimilarity between those which were low and level and others which were high and peaked. On Preservation Island he set off on an extensive exploration. Like the other islands of the group it was granitic, as he recorded, rising to no more than about 80 feet, the rock thinly patched with sandy soil. He was greatly puzzled by large blocks of stone that lay apparently unattached upon the rocky ground and speculated on a 'subterraneous or volcanic fire' having caused them.[8] Also intriguing were areas of chalky rock formed, as he believed, from the remains of shellfish 'when the island was yet beneath the surface of the sea'.[9] Shiny black metallic specks found on the beach, and apparently also embedded in the granite, he assumed to be tin. Particularly curious were some brittle, white, chalklike stumps and short branches found among the remnants of dead trees. Bass dug around the roots of the stumps, broke the twigs to examine their core and tested them with acid, and could only assume that some kind of petrification had taken place. The *Sydney Cove* castaways believed that they had been adversely affected by drinking the island's water, thought to contain arsenic. Bass experimented with the water and the metallic particles he believed were tin, and concluded that this was possible. Rainwater collected in ponds was substituted. He gave considerable attention to examining the soil, with future cultivation in mind, and seems to have had a particular interest in rocks. Unfortunately geology was a subject on which there was little scientific knowledge at the time.

Bass also investigated the southern shore of the nearby Cape Barren Island, where he found varied elevations, a coarse wiry grass, some small to medium-height gum trees, a species of tall straight 'fir' and small areas of 'flowering heath'. Much of the island, however, had a 'dark, sombre aspect, too much like the barren heath of Hampshire'. In view of the sparse vegetation, Bass found it

> singular, that a place where food seems to be so scarce, should be so thickly inhabited by the Kangaroo, which is of the small brush kind; and by the new Quadruped the Whombat [sic], which is likewise a grass eater. This Whombat [sic] is a squat, thick, short-legged, and rather inactive Quadruped, with great appearance of stumpy strength, and somewhat bigger than a large turnspit dog. Its figure & movements, if they do not resemble those of the Bear, at least, remind one of that Animal.[10]

Subsequently Bass wrote the first complete scientific description of the wombat:

> Its length, from the tip of the tail to the tip of the nose, is thirty-one inches, of which its body takes up twenty-three and five-tenths. The head is seven inches, and the tail five-tenths. Its circumference behind the forelegs, twenty-seven inches; across the thickest part of the belly, thirty-one inches. Its weight by hand is somewhat between twenty-five and thirty pounds. The hair is coarse, and about one inch or one inch and five tenths in length, thinly set upon the belly, thicker on the back and head, and thickest upon the loins and rump; the colour of it a light sandy brown, of varying shades, but darkest along the back.
>
> The head is large and flattish, and, when looking the animal full in the face, seems, excluding the ears, to form nearly an equilateral triangle . . . The hair upon the face lies in regular order, as if it were combed, with its ends pointed upwards in a kind of radii, from the nose their centre.
>
> The ears are sharp and erect, of two inches and three-tenths in length, stand well asunder . . . The eyes are small, and rather sunken than prominent, but quick and lively. They are placed about two inches and five tenths asunder . . .
>
> The nose is large and spreading, the nostrils large, long, and

capable of being closed . . . The whiskers are rather thick and strong, and are in length from two to three inches and five tenths.

The opening of the mouth is small; it contains five long grass-cutting teeth in the front of each jaw, like those of the kangaroo; within them is a vacancy for an inch or more, then appear two small canine teeth . . . eight molars . . . The whole number in both jaws amount to twenty-four.

The neck is thick and short, and greatly restrains the motions of the head, which, according to the common expression, looks as if it were stuck upon the shoulders.

From the neck the back arches a little as far as the loins, whence it goes off at a flat slope . . . A tail . . . may be found by carefully passing the finger over the flat slope in line with the backbone. After separating the hairs, it is seen of some five tenths of an inch in length . . .

Bass went on to describe the forelegs as strong and muscular, the paws fleshy, round and an inch and nine tenths in diameter, each with five claws.

The hind legs are less strong and muscular than the fore . . . The claws are four in number . . . there is a fleshy spur in the place of the thumb claw . . . In size the two sexes are nearly the same, but the female is perhaps rather the heaviest.[11]

The wombat's pace was somewhat like a 'shuffle', and Bass chased one, ran it down and picked it up with his hands under its belly.

Carrying it on his arm and sometimes laying it on his shoulder as one would a young child, he described its placid acceptance of being handled, except when on going into the brush for a specimen of wood, he was obliged to secure the animal's legs. Evidently the twine pinched, and kicking and scratching furiously, the creature bit off a piece from the elbow of Bass's jacket and remained 'implacable all the way to the boat'. It seemed that 'with kind treatment the Wombat might soon be rendered extremely docile, and probably affectionate; but let his Tutor beware of giving him provocation'.[12] Bass also performed an autopsy on a wombat, but did not record these details in his journal. He found Cape Barren Island inhabited as well by echidnas, a web-footed rat, birds—some very beautiful, others unknown at Port Jackson—and black snakes 'with venomous fangs'. That the islands contained much more in terms of remarkable animal life, Bass was convinced. Of human occupation, however, there were no signs.

Although he would not have thought in those terms, Bass's anatomical examination of the wombat was in line with the science-oriented approach of the Enlightenment and in particular with the contemporary work of the anatomist and palaeontologist Georges Cuvier, who published a study of mammalian classification in 1795. In a minor way Bass's investigation of Australian fauna was a precursor of the work that would be done in the next generation by other zoologists and anatomists.

The *Norfolk* followed the *Nautilus* to more secure moorings at Kent's Bay, within better reach of the sealing grounds. About a mile north of the anchorage Bishop and his men pitched tents beside a freshwater stream and planted a vegetable garden. Rain and westerly gales made the *Norfolk*'s sailing westward impossible, and Bass pursued his onshore investigations, while Flinders, sounding the nearby channel, improved his survey. There was also time to get 'a few sealskins dried to make us good warm caps'.[13]

On 31 October the winds moderated to a light breeze and on a flood tide the *Norfolk* sailed for the Swan Isles, a cluster of rocks and islets off Van Diemen's Land's northeast point which Flinders had named on his journey on the *Francis*, having been told that there were great numbers of breeding swans upon it. At three in the afternoon the sloop anchored in a little bay at the southeast end of the largest island, and Flinders and Bass landed, Matthew to take angles and George to pursue his research.

The island was much like those in the Furneaux Group, the principal difference being in the rock, which was of a kind Bass had not encountered before—varicoloured, although mainly grey or light brown, lamellated in part, with rusty streaks. Struck with steel it gave off sparks, and Bass believed it to contain both iron and flint and perhaps other metallic substances. There was little wildlife. The explorers saw neither kangaroos nor seals, and no evidence of human visitors. The reputed swans turned out to be geese, later known as Cape Barren geese (*Cereopsis novae hollandiae*), dove grey with black spots and a deep, hoarse voice. Bass shot two. 'The flesh was excellent.'[14]

Early the next morning the *Norfolk* weighed, and on a high tide
Flinders steered her west towards islets at the northeasternmost point
of Van Diemen's Land, which Hunter would later name Cape Portland.
The anchor was dropped at about five o'clock in the afternoon,
approximately one mile west of Cape Portland. Before them lay an
unrecorded coast and an uncharted sea. Flinders felt the thrill of
guiding his first command into the unknown. For Bass there was
the magic of a new natural world. Alert and watchful, he scanned the
islets, the rippling and direction of the tide and the westward trending
shore—beaches, a grassy headland dotted with trees, hills rising into
mountains 'whose parallel edges were lying elevated one above another
to a considerable distance inland'.[15] In the distance clouds of smoke
rose into a quiet sky.

In the afternoon of 3 November the *Norfolk* entered a deep inlet
that narrowed, then opened into a basin-like bay with several exten-
sions reaching into hilly, wooded country, and a broad river flowing
into it from the southeast. Sundown overtook the *Norfolk*. The forest
around them darkened and the green of the water deepened. In the
dusk Bass went off in the boat and returned with four black swans,
fresh food for the evening meal. Bass and Flinders had found the tidal
estuary of the Tamar River, to be so named by William Paterson when
he established a settlement there in 1804.

At daybreak the *Norfolk*'s company surveyed their surroundings
with delight. Grass and trees grew luxuriantly down to the water's
edge, a marvellous contrast to Port Jackson's dry and stony shoreline.
Flinders wrote that 'it spoke favourably for the country, and added to
the satisfaction we felt in having made the discovery'.[16]

Bass and two crewmen landed. The necessary search for water was
made and a little stream with excellent water was found running into
a deep gully. The bay here was very shallow, and the water casks had
to be rafted in and off at high tide.

The expedition spent seventeen days in the estuary, the weather,
despite mild temperatures, varying from strong squally winds with rain
and hail, to thick fog and calms that made it necessary to man the
sweeps in order to shift the *Norfolk*. From the sloop and from the boat,
Flinders mapped the arms of the inlet and some distance up the river.
His calculations of latitude, often done with the artificial horizon, were

reasonably accurate, but longitude, observed by sets of lunars when the clouds parted sufficiently, was frequently out by many miles. The lack of a chronometer was a constant annoyance.

Bass ranged along the river banks, over the many fingers of land that jutted into the bay and inland to the hills and valleys beyond. He found rich, verdant vegetation, grass overlying the slopes like green coverlets, tracts of colourful, scented flowers and trees varying from tall eucalypts and spreading casuarinas to very small, gum-producing varieties. 'The grey kangaroo of a very large size, abounds in the open forest; the brushes are tenanted by the smaller Wallabah.'[17] He noted the many types of aquatic birds in the smaller coves, and was astonished at the numbers of black swans. He made 'a rough count of 300—swimming within the space of a quarter of a mile square: we heard the <u>dying song</u> of some scores;—that song, so celebrated by the Poets of old.—It exactly resembles the creaking of a rusty <u>Signe</u> on a windy day!!'[18] He followed the swimming birds in the *Norfolk*'s boat, watching their efforts at escape without leaving the water, moving 'in the most artful manner to gain the wind', which put the boat at a disadvantage. 'Is this reasoning?' asked Bass.[19] Birds were regularly shot for food. Bass dissected many, and to discover what they ate examined the swans' gizzards, finding only small water-plants and a little sand. He also worked with Flinders in exploring and charting the waterways, easily taking charge of the sloop while Flinders moved about in the boat taking angles.

There were brief glimpses of the Aborigines. The explorers watched as a man set fire to the grass abreast of the sloop, but he ran off as the visitors approached in the boat. A man and woman wrapped in small cloaks of skin, and a boy, were seen at a distance.[20] Bass examined the deserted huts, which he found made of strips of bark laid across bent dead branches and sometimes sprinkled over with grass. These were usually in groups of seven or eight, 'like a little encampment'.[21] Mussel-shell middens stood near each hut, and among the ashes of their fireplaces Bass found a few bones of possums, a 'squirrel' and a small kangaroo, but to his surprise no remains of fish. There was a sort of basket made from bunches of long grass, and notches left on the bark of trees suggested a very rough-edged stone hatchet. 'We never saw a canoe.'[22]

The expedition's assigned duration of twelve weeks made it necessary to move on, and Flinders's wish to explore the river as far as it was navigable had to be abandoned. Instead, the *Norfolk* was brought closer to the inlet's entry to await the first favourable wind, as for several days strong westerlies frustrated any attempt to leave. Despite recurring rain, Flinders made additional astronomical observations and refined his survey, Bass explored the countryside further and the crew hunted swans. On 20 November, as the wind veered to the northwest and moderated, the *Norfolk* beat out of the inlet. Briefly the men were concerned by curious dark patches in the water which suggested shoals, but there was no chance to examine them, and the little sloop headed west.

With the coming of night the wind strengthened, driving heavy rain before it. Throughout the next day a high sea poured thick spray over the *Norfolk*'s bows as under a close-reefed mainsail and jib her men struggled to keep away from the dangers of the coast. Towards evening the storm jib split and the sea mounted—but, as Flinders wrote, 'Seas that were apparently determined to swallow her up she rode over with all the ease and majesty of an old experienced petterel.'[23]

It was now impossible to hold their course westward. Driven by strong winds and an angry sea, the *Norfolk* headed back towards the Furneaux Group, reaching the safety of Preservation Island before dark. With enormous relief the men dropped anchor.

The next day the sails were dried and repaired on the windy beach. There was an eclipse of the moon that night. Flinders took astronomical observations, using the altitude of the stars Rigel and Sirius to obtain the island's longitude of 148° 37' 30" east of Greenwich.

A day later the *Norfolk* joined the *Nautilus* in Kent's Bay. Bishop's sealing was proceeding well, and as he expected to bring a load of skins and oil back to Port Jackson at about Christmas, Flinders entrusted him with a report to Hunter on the river and the bay that had been discovered. Hunter would later name the estuary Port Dalrymple for the navy's hydrographer, Alexander Dalrymple.

That evening a light breeze sprang up from the northeast. Despite the hazards of sailing by night, the *Norfolk* headed back to Van Diemen's Land. Once again contrary winds hindered her progress westward. By 3 December the explorers had regained their position off the estuary of the Tamar River, where they briefly sought shelter. At the inlet mouth they found that the dark patches in the water which had looked suspiciously like shoals were in fact seaweed. 'In steering through these', Flinders wrote, 'we yawed to one side and then the other, to prevent running over any of them.'[24] The next day they resumed their course westward. In light and variable winds and sometimes in calms they moved only slowly, now a matter of serious concern. Of the twelve weeks allotted for the voyage eight had now expired, and Flinders cut back on the company's daily rations, lest the voyage take longer than the time for which they were provisioned.

Anxiously, Flinders and Bass watched the coast trend northwest, as if it would connect with the coast of New South Wales. The water discoloured, suggesting that they were approaching the head of a bay. When the wind freshened and the sea began to rise, they considered steering north towards Western Port, but its precise location was uncertain and the idea was abandoned. Instead they sought shelter in the lee of a small island, where the two men landed to look for something edible. Brushwood growing right down to the beach was so impenetrable that even the dogs could scarcely get through, but although there was no visible source of food, a few old fireplaces indicated that men had been there. This surprised them. The island lay some three miles from the coast, and they had so far seen no sign that the people in the area had canoes. No food was found, but the explorers made an intriguing observation. Although 'the tide had been running from the east all afternoon' there was 'near low water by the shore'. The flood tide therefore had to come from the west, which seemed to them 'almost a certain proof that there was a passage through between this land and New South Wales' and that they could not be far from an opening into the Indian Ocean.[25]

The wind died away during the night, but with a light breeze from the southeast at daybreak they got under way. As they were preparing to do so, a large flock of gannets emerged from the south and flew overhead, followed to the explorers' utter amazement by a dense mass of petrels flying westward in a continuous stream for an hour and a half: 'the number could not have been less than a hundred millions'.[26]

Then, as the Norfolk rounded a point of the mainland, a long deep swell was seen rolling in from the southwest and breaking heavily on a small reef, against a little island and on the nearby shores. Such breakers could only come from an open sea, and the *Norfolk*'s men broke into joyful cheers, heralding 'the long-wished-for discovery of a passage into the Southern Indian Ocean'.[27]

The need for food remained. The summit of the small nearby island was whitened over with birds, and Bass and some of the crew pushed off in the ship's boat. Getting to the beach through heavy surf washing over loose stones was difficult but, wrote Bass:

> 'Two of us landed . . . and after a little <u>rencontre</u> with some Seals, that stood above; reached the Top. The birds, were Albatrosses, innumerable. Their spread of wing, was from seven to nine feet; their colour, more white, than black: the sight of us, occasioned little, or no disturbance; no one made off even, when we approached close to them: but they yet knew nothing of the power and disposition of Man. They were breeding; the females sat upon nests . . . built of muddy earth and a little common grass, raised about four inches from the ground, and formed into a concavity of nearly that depth . . . One young bird only, was in each nest . . . about the size of a young Pullet . . . coated in beautifully white down . . . that, at a distance, resemble balls of Cotton . . . The nests were so near each other, and the birds so conscious of the vast strength of their sharp bills, that, in going through them, we were kept upon a continued, lofty caper, by their <u>posterior</u> and lateral attacks: but this could not last long; our legs and humanity soon grew tired of this dancing march. The cloven foot (of this Devil, Man) appeared: we made a road with our Seal clubs and soon taught them to <u>respect</u> our Species: the little Cotton Balls did not neglect us: they, as their part of the fray, spouted plentiful squashes of oil, not inodorous, upon our feet and trousers.[28]

That the expedition was at the edge of an open sea was additionally evident from the top of the island. The coast could be seen to stretch southward, with islands leading off in the same direction. At half past two in the afternoon Bass returned to the sloop with a boatload of seals and albatrosses.

The *Norfolk* passed several other small, mostly barren islands and projecting rocks, the peaks of submerged mountains which once towered over the plains that connected Tasmania with the continental mainland until the sea level rose perhaps 14 000 to 15 000 years ago. Flinders later named the group Hunter's Isles. Continuing south, they saw the steep black headland that Flinders named Cape Grim, which they soon understood to be the northwesternmost point of Van Diemen's Land. They were now without question in the Southern Indian Ocean. For Bass there was a profoundly satisfying sense of having successfully completed the voyage of discovery which he had begun in the whaleboat a year before.

Under an opaque sky the *Norfolk* ran south, driven by the west wind along a bleak and often hazy coast. The craggy shore rose into rugged mountain chains which the men from the level Lincolnshire fenlands viewed, in Flinders's words, as 'stupendous . . . and, at the same time . . . the most dismal and barren that can be imagined. The eye ranges over these peaks . . . with astonishment and horror'.[29] There were only two sightings of smoke, suggesting that the land was sparsely populated.

Keeping at some distance from shore, they nevertheless watched for possible shelter should a rising wind force them towards the land. They saw none 'and we therefore carried all possible sail to get past this dreary coast'.[30] Bass speculated upon the effects on the coast of heavy swells continuously surging in from the ocean. Flinders was able to produce only a running sketch survey.

In the faint light of the approaching dawn of 13 December 1798, the men of the *Norfolk* were steering for a jagged, sheer-sided point that ran tail-like into the southern sea, the Southwest Cape of Van Diemen's Land, seen by Tobias Furneaux aboard the *Adventure* in 1773. Flinders wrote, 'from a totally unknown coast we were now come to a part of the island that had often been visited before'.[31] A coastline of some 460 miles hitherto unknown to Europeans had been recorded.

By eight o'clock the *Norfolk* had passed the Cape and steered in among the rocks and islets of the Maatsuyker Group, which Flinders referred to as the De Witt Isles, both names derived from Abel Tasman's account. A large cloud of smoke hung over the mainland, testifying to its being inhabited, but what puzzled Bass and Flinders were vestiges of fire on two islands at some distance from the shore. Neither they nor any previous explorers had seen canoes among the people of Van Diemen's Land, and their conjectures included lightning strikes or people swimming or using logs to get across.

By six o'clock the *Norfolk* was a mile off modern Tasmania's South Cape. Suddenly the wind died. In the west the sunset sky vanished behind dark masses of grey and purple cloud. As gusts of wind began coming over the water at shorter and shorter intervals, the men rapidly took in all the canvas but the foresail. Then the storm burst upon them with branching stabs of lightning, peals of thunder and pouring rain. Fortunately the storm came from the west; had it come from the south, the little craft and its crew 'would have been left to bleach under the high cliffs of the South Cape', their discoveries unreported.[32] The tempest was brief, but strong winds and heavy rain continued through the night. By noon the next day the weather had cleared, but contrary winds made their entry into the large sheltered inlets of southeast Van Diemen's Land difficult. By half past six in the evening, however, they had anchored in Tasman's Frederick Henry Bay.

Bass had been much intrigued by the spectacular headlands that jutted into the Southern Ocean from the steep barren ridges of Van Diemen's Land. He saw in them similarities to what he knew of South America's far southern Tierra del Fuego and Africa's Cape of Good Hope, and theorised:

> The relative situations of these three points . . . is particularly striking: they lay at nearly equal distances from each other . . . and each extends itself, so directly towards the South, that if continued in the same lines, they would certainly meet somewhere near the Pole. The effect that is produced upon the whole Globe, by this peculiar disposition, of three of its principal Points, seemed indeterminable. Like that of Terra del Fuego, this extremity of Van Dieman's Land, presents a rugged and determined front, to the icy regions of the South Pole.

He continued:

> Lofty ridges of mountain, bounded by tremendous cliffs, project two to four miles into the sea . . . These buttresses appear to be the southern extremities of the mountains of Van Diemen's Land; which, it can hardly be doubted have once projected into the sea far beyond their present abrupt termination, and have been united with the now detached land, De Witt's Islands.[33]

As the *Norfolk* passed these islands Bass had tried to compare the various exposed strata, finding some of the same appearance but not enough 'correspondence' to formulate a convincing theory on their having been originally connected.

On the morning of Saturday 15 December, Flinders and Bass began their exploration of Frederick Henry Bay, the connecting Norfolk Bay—named by Flinders for the sloop—their shores and islands, a coastline seen in various parts by Tasman, Cook, Hayes, Furneaux, Bligh and D'Entrecasteaux. There was evidence of Aboriginal visits on several islands, but again no sign of canoes.

Four days later they began steering for the Derwent River, reaching its entrance on the 21st. Flinders took the boat to lushly green Betsey's Island to take bearings, while Bass brought the sloop into the river's estuary, where Flinders rejoined him. Their progress up the Derwent was slow. The river was little affected by tides and the weather was erratic. They found themselves passing gently sloping hills, lightly timbered, but grown with thick rich grass and watered by ponds and creeks. A height some three miles to the west stood out so prominently that Bass decided to climb it. This was Mount Table, today's Mount Wellington. He found it forested with exceptionally tall, straight eucalypts, and saw to the north hundreds of acres of what appeared to be good pasture land. Evidence of past geologic upheavals continued to fascinate him—disjoined strata in a cliff face, pieces of petrified wood embedded in rock, stone surfaces divided into rough squares by intersecting lines of what seemed to him to be 'iron-tinged' stone.

The *Norfolk* continued upstream, contending with shoals and bursts of rainy, blowing weather. When the river became too shallow for the sloop, Bass and Flinders pushed on in the boat. They saw numerous deserted huts along the river banks, and Bass found their fireplaces to contain mainly the bones of small forest animals.

Suddenly someone called out from the direction of a nearby hill. The explorers landed and, carrying a swan that they had shot, walked up the hill. Two Aboriginal women wearing short skin capes over their shoulders snatched up two small baskets and fled, whereupon a middle-aged man approached, showing no sign of fear or distrust. He accepted the swan with pleasure, but no conversation was possible. His language was unintelligible to the Englishmen, and he understood none of the New South Wales dialects or South Sea island words they tried. Their muskets apparently meant nothing to him; only the red scarves the strangers wore around their necks were of interest. This was the expedition's only meeting with a native of Van Diemen's Land. Bass and Flinders conjectured that the man's peaceable acceptance of the visitors may have resulted from the fact that in his excursions on shore, Bass had almost always been alone except for his two dogs and so had posed no threat. Observing the people's very basic way of life, Bass thoughtfully contrasted this 'equalised poverty' with the extremes of wealth and want in some of the world's other countries. He wrote at some length on the island's characteristics—its soil, animals, water resources and the two rivers known to him, the Port Dalrymple, later the Tamar, and the Derwent, with the possibility of there also being a river behind Point St Vincent on the southwest coast. In this last supposition he was right. The Davey River empties into the large inlet of Port Davey, sheltered by the rocky headland.

Through the last day of 1798 and the first day of the new year the *Norfolk* beat down to the entrance of the Derwent. The twelve weeks allotted to the expedition had expired and provisions were nearly gone. Bass had wanted to land at Adventure Bay, where several previous explorers had gone ashore, and Flinders wrote, 'It would have been worth some trouble to ascertain whether the hogs and goats which the philanthropy of navigators had placed here are yet remaining.'[34] There was, however, no real option but to head for Port Jackson. On 3 January 1799, having stopped for fresh water at a cove near the top of the D'Entrecasteaux Channel, the *Norfolk* crossed Storm Bay and sailed past Cape Raoul and subsequently Cape Pillar. These headlands, towering rock masses fluted so they looked like huge, closely clustered columns rising from the sea, filled Bass with wonder and questions. 'What is become of the part, that was once connected with it?' he asked. 'Did it sink into the sea suddenly? Or was it worn away by the gradual attrition of the water?' Were these promontories the monumental remains of the 'sudden and awfull changes' the planet had undergone?[35] None of his studies so far provided any answers.

By 7 January, in thick haze, the *Norfolk* was east of the Furneaux Group, and early the following morning Bass landed on one of the small, rocky offshore islands. He found himself in a world of birds—

gulls, shags, geese, penguins, sooty petrels, redbills, gannets and quail, many of them nesting in their own sections of the island, some of them unbelievably 'fearless and pugnacious', all raising a deafening clamour of cries and shrieks, for which Flinders called the island group the Babel Isles. In addition, the rocks along the shore were occupied by seals, and while many slithered away on the men's approach the big males, surrounded by their harems and young ones, held their ground, emitting menacing roars, clearly prepared to attack. Bass reflected on the popular belief that seals were stupid animals, but did not agree. He saw what he considered to be signs of intelligence. Seals could perhaps be trained to fish for man. Hawks, after all, could be trained as fowlers. The immediate result of his visit to the island was, however, a welcome boatload of seals and gannets, fresh meat for the remainder of the journey.

At ten o'clock in the evening of 11 January 1799, in strong winds, the *Norfolk*'s anchor splashed down at the entrance to Port Jackson. She had exceeded by eleven days the time fixed for her return. The next morning the little sloop continued into the harbour and drew alongside HMS *Reliance*, moored in Sydney Cove.

Bass's journal of the voyage consists of 46 pages of clear, handsome script, each full stop ending in a minute flourish and the word 'anchor' indicated by a tiny, precisely drawn image, one fluke neatly embedded in the seabed. Locations were given in terms of latitude and longitude, dating was switched from naval to civil time as he thought appropriate, and referrals to Matthew Flinders's charts were made from time to time. Some of Bass's speculations were well ahead of any knowledge of the period.

8

A Change of Course

On 15 August 1799, seven months after the return of the *Norfolk*, Governor Hunter wrote to Secretary Evan Nepean on the condition and availability of the ships serving the colony. He concluded with a postscript:

> P. S. I transmit by this conveyance a copy of the rough survey which I have had made of the strait which I in a former letter had occasion to say I believ'd to exist between Van Diemen's Land and the southern promontory of this country. Lt. Flinders and Mr. George Bass, late surgeon of the Reliance, were the officers I employed upon this service, and they completely circumnavigated Van Diemen's Land, former consider'd a part of this country.[1]

It was scarcely a message reflecting the importance of the discovery that had been made. The voyage of the *Norfolk* and her company had added to the map of the Australian continent the significant geographical fact that Van Diemen's Land, in 1855 renamed Tasmania, was an island, not an adjunct of the mainland. It created important advantages for shipping at the time and in the years to come. Ships making the passage from Europe and the Cape of Good Hope to Sydney and the East, or the reverse, had been rounding the big island to the south, at times encountering the Southern Ocean's subantarctic storms. As Governor Philip Gidley King noted later, 'every seaman knows the difference there is in the weather in that latitude [39° in the strait] and in 45°, in which ships must necessarily get into to round Van Diemen's Land'.[2] The strait route could save a week or more in sailing time and serious wear on the ship and its cargo, which often included convicts. While westerly winds provided optimum conditions for a west to east passage, Hunter believed that in the southern summer the possibility of easterlies provided a chance to sail westward as well, and by 1803 a number of vessels from the east coast had successfully negotiated the strait. There was an additional element of safety in that a vessel using the strait could remain closer to land for a longer period of time than one sailing into and across the Southern Ocean. Wartime concerns and international commercial rivalries throughout the 1790s and early 1800s gave the route important strategic significance as well. The discoveries made by Flinders and Bass firmed Britain's claim to that part of the Australian continent. Largely on the basis of Bass's favourable reports on agricultural possibilities, settlements were established on the Derwent River in 1803 and 1804 and at Port Dalrymple in late 1804, while charting and exploration of the mainland coast along the strait further strengthened British hold upon the region.

Hunter was not, in fact, unappreciative of the discoveries made by George Bass and Matthew Flinders. He would have studied their journals and Flinders's charts with a navigator's comprehension and a governor's eye for potential. On Flinders's suggestion he named the strait for Bass, whose whaleboat voyage had presented the first possible proof of a sea passage. The *Norfolk*'s achievement was a bright if brief opening in the darkening clouds of frustration and defeat that Hunter saw gathering about him as governor. His letter of 15 August also reveals his profound personal concerns. He wrote of the lack of prospects of promotion for naval officers serving in the colony, including himself, and his comments on the contrasting situations of military and naval officers betray additionally the growing antagonism between himself and the men of the New South Wales Corps. Naval officers, he wrote, suffer 'the additional mortification of observing rapid promotions amongst the military serving in this country, whose duty in point of severity cannot be compar'd with the sea officer'.[3]

Bluff, approachable, courageous and conscientious, John Hunter had spent 41 years in loyal active service when at the age of 58 he arrived at Port Jackson to undertake the governorship. His dedication to the welfare of the colony was deep and sincere, as was his loyalty to the service of his King and country. He had shared the colony's earliest days with Arthur Phillip, surveyed the inlets known to the British and carried out legal duties.

Now, however, he found a community very different from the settlement he had left in 1791. Civil government had been replaced by a military administration that had provided itself with numerous advantages. In the closely guarded and supervised penal colony that he had left, there was emerging a core of free people—public servants, emancipists and settlers as well as the military—determined to improve themselves through private trade and agriculture, to the detriment, in Hunter's eyes, of the common good. These private activities fostered the mercantile success of such men as Simeon Lord and drew outside investment, such as that of Campbell, Clark and Co. of Calcutta. The colony was acquiring an independent economic base but, indulged in by a few, it led as well to the serious neglect, even abuse, of the ordinary person, convict or free.

It was Hunter's assigned task to restore civil government and to deal with the well-enrenched abuses of men who would not readily surrender them. He came to see the military and others, men who ranged from the wealthy landowner, pastoralist and officer of the New South Wales Corps, John Macarthur, to his own new judge-advocate and secretary, Richard Dore, as the destroyers of his administration. Nor did he receive the support he desperately needed from a government on the other side of the globe. Changing conditions in the faraway penal settlement were not of primary concern nor even understood by ministers under the pressures of a war of survival in Europe. Even his friend and supporter, Joseph Banks, could only respond to his letter of bitter complaint with the assurance that Hunter's colony was already 'a most valuable appendage to Great Britain and . . . we shall before it is long see her Ministers made sensible to its real value'. For the present, Banks could only write, 'Persevere . . . my good sir . . . and you must in time prevail.'[4]

Nature itself seemed to stalk the colony. Suffocating summer heat, 107° Fahrenheit in the shade, seared the land. Months of drought, a relentless sun and hot northerly winds had sucked all moisture from the earth, and bushfires flamed through the parched countryside. The wheat harvest had been a third of what was expected. The maize crop failed completely. Dysentery broke out, attributed to the drying-up of the springs and small streams.

On 11 February 1799 a fiery midnight sky reflected the flames that enveloped Sydney's new log gaol, deliberately torched. The gaol at Parramatta burned in December. Various offenders were before the criminal court, while another, convicted of perjury, stood in the pillory near the Tank Stream bridge. There had been deaths—a woman died of snakebite, another drowned at Norfolk Island, a Mr Stephenson, an emancipist and Sydney's storekeeper, had died suddenly of unknown cause. Hunter had been personally stricken by the suicide of his steward. Discovered to have been robbing the Governor, he went into the Government House garden and shot himself in the head.

In March the trial of Isaac Nichols, an emancipist of previous good conduct but now charged with having accepted a basket of stolen 'Brazil Tobacco', attracted considerable attention. As was normal procedure, naval and military officers constituted the court, in this case three officers of the New South Wales Corps, who found Nichols guilty, and three men of the Royal Navy, Flinders, Kent and Waterhouse, who declared the evidence to be either false or insufficiently substantiated. The colony's new deputy judge-advocate, Richard Dore, sided with the military and Nichols was convicted. Governor Hunter was outraged by the entire proceeding and ordered a court of inquiry, of which George Bass was a member. Bass served as required. Flinders, however, wrote a lengthy memorandum in defence of Nichols, whose sentence was suspended by the Governor and who eventually received a full pardon from the King.

There was also progress. The foundation stone for a new church, St Phillip's, had been laid by the Governor in October 1798. The men of the condemned *Supply* finished building a semicircular battery mounted with some of the vessel's guns at Cattle Point, where Sydney's opera house now stands. A new government house was erected at Parramatta on the site of the one built by Arthur Phillip, which had collapsed. Apparently at about this time George Bass considered writing a book about the colony. Matthew Flinders referred to it in a letter, but it was almost certainly never written.

Bass's concern at this point was his own future. The Van Diemen's Land voyage had undoubtedly been the highlight of his life, an exciting adventure and an opportunity to use his skills and intelligence to investigate and draw hitherto unrecorded knowledge from a strange new natural world. It appears that the trip had encouraged him to think of developing plans for a new kind of settlement and to consider exploring coal possibilities and the hinterland at Port Stephens. Progress was intrinsic to the beliefs of the Enlightenment, but Bass would have known, too, that such endeavours were unlikely to receive support in the prevailing conditions of New South Wales, and that the *Norfolk* journey was probably the climax of his opportunities as an explorer. Realistically, what remained for him was the mundane, ill-paid career of a naval surgeon with no prospects for advancement. Almost carelessly, he gave his narrative of the *Norfolk* voyage to David Collins, who incorporated it into his own work on the colony. In the words of an unnamed contemporary, Bass 'was a man possessing very great strength of mind, and of a strong robust habit, fond of enterprise, and despising danger in any shape'.[5] His medical career offered little for such a person. And with the same determination that he had used to enter the navy, he now planned to leave it. His goal remained a life at sea, but one that would give him independence and a lucrative future.

Thus, a month after his return, he was again writing to Thomas Jamison on plans for a commercial venture. He expanded his prospects to include James Williamson, the Deputy Commissary, and William Kent, captain of HMS *Buffalo*, a long-time friend, an outstanding seaman and one keenly interested in improving his financial lot. Kent had mercantile connections in London, with contacts in 'distant parts of the world', Bass wrote. 'Our views are extensive . . . the west side of the Southern Atlantic Ocean the whole South Seas and coast of America,—the Indian Ocean China Sea &c.'[6] Countries in these regions would pay in cash or bullion, an advantage in uncertain times. These were intensely ambitious, wide-ranging goals, characteristic of George Bass.

Bass discussed with Jamison the international situation, which was not conducive to commerce. However, typically optimistic, he believed that the war with France, 'this blasted Pitt's war',[7] would be almost over by the time he had returned to Europe to prepare for trading, as he now intended to do. Kent would then be free to leave the navy to captain one ship, while Bass commanded another, to bring merchandise to a Sydney where, Bass was sure, a paucity of sale goods would have set in. Peace would further expand his endeavours. In May 1799 he wrote, 'the peace will commence our grand operations: The sale of european goods upon the coast of Chile and Peru is our market. We have ample information upon this subject. It is altogether infallible'.[8] Unknowingly he again foreshadowed the course which would take him into oblivion.

Nevertheless, Bass still felt some uncertainty as to the wisdom of his plans. Only six months earlier he had written to his mother passionately expressing his resentment of the navy, yet he acknowledged that his mind was not entirely made up. Now he clearly wanted the freedom to act independently, but without entirely cutting his naval ties. If necessary, he wrote to Jamison, he would 'be sick'.[9] On 10 May 1799 George Bass was invalided from HMS *Reliance*, and in the ship's muster book was recorded as 'unserviceable', that is, physically unfit for duty. No word of explanation seems to exist. On 27 May 1799 Bass said goodbye to the assembled company of the *Reliance* and was rowed ashore from the ship for the last time. With him was his servant, William Martin, now a young man of eighteen—of whom there appears to be no further record.

On the day he left the *Reliance* Bass wrote to Joseph Banks, apparently for the first time. He introduced himself with a reference to the letter of recommendation written for him in 1794 by Christopher Nevile. Passing briefly over the discovery of Bass Strait, he went on to describe his interest in natural phenomena and his efforts to collect plant and animal specimens, which he was sending to Sir Joseph in a box by the homeward-bound *Reliance*. With apologies for their less than professional preservation, he listed plants, specimens of the brushwood he believed to be petrified, the skin and skull of a wombat, the skins of two birds and a canister of 'metallic' particles from the Furneaux Group. He concluded by saying that his health did not permit his return to England by the Cape Horn route with the *Reliance*, and he was travelling instead by way of China, so as to remain in a warmer climate.

Bass's reported state of ill-health at this time needs to be examined carefully. At no point is his sickness given either a name or a description. Some historians have cited the strenuous activities of his three and a half years in New South Wales as having taken their toll on a notably strong young body. Other writers have considered the fact that in Sydney at this time a number of people were afflicted with painful eye inflammations.[10] Conjunctivitis was, in fact, endemic. An eye problem is also brought up in connection with his comment in a letter to William Paterson in 1797. Describing a tree he had not seen before, he mentioned the 'long sharp prickles' on the smaller branches which 'in the blindness of my eyes I seized . . . and was handsomely repaid for my hasty curiosity by a handfull of them'.[11] Was this 'blindness' a figure of speech? Or was Bass suffering from failing eyesight two years before he contemplated leaving for England? If he was, there is no mention of it in his accounts of either the whaleboat or the *Norfolk* voyages. On both expeditions Bass, sextant in hand, took bearings and astronomical sightings, observed the characteristics of land and sea and was able to describe in detail the plants, animals and people he saw even at a distance. By 1803, two years after his invalided departure from the navy, Bass was wearing glasses, but without any reference to blindness. Nor did he seem to show any physical weakness during the long voyage to England via China and India. His activities in England were characteristically full of almost unbounded energy and enthusiasm. Some months later he was sailing the Pacific as his ship's commander and navigator with no reference to a handicap of any kind. Combined with his remarks to Jamison, which at no point cited health as a reason for journeying by way of China, the veracity of his claim to being 'unserviceable' seems open to question. Whatever his state of health, in his letter of 26 May Bass announced to Jamison that he had quitted the *Reliance* and was on his way to China aboard the *Nautilus*, adding with a flourish, 'Behold me embarked in trade'.[12]

Bass's plans to engage in trade had coincided with those of Charles Bishop, with whom he so far seems to have had a fairly casual relationship despite their vessels having sailed in company to the Furneaux Group the previous year. At Christmas Bishop had returned to Sydney with some 5200 seal skins and about 300 gallons of seal oil, and in February he delivered a second shipload of skins. In March and April the *Nautilus* was chartered by Captain William Campbell of the ship *Rebecca* to deliver a cargo of general merchandise to Norfolk Island. The brig returned to Port Jackson on 24 April 1799.

Bishop was desperately anxious to succeed honourably and financially for himself and for his employer, Sidenham Teast. In his frequent letters to Teast he apologised repeatedly for the years of business reverses he had incurred, protesting his loyalty and promising better results. He had a plan, as he wrote in January, 'of redeeming all the failures of the sad 5 years adversity —'. With his 'Knowledge of the seas and Commerce of the great Pacific', he was certain that in one two-year voyage fitted out with trade goods from England he could recover all past losses. As a first step towards this goal, he intended to sail the *Nautilus* to Macao or Guangzhou, where he would sell both ship and cargo. Possibly encouraged by the example of James Ellis, John Boston and Thomas Fyshe Palmer, small but active traders, Bass and Bishop arrived at tentative plans for certain joint commercial endeavours. Bass wrote exuberantly to Jamison that he was 'bound for China, where I expect my first mercantile essay will commence'. Already he had secured funds of his own and from two partners, sufficient, he said, to buy Bishop's half ownership of the *Nautilus*, which he would then 'cram' with a suitable cargo for Norfolk Island and Port Jackson. In the following December or January, hearing that a brig was approaching Norfolk, Jamison was to 'hurry down to the beach, have the then prices of tea, nankeens, china ware at your tongues end or on a bit of paper ready to give me the cue'. Alternatively, Bass thought he might be able to purchase the *Nautilus* in its entirety or possibly some larger vessel. Should these China plans fail, he would 'push for England, purchase a ship there, lay in such an investment as will answer Port Jackson Brazil and the NW of America . . .'.[13] These expansive, ebullient notions were typical of Bass. The extent to which they were Bishop's is not clear, but obviously he and Roger Simpson were at least in general agreement. From his letters and personal journal, Charles Bishop emerges as an intelligent, competent seaman, essentially gentle, good-natured and, it would seem, emotionally vulnerable. Very likely he found renewed optimism and a certain affective support in the company of the energetic and charismatic Bass.

Shortly before leaving Port Jackson, Bishop received from Governor Hunter a letter of marque, under which he could seek 'reprisal against the subjects of the King of Spain the enemies of my King and Country', in effect, permission to raid and capture Spanish ships and ports.[14] For this purpose Bishop listed the *Nautilus*'s armament as including six brass cannon, six and a half swivels, fifteen muskets together with bayonets, pistols and cutlasses, and 25 men exclusive of himself. Kent and Williamson gave their names as certifiers for Bishop's conduct according to the terms of the commission and it seems probable that Bass had warmly encouraged the idea.

In making Bishop his partner, Bass bypassed the interest of his friend Matthew Flinders in joining him in business. Flinders was at this point similarly disillusioned with his naval career and yearned for independence and a better income, possibly operating his own ship in trade with China and India. Flinders wrote to Bass of his hopes to obtain money from his father and other sources in England, unlikely possibilities at best. Perhaps Bass recognised this, at a time when Bishop provided a more realistic prospect. Whatever his reasons, Bass's decision did not impact upon the two men's friendship. Flinders provided Bass with a warm letter of introduction to a friend, the botanist Christopher Smith, then working at the Botanic Gardens in Calcutta. A year later, on the way to England aboard the *Reliance*, Flinders created his own bold plan, the circumnavigation and close charting of the entire Australian continent, which brought about his great voyage of exploration aboard HMS *Investigator* in 1801–03. The two friends continued their correspondence but probably never met again.

On 29 May 1799 George Bass sailed from Port Jackson aboard the *Nautilus*, heading northeast into the Pacific. Throughout the late 18th century ships returning to Europe from New South Wales had been almost literally feeling their way along various possible routes. The Torres Strait passage, which James Cook had pioneered, was the shortest, but rarely attempted because of the uncharted perils of the strait and of the Great Barrier Reef that guarded its eastern entry. More frequently, ships sailed west in a slow wide arc well north of New Guinea and then south to Java and beyond. Others, leaving the colony in ballast, headed for China to seek cargoes for the return trip. Dependent on winds and currents, some of these vessels did so by way of the island-strewn eastern Pacific. In May 1788 the First Fleet convict transports *Charlotte*, Captain Thomas Gilbert, and *Scarborough*, Captain John Marshall, departed from Sydney on this route, 'the outer passage' as it was known.

The *Nautilus* steered the same course. Her company sighted some of the islets of Tuvalu, formerly the Ellice Islands. Five weeks after leaving Sydney they crossed the Equator and at the beginning of July moved through the Gilbert Islands, now part of Kiribati, and subsequently through the Marshall Islands. These are reef islands and atolls, coral formations capping volcanic cores that rise from ocean depths to near the surface. The *Nautilus* steered cautiously among them, standing off and on after dark and resuming progress at daybreak. At Tabiteuea the brig dropped anchor and the men went ashore on the thinly wooded atoll. Bass's enjoyment of the islands is evident in his comments: 'These Islands are, for the most part extremely low, and sandy; abound with Coconut Trees, but produce also Bread Fruit, Plantanes, Bamboo, Tarrow &c; and are inhabited: The Larger islands, thickly, by a brown, handsome and courteous People.'[15]

A few of these islands had been sighted and even visited by European navigators for over two centuries before the arrival of the *Nautilus*. Unaware that some of these explorers, including Captains Gilbert and Marshall, had given names to their sightings, and ignorant of native names, Bass and Simpson put their own light-hearted appellations to those they charted. Thus the Gilbert Group acquired Bishop's Islands, on one of which the adventurers went ashore; Sidenham Teast's Islands, which included Dog Island; Roger Simpson's Islands and Two Tree Island; while in the Marshall Archipelago they recorded Bishop's Junction Island and George Bass's Reef-tied Isles. The last, actually Maloelap Atoll, is a chain of islets thickly grown with coconut palms and other trees, along which the *Nautilus* sailed for almost an entire day. Then, altering her course to northwest, the brig sailed through the Marianas Islands for the Asian mainland.

On 18 August 1799 the *Nautilus* arrived at Macao after a voyage of almost exactly three months. Ten days later Simpson and Bishop sold their cargo of 9000 seal skins to 'Ponqua, Houng Merchant of Canton' for $14 000, presumably the so-called Spanish dollars, the peso or peseta, the principal commercial currency of the time.[16] On 5 September Bishop applied to the East India Company, under whose licence he sailed, for permission to sell the *Nautilus*. This received, he sold the vessel for $4000 to Robert Berry, a merchant of Macao. The *Nautilus* venture ended in financial loss for both Teast and Bishop, as well as for Conseequa, the Guangzhou merchant who had backed the purchase of trade goods for the *Nautilus* at the outset of her long voyage. Bishop's journal ends with the settlement of these final transactions. Without doubt this additional financial failure was an agonising blow. Very likely Bishop now saw his partnership with Bass as a lifeline in the morass of his financial troubles. They evidently arranged to meet again in England, where under Bass's forceful leadership their joint endeavour was set in motion.

Bass himself was deeply disappointed in his plans to purchase merchandise in China for sale in Port Jackson. During a stopover at St Helena on the way to England a few months later, he wrote to Jamison that he had sent him a letter 'from China of my blighted prospects there'.[17] The China letter with its account of Bass's failed expectations appears to have been lost. Thus we know only that during a hot and probably rainy summer, Bass was in Portugal's Far Eastern outpost, Macao, the crowded Chinese city on a hilly peninsula west of the Pearl River estuary, with his plans somehow stalemated. Possibly he travelled upriver to Guangzhou, a teeming commercial city on the river over 90 miles inland from the South China Sea. Here in 1685 the English East India Company had established its factory, that is, its warehouses, offices and residences. The factories of other nationals as well now lined the waterfront of a river thronged with boats and ships, especially during the seven-month trading season. Bass would have been familiar with Bishop's recent contact with the East India Company, and quite likely he visited the Company's factory and its supercargo, Richard Hall.

Shortly after, Bass obtained passage from Macao to Bombay, today's Mumbai, by way of the Singapore and Malacca, or Melaka, Straits. Watching the low-lying shores grown with sedge, pandanus, ferns and rattan, he produced a sketch map showing the island of Batam and across a narrow strait Bintan Island and its settlement of Riau, which he wrote as 'Rio', briefly held at this time by the British. What is today the island of Singapore Bass labelled 'Peninsula of Malaya' and drew in a cluster of offshore islets. The map was published by Dalrymple in 1805 as 'Plan of the Entrance to the Strait of Malacca and Port of Rio by George Bass'. The following year a more precise chart of the area was completed by Captain James Horsburgh, the East India Company hydrographer.

Interesting light is thrown on Bass's stay in Bombay by a letter written to him about two years later by Robert Shepherdson, a merchant ship's captain who traded between Indian and Chinese ports, and with whom Bass struck up a friendship while in the city. The two men discussed business prospects and Shepherdson, like so many, was very much impressed by Bass. He wrote, 'I have so high an opinion of your diligence and application, as well as great talents, that I am satisfied of your excelling at any one trade or profession that you turn your hand to.' Bass's interest in languages astonished him: 'at this instant I have you in the pupil of my Eye—an Arabic phrase—Studying the Arab grammar in a low little room-corner of the Macleans hotel in bombay [sic]'. As apparently he had read his medical books in the crowded gunrooms of his early naval career, so Bass now ignored the bustle of the hotel around him to immerse himself in the study of a new and disparate language. Literature too was evidently a topic of conversation between the two men, for in his letter Shepherdson listed several books on history and philosophy, including Gibbons's *Decline and Fall of the Roman Empire*, with which he was trying to improve his education. He concluded his letter saying that he had recently heard of Bass and Bishop's arrival at the Cape of Good Hope in their vessel, the *Venus*, and wished that 'Fortune may take you in her good keeping—for next to Health good fortune is the most desirable thing in our short residence in this Theatre—Adieu I am your Friend & Constant Well Wisher, Robr Shepherdson'.[18]

Bass had hoped to continue his journey overland, a more interesting and possibly quicker route, but for reasons he did not explain he embarked instead on the East India Company's ship *Woodford*, which sailed from Bombay on 23 January 1800. First steering south, the ship quitted India's Malabar Coast in mid-February and crossed the Indian Ocean to double the Cape of Good Hope. In late May the little mid-South Atlantic island of St Helena was sighted, perpendicular cliffs rising 1600 to 2300 feet above the sea. The *Woodford* dropped anchor at Jamestown, the island's only port, and Bass wrote to Jamison, mentioning his 'blighted prospects' in China. 'Thus far am I', he said, uncharacteristically despondent, '. . . and no further on my way to England'.[19]

On 4 August 1800 *The Times* newspaper reported that the purser of the India Company ship *Woodford* had arrived at London's India House with a record of the journey and a list of passengers. Among them was 'Mr. George Bass, Surgeon, Navy'.[20]

9

The Venus Venture

In the course of the long voyage home, Bass obviously clarified in his mind precisely the commercial goals he wanted to achieve and the means of doing so. On his arrival he took lodgings in Arundel Street, a short roadway built by the Earl of Arundel which ran from the broad and busy Strand, with its carriages, pedestrians and fashionable shops, to the Thames, where steps led down to the water. The disappointments of China evaporated. With immense energy and purpose, Bass plunged into a spiral of hyperactivity that in just eighteen months culminated in the formation of a trading company, the purchase of a ship and cargo and the start of a return voyage to New South Wales.

With the report on his poor health from Sydney, Bass obtained from the Admiralty's Sick and Hurt Board a 12-month leave from the service, commencing on 22 November 1800. Later correspondence with his London agent, James Sykes, confirms that in due time he requested and was granted an additional year's extension of his leave. While this gave him the time to organise his new enterprise, in terms of income he was on half pay, which amounted to approximately six shillings a day, bare subsistence, probably paid semi-annually. Bass received no recognition of any kind from the British government for his exploration work in New South Wales. While at the time he appears to have expressed no resentment over this, it is clear that it later became a source of some bitterness. Any prospect of success or betterment for himself had to come from his commercial endeavours, and for this he had to find investors.

It is obvious that Bass left Port Jackson with commitments from several individuals. Speculation was virtually a way of life for many in the colony, and there seemed little likelihood of anything but success and profit resulting from bringing a shipload of attractive merchandise into Sydney. Bass's earlier negotiations with Thomas Jamison, William Kent and James Williamson now resulted in substantial investments by all three. In the company that Bass now formed Jamison was the largest shareholder, having made available £2705. Kent invested £1686 and Williamson £925.

On 27 August, less than a month after Bass's own arrival, HMS *Reliance* reached Plymouth and subsequently anchored at Portsmouth with Matthew Flinders and Henry Waterhouse on board. Flinders had come to his own decisions on his future. Determined to find fame and fortune through maritime exploration, he was approaching Sir Joseph Banks with a proposal for a naval expedition of discovery along the coasts of Terra Australis, which he would command. Whether Bass and Flinders met at this time is not recorded. Both men were much involved in their separate projects. Waterhouse, however, was always interested in business opportunities, and evidently enlisted his father's support for Bass's company. William Waterhouse invested £800, which he followed with an additional £100.

Another matter required Bass's attention. The box of natural history specimens that he had sent with the *Reliance* for Sir Joseph Banks had arrived, and Bass completed his descriptions of its contents and a scientific paper on 'the quadruped called Wombat'. Did Bass meet with Banks? Comments in a letter from Banks to Governor King and a later newspaper article suggest that they met, but no certain evidence exists.

Bass now travelled to Lincoln to see his mother. Sarah Bass had boarded for some years with the Calder family at their home, evidently located towards the lower end of The New Road, now Lindum Road, as it ran downhill below the soaring spires of the great cathedral. Probably sitting with his mother in the Calder parlour, Bass outlined his project. Sarah Bass was then in her mid-sixties, a woman of 'a most imposing presence, very stern looking', according to one of the Calders.[1] Rejoicing at the sight of her handsome son, impressed with the competence and boldness of his plans, perhaps at this point unable to deny him anything, she gave him £200 to invest in his scheme and subsequently, together with her sister Eliza, provided an additional £150. In 1798 Bass had written to her of his hope of adding a room for her to a house of his own or to build a home for her. Perhaps now they both believed that the dream could become a reality.

Did George visit Sally Aked? At one point Sarah Bass had complained in a letter to him of disrespect and ingratitude on the part of the Akeds. 'I have be in general composed respecting you', she wrote, adding, 'I always thought it an unprofitable Plan and I fear you now think so too . . .'.[2] Was this a reference to marriage intentions on Bass's part? Sarah Bass said no more on the subject, and Bass's response at the time was that he would not write to Sally but would leave the Aked affair to his mother. What the situation was now, three years later, seems to be unrecorded.

Back in London Bass's search for investors was yielding good results. Robert Berry, the Macao merchant who had bought the *Nautilus*, contributed £1500, as did James Crichton, an Edinburgh merchant. Charles Bishop, meantime, had arrived from China. Apparently he settled his obligations to the East India Company and to Sidenham Teast. The *Nautilus* enterprise had cost its backers a net loss of some $10 500, of which about $450 was borne by Bishop, evidently leaving him with nothing for further investment. Nevertheless, he resumed his association with George Bass, and his brother William invested £443 in the new enterprise. Additional sums came from others, including Robert Scott, who would become first mate of Bass's ship. The total sum raised was £10 890.

A printed prospectus now appeared, announcing the sale by auction of 'the good brig Venus' at Lloyd's Coffee-House, Cornhill, at half past two on 18 September 1800. She was described as of about 140 tons burden, built in India of teak, coppered, square-sterned, with a figure-head, and fitted to mount twelve carriage guns. She was 'reported to sail extremely fast, and is one of the most compleat, handsome, and strong built Ships in the River Thames', to be sold as she lay 'at the Swinging Chain of East Lane'. An inventory listed anchors, cables, sails, and chandlery that included horn and tin lanterns, compasses, an ensign, jack and pennant, and 'about 6 or 7 tons iron ballast', in addition to boatswain's, carpenter's, cooper's and cook's stores.[3] Probably Bass travelled down the Thames in one of the river's countless wherries, passing under one of the graceful arches of the Blackfriars Bridge of the time, with the dome of St Paul's against the sky, to where the *Venus* was moored off East Lane. Boarding, he would have inspected the little brig throughout, and no doubt had himself rowed around her, studying her from stem to stern. There was much to commend her. The iron ballast alone was a bonus, a cleaner alternative to shingle, gathered wave-washed off England's beaches but impossible to clean of the filth that accumulated over time. Bass was delighted with the ship, and with the assistance of James Crichton he bought her. On 8 November the *Venus* was registered with Lloyd's of London and 'insured for £7,650 at the rate of four guineas per cent, for Botany Bay, Port Jackson, or all or any ports and places in New South Wales, New Holland, Van Diemen's Land, and in the islands adjacent'.[4] The reference to the islands related to the territory claimed by Britain in the commission given to Governor John Hunter, which somewhat vaguely included 'the islands adjacent in the Pacific Ocean'.[5] From the evidence, she was insured further on 3 July 1801 at Simon's Bay at the Cape of Good Hope. After the disposal of his English merchandise principally at Port Jackson, Bass intended to pick up new cargoes in New Guinea, the East Indies and wherever else he could find them, and with certain of his European goods sail for the markets of Guangzhou.

Much remained to be done. To the stores and equipment that came with the ship, countless additions and replacements were needed. Almost 30 tradesmen spread through the vessel, working at repairs and alterations and generally preparing her for sea. Although the brig was equipped to carry twelve guns, Bass had her fitted with eight. Bass and Bishop visited the East India House, passing through the high, columned portico below the sculptured pediment symbolising the company's worldwide commerce. Their errand was to apply for a licence to trade within its chartered areas, for the company held a nominal monopoly over the entire region from the Cape of Good Hope to Cape Horn. Trade goods had to be selected, purchased and made ready for loading. A crew had to be assembled. Throughout November and December Bass was almost frenetically busy. Bishop apparently participated in all of this. His experience in trade with Pacific islanders was valuable in the selection of merchandise. In Sydney as well he would have observed people and conditions from a merchant's point of view.

On 8 January 1801, 'and in the forty first year of the reign of our Sovereign George the Third over Great Britain and Ireland King and the first year of his reign over the United Kingdom of Great Britain and Ireland', the association became official. Bass and Bishop committed themselves to a mercantile partnership in signed, witnessed and duly stamped Articles of Agreement. Bass was termed merchant and managing part owner of the ship, agent for the company's investors and second commander. Bishop was designated merchant, part owner and commander. George Bass and James Crichton, however, remained the registered owners. Bass and Bishop had what was in effect a veto over each other, and their wages and other moneys were to be equal. Essentially the agreement was for 'Twenty Pounds Sterling p. Month as for their joint Wages . . . Together with Four P. Centum, each, commission, on the gross proceeds of all merchandize sold and freights obtained during the said voyage' together with certain other minor arrangements. Each was to take over the duties of the other in the event of death or incapacity, no secrets were to be kept between them, and disputes were to be put before self-appointed adjudicators.[6] Meantime, permission to trade within their chartered areas was received from the East India and South Sea companies.

Bass's personal life also took an exhilarating if unexpected turn. He had been welcomed at Henry Waterhouse's home, the Piccadilly residence of his parents Susanna and William Waterhouse, their twelve children and Henry's little daughter Maria. Tichborne (or Titchborne) Street ran into Piccadilly Street at its junction with the Haymarket, roughly along a section of what is today Regent Street. Only a few houses away from the junction and the daily rumbling of wagons carrying hay and straw to feed London's thousands of horses, 29 Tichborne Street was probably a typical narrow-fronted Georgian residence. No doubt of red brick, possibly three or four storeys high, it probably gave directly on to the street through a doorway flanked on either side by a white column. The family might have attended the nearby St James's Church, Piccadilly, a slender-spired brick and stone dressed building evidently designed by Christopher Wren, which drew a fashionable congregation.

Extant letters show a close, affectionate family, apparently well connected and reasonably prosperous, despite references to recent financial losses. William Waterhouse had been a page to William Augustus, the Duke of Cumberland, brother of King George III, for

24 years; Cumberland became Henry Waterhouse's godfather. Thomas Townshend, Viscount Sydney of St Leonards and twice Secretary of State for the Home Department, was a friend who apparently shared his letters from Henry with the family, and whose patronage Henry expected in the matter of his promotion.[7] Arthur Phillip, now a ship commander, was also a personal friend who was often in touch.

The eldest of the children was Elizabeth, then 32 years of age. There is no known existing picture or detailed description of Elizabeth. George Bass later possessed a portrait of her, apparently a miniature, which he called Little Bess, but it did not survive. Bass, however, mentions her large eyes and a roguishness in her expression, perhaps reflecting the mischievous sense of humour that he so appreciated. She was short. Bass himself was tall, and teased that unless he stood close to a chair for her to stand on she could not reach him to be kissed. Educated to the extent expected of a woman of her time and class, she wrote letters at length, with warmth and dignity. Her letters also reflect a courageous young woman who was capable of profound devotion and loyalty. The family sometimes mentioned her sharp tongue, and Bass wrote of her 'chatter' and urged her to say 'kind things' to her younger sisters. Yet obviously she possessed the charm that would elicit from George Bass repeated avowals of his love and, from the evidence, his fidelity through the years of their separation. The attraction between Elizabeth and the 29-year-old Bass was apparently immediate. Their letters show clearly that Bass had fallen very much in love and that Elizabeth idolised this clever, handsome man. A portrait of Bass which may date to about this time shows a well-dressed young man, hands resting casually on the head of a walking stick, the face calm, even-featured, the eyes quietly observant, with thick hair, possibly powdered, fashionably cut below ear level. There was no question of Bass giving up the enterprise to which he was so deeply committed, or of the possibility of Elizabeth accompanying him in a small, excessively crowded ship on a commercial adventure fraught with risks and uncertainties. A successful voyage would bring him back to England possibly within three years, and Elizabeth was prepared to marry him and wait for his return. With a future that could keep them apart for years and all Bass's resources invested in a ship and in a highly speculative enterprise, they were apparently unsure of her parents' reaction. Thus Bass seems to have obtained a special licence that required no reading of banns in church, and on 8 October 1800 they were married under the fine vaulted ceiling of St James's Church, a short distance from the Waterhouse home, with only Henry and his sister Maria as witnesses.[8] Immediately afterwards Bass wrote to Elizabeth's father:

> Dear Sir,
>
> Your daughter Elizabeth and myself were this day married at St James's Church. May it be an increase of happiness to us both, as well as to our friends. Pray present my most kind compliments to Mrs. Waterhouse and kind remembrance to Miss Maria and believe me to be yours truly in friendship,
>
> Geo. Bass
>
> My wife requests me to present her love and duty but she cannot write herself. Elizth. Bass.[9]

On the reverse of the same sheet of paper, Henry Waterhouse added:

> My Dr Father,
>
> You will certainly think me an impudent fellow when I inform you I this day gave irrevocably away your daughter formerly Eliz. W — now E. Bass.
>
> My long knowledge of the worth of Mr Bass to whom she has united herself makes me congratulate you & my Mother on the occasion—of my own concerns I can say nothing.
>
> Yours affectionately,
>
> Waterhouse[10]

The marriage was noted in the *Gentleman's Magazine* of 1800, and the young couple moved into Bass's accommodations in Arundel Street, Strand. Despite their undoubted surprise, Elizabeth's parents received the news graciously and welcomed Bass into the family. For his part he quickly referred to Elizabeth's siblings as his brothers and sisters. There was clearly between William Waterhouse and his eldest daughter a special bond, and a particularly firm friendship developed as well between Waterhouse and his son-in-law.

The weeks that followed were centred upon preparing the *Venus* for her voyage. Few letters and no personal journals make a detailed reconstruction of the events of the next three months difficult, but the picture is one of intense activity, much coming and going and the excitement and good humour of high hopes. Sarah Bass came to London, and the fond relationship between her and Elizabeth that is soon evident would have developed at this time. Charles Bishop seems to have become a part of the family circle and, perhaps at times serving as Sarah Bass's escort, was jokingly referred to as the elderly lady's 'husband'. Family letters written to Bass during the voyage regularly included greetings to 'Captain Bishop'. Elizabeth was ill during part of this time but, as she later wrote, she had a dear husband to comfort her as he sat beside the bed.

Expenditures for the voyage mounted. The ship was packed with merchandise. Among the thousands of different items listed were various types of fabric and items of clothing including boots and shoes, hats and feathers. There were paints, oils, glue, looking-glasses, 'musquets' and flints, pencils, cutlery, beads and 'trinkets', blankets, candles, Jamaica rum, swords, pistols, and quantities of ironware, including tools, different kinds of nails and screws, pots and kettles, and furniture fittings. Books were included, some selected by Bass for himself and probably others for sale in Sydney. There were several volumes on travel and exploration, including the voyages of Vancouver and Cook, and some on law, others relating to insurance and bills of exchange. Aside from four volumes of the works of the feminist Mary Wollstonecraft, there were such philosophical works as *An Enquiry Concerning Political Justice, and Its Influence on General Virtue and Happiness* by the social philosopher and religious dissenter William Godwin, and *An Essay on Crime and Punishment* by Cesare Beccaria, who advocated the use of scientific methods in criminology, notably observation and punishment calibrated to the crime. Bass's strong interest in abstract ideas and the influence of his experience in a penal colony can be seen in this choice of subject matter.

Almost £11 000, a huge sum at the time, was spent on cargo.[11] Provisions for months to come, firewood and livestock had to be purchased. On a list of tradesmen the wages owing to them totalled £5645 19s 2d.

As sailing time approached, Sarah Bass returned to Lincoln. In addition to the heartache of having her son once again cross the oceans to a strange and distant world, she clearly had been shocked and deeply worried by the size of his expenditures and the debts he had incurred. Her worry over his finances, which included her own small investment, spilled over into a letter in which she expressed her concern that he had exhausted his funds and she in turn would lose her 'comforts'. Exasperated, George wrote back on 8 January, the day before he sailed. She was mistaken, he said. He had left with his agent and another person nearly £300 as a 'resource' against any accident befalling the *Venus* before she began to produce a financial return. He did not feel himself 'straightened in circumstances', adding, 'If my numerous Creditors in London had no more confidence in me than you I should now cut but a sorry figure'. As to the loss of her comforts, he was 'upon the point of setting out to acquire the means of making us all <u>more</u> comfortable'. The letter ended affectionately and with a promise to write her 'by all opportunities'.[12]

With Elizabeth on board, Bass had taken the *Venus* down the Thames and through the Channel to Portsmouth, where the brig joined a fleet of ships at the Spithead anchorage and arrangements were made for her departure with Lord Garlies's convoy. This provided an impor-tant—and required—element of protection against possible French attack, and reduced Bass's insurance premium significantly. Dwarfed by great warships and large merchantmen, the little *Venus* rode rest-lessly at her moorings. A cold, capricious wind was blowing. Wintry skies and chill, choppy waters were shifting shades of grey. Elizabeth was established in warm lodgings with a Mrs Dozells at Gun Wharf in nearby Portsea. Here she stood on a chair to kiss George as he took leave in the morning, and waited for the sound of his voice on the stairs as he came home, sometimes to her immense joy unexpectedly. Christmas Day they dined together alone at an inn, one of the 'two happiest Days I ever remember to have spent. your poor Bess always wished to be alone with you, but seldom had that wish gratified . . .'.[13]

Merchant vessels carried far smaller complements than warships and generally offered better pay, so by 2 January 1801 Charles Bishop was able to write out the completed list of the brig's nineteen officers and crew. Aside from Bass and himself they included Robert Scott, Chief Mate; Jacob Tibbots, Second Mate; seamen, landsmen and two appren-tices. Very little is known of these men. As chief mate Scott would have had the education to take over from a captain in the event of his death or incapacity. His interest in the voyage and that he had some financial resources are evident in his investment of £260, which placed him on the list of the brig's proprietors. Whether this had influenced Bass and Bishop in selecting him as chief mate remains a question. As second mate Tibbots took charge of the watch and supervised the seamen, but his ability to navigate or do the ship's accounts is not known. Bishop was fortunate in securing four able seamen, an ordinary seaman and the specialists—the boatswain, gunner, carpenter and cook, presumably men of experience. Their names are recorded, nothing else. One man is listed simply as 'Sandwich Islander'. What were the landsmen? They were just that, landsmen with little or no experience of the sea, who would be carrying out the necessary menial tasks on and below deck. Of the apprentices nothing is known beyond their names. Probably they served to some extent as servants for Bass and Bishop. In appearance the crew were undoubtedly a typical lot—weathered, sunburned faces, hair in long, tight plaits or perhaps cut short in the newer fashion, wearing the loose trousers and striped or checked shirts preferred by sailors, woollen caps or narrow-brimmed hats.

Final provisions and water were rowed out to the brig. A letter to William Waterhouse described last-minute financial arrangements. Later Elizabeth wrote to her mother-in-law that George had been 'so much busied ever since you went I have scarcely had a moments time to speak to him'.[14]

On 9 January a favourable wind seemed to be holding long enough to carry the convoy out of the Channel, and it was imperative to sail while the chance was there. Bass scratched out a final note to Henry Waterhouse: 'My dear friend, adieu Every success and much happiness attend you. Geo Bass.'[15] In his hurry he misdated the letter to 9 January 1800.

Later Elizabeth wrote to Sarah Bass:

> . . . our dear George left me on Friday last the Ninth at Nine in the Morning, I can hardly describe what . . . I felt and in short ever since it seems as if I had lost all I care for in the World indeed I love him most sincerely and three years is a great while to look forward too.

She added, 'he only just came in with the Boatman to fetch his things and just said good by'.[16] Some money matter seems to have been left unfinished. Aboard the ship Bass somehow found a moment to scribble a last word to his wife:

> Venus, Jan 9 1801
> My dear Bess
>   I have no cash to entrust to your care. and have only time to say God bless you my love. Remember me to our father most kindly Adieu adieu
>   Yours most affect'ly
>   Geo Bass[17]

Later Elizabeth wrote:

> My ever Dear George,
>   How shall I describe my feelings when you left me. I had stifled my Tears that I might not distress you it seemed as if I had lost every friend I had in the World, I watched the Boat till it was quite out of sight when the Waterman brought your little Note . . .[18]

By the waterman (or boatman) Elizabeth sent back to George a little 'scrap' of a note. This Bass received but was unable to answer 'for', he wrote later, 'as he came alongside the signal was just thrown out for the fleet to make all sail and we were every soul of us fully engaged. I have preserved your little scrap . . .'.[19] By ten o'clock the fleet was under way, hundreds of white sails filling and signal flags whipping in the wind. Knowing that the breeze might yet turn and the ships could be forced back into port, Elizabeth waited. But the wind held. The convoy moved on, out of Spithead and into the Atlantic, the little *Venus* third in line. Despite invitations from friends, Elizabeth did not leave her lodgings until a week afterwards when it was certain that the *Venus* would not return. She was also ill for several days, an indisposition she linked to evidently having failed to become pregnant. 'O my dear George', she wrote, 'it will hurt me more than I can discribe being obliged to disapoint your hopes'.[20] She was further distressed by the arrival just after Bass's departure of charts from the navy's hydrographer Alexander Dalrymple, that George had wanted to take with him.

In the view of the time a lady's health was a delicate affair, easily affected by circumstance, and Elizabeth later wrote that she had been

unwell for some months after Bass's departure. Returning to her disappointment in not falling pregnant, she said that initially she had
'pleased myself with the hope there was a little one on the Road that
would be able to call you Father on your return, but in that I am disapointed'. Rosemary tea and port wine had been prescribed, a doctor
had promised to take care of her health until Bass's return, and by
April she was 'so much better'.[21] Anxiety for Bass's safety had been
heightened by knowledge of very strong winds assailing the convoy. By
July, however, Henry Waterhouse was able to obtain a naval report
that although the *Venus* had been separated from the convoy, a brig of
her description had been seen past Madeira, heading south.

10

Adversity and Solutions

A few hours after the fleet left Spithead the wind rose to gale force. Steering south into the Bay of Biscay, the ships slid into dark watery pits, staggered and struggled upwards again on white-crested ridges that poured foaming torrents over the decks, while bare masts inscribed erratic patterns against a leaden sky. Blown from her place in the convoy, the *Venus* managed for some eleven or twelve days to keep company with HMS *Hussar*, but off Spain's Cape Finisterre in heavy winds from the north she dropped behind and fought on alone. With skill and determination, however, Bass and Bishop brought her safely into the port of San Salvador on the coast of Brazil at the beginning of March. Bass wrote to Elizabeth:

> We are arrived here all safe after a passage of 45 days from the spot where last we parted, that is, my dear Bess, you and I . . . Little Bess is well . . . she hangs up over the foot of my bed, and looks quite roguish. let the winds blow high or low, even the excesive heat of St Salvador are not able to put the waggery out of her countenance. Adieu little Bess; adieu, adieu to her original!! Pray write to me at China, write several letters; open all your soul to me; tell me all that grieves you, all that delights you. Yes, my Bess Bass. I will return; return to you, and that as speedily as possible.[1]

His letter reached Elizabeth seven months to the day after his departure. Ten days after writing his first letter from San Salvador he wrote again, full of yearning for a return of their brief happiness together — 'Oh Bess, may nothing prevent a renewal of those short lived happy days!' — and his hope for a quick and prosperous voyage that would enable him to acquire a ship big enough for her to accompany him on future voyages.² Letters to Henry and William Waterhouse apparently never arrived.

Sales did not go well in San Salvador. Bass and Bishop displayed their wares, but European manufactures were already plentiful in the hot, humid seaside town. The *Venus* then spent 23 days at the Ilha de Sao Sebastiao, 'a little, paltry place . . . some 10 score miles westward of Rio Janheiro', where wood and water were taken on and Bass worried that his letters might not be forwarded by 'these false, deceitful Portuguese'.³ That Bass himself had planned some duplicity seems likely. Among the trade goods listed in England were 'two Uniforms to humbug the Brazilians', suggesting that he intended to present a naval front to facilitate his sales.⁴ There is no further word that relates clearly to this scheme. His record of expenses at Sao Sebastiao includes gifts to the local commander 'for his winking at our trade', but Bass did not detail the circumstances.⁵ In both Brazilian ports he took on board a substantial quantity of tobacco.

There had been other disappointments. As they passed the Canary Islands the chance of capturing a Spanish prize, for which they evidently carried letters of marque, eluded them. On board rats became a plague, eating, among other things, the store of raisins. The ship's company, however, was apparently congenial and the *Venus* was, in Bass's words, a 'happy little vessel'.

The *Venus* quitted the Brazilian coast on 30 May, and on the eastward flow of winds and currents crossed the South Atlantic to arrive at the Cape of Good Hope without incident on 3 June 1801. The Cape, with its large British naval and military establishments and busy shipping activities, was a lively and prosperous place. Cape Town's wide, straight streets and large white and green Dutch residences would have revived pleasant memories of Bass's stay in 1797, when with William Paterson he visited local Dutch families. Now, however, his mind was on his enterprise. He wrote to William Waterhouse that with the addition of Brazilian goods, 'Our cargo . . . is now one of the most complete that was ever carried there [Port Jackson], and the little brig is as deep as she can swim, and full as an egg'. He added, 'She turns out very sound and tight, and bids fair to remain sound much longer than any of her owners.'⁶

Word from Port Jackson, however, was not encouraging. Changes in government regulations and the arrival of other merchant ships dimmed Bass and Bishop's brightest hopes. There were warnings too about attempting trade in New Guinea. Bass remained optimistic. 'We are, however, sanguine and sure of a successful voyage upon the whole', he wrote to his father-in-law. But the uncertainty of how long the voyage would now take firmed his determination not to be parted again from his wife. He added, 'The next voyage I believe she must make with me, for I shall but badly pass it without her.'[7]

To Elizabeth he was more explicit:

> I think my love this voyage once done we shall then have a fair chance of living together the remainder of our days. Not on shore Bess for I fear we must beat the wave in company and seek our bread on many & distant shores. Hard lot for thee! But thou mayest be happy even under such circumstances ... I will return to thee my dear Bess but there is yet a long round of voyage to make & much to be done.[8]

Clearly Bass saw his future upon the sea.

The *Venus* crossed the Indian Ocean and made her way through Bass Strait—'a good and perfectly safe passage'—and up the coast of New South Wales, with for Bass many reminders of his whaleboat and *Norfolk* voyages.[9] No doubt those first adventures now seemed far in the past.

On 29 August 1801 the *Venus* sailed between the massive promontories guarding the entrance to Port Jackson, and hours later splashed her anchor into the deep, quiet waters of Sydney Cove. The settlement had grown since Bass had seen it from the deck of the departing *Nautilus* over two years before. Houses of whitewashed brick or painted timber had spread farther over the hillsides. Government House on its rise had acquired a one-storey extension at its eastern end. To the west a windmill and the tall tower of the unfinished St Phillip's Church stood against the sky, while a new wharf and warehouse, built by the Calcutta merchant Robert Campbell, occupied part of the western foreshore. Lighters and flats moved among the several ships at anchor, unloading, among them the brig *Harrington* from Madras and Calcutta and the *Earl Cornwallis*, which had arrived from Britain with prisoners and miscellaneous freight. For Bass this was immediate confirmation of the word he had received at the Cape of a glutted market.

Since early January eleven ships had delivered general merchandise to Sydney, and only days after the *Venus*'s arrival the brig *Nautilus*, now owned by Robert Berry and with Roger Simpson in command, arrived from China with additional goods. There was more merchandise for sale than could be absorbed by the population of an estimated 5945 colonists, most with limited financial means. Food, specifically salt meat, was the commodity in which the colony remained in serious need.

The economy was slow for another reason as well. New South Wales had neither a treasury nor an official currency. The government and the military's paymaster paid with bills to be drawn on the British Treasury, the Navy Board or regimental agents in London. The Commissariat Store purchased local supplies by issuing store receipts. While an amount of diverse coinage—guineas, shillings, pence, Portuguese Johannas, guilders, Indian pagodas and Bengal rupees, ducats and, most importantly, Spanish dollars—reached Sydney with new arrivals or as change from purchases made from incoming ships, these amounts were relatively small. Government bills and receipts were in fact the colony's currency. The arrival of government supplies from England had at this time become more regular than before, necessitating fewer purchases from other sources and thus fewer bills to be drawn on the Treasury. In addition, the new governor, Philip Gidley King, was under pressure from London to reduce public expenditure, and through his efforts at greater government economy the circulation of bills and receipts was further reduced. The result was a deflationary situation, which lowered prices and slowed the movement of goods. '. . . glutted market, empty purses, treasure house dry. Hands full of goods, all sellers, no buyers. Distraction!' Bass later wrote to Jamison.[10] Containing his exasperation better, he wrote to his brother-in-law, Henry Waterhouse:

> Everything went on well until we arrived here, and since all things have gone bad. This market is glutted with goods beyond all comparison; glutted even on two accounts a natural glut from the quantity of goods far exceeding the consumption, and glutted also because the new system of Government is built upon a plan of the most rigid economy. It issues very little or no bills. We can sell very little of our cargo here

and what we do sell is to but very little advantage. Our wings are clipped with a vengeance, but we shall endeavour to fall upon our legs somehow or other. Our dear Bess talks of seeing me in 18 months alas poor Bess the when is uncertain, very uncertain in every thing but its long distance.[11]

Bass's plight was confirmed by Thomas Rowley, an officer of the New South Wales Corps who had resigned his commission to engage in farming. He wrote to Henry Waterhouse, 'There has been so many ships from England, India, America, &c., articles are wonderfully cheap . . . Liquor at 5s. p'r gallon, everything else in proportion.'[12] Even if cheaply, liquor, at least, was selling. An entry in the government's account of bills paid notes that on 14 October 1801, £122 17s od was paid to Bass and Bishop for '409½ gals. spirits @6/'.[13]

In desperation Bass conferred with Governor King, suggesting that the *Venus*'s merchandise be taken into government store to be offered at a 50 per cent reduction in price. King, however, declined for, he said, lack of authority. Bass immediately began looking for other means of salvaging his finances. He considered sealing on the American north-west coast, something with which Bishop had experience, but word was that the Chinese market for seal skins had collapsed. He turned towards possible trade with the Pacific islands.

Tentative plans to develop trade between New South Wales and the Pacific islands had existed virtually since the founding of the colony. An element here was the influence of the London Missionary Society, which wanted to establish stations on Tahiti and Tonga and in the Marquesas Islands, for which both King and Sir Joseph Banks had promised support. Another factor was the possibility of a food source much closer than England. Governor Arthur Phillip had been urged to import island live-stock, but did not do so. On the arrival in the colony of Governor King, however, the idea gained impetus. The islands, specifically Tahiti, were seen as a likely source of much-needed salt pork. Matavai Bay on the island's north coast had been the main anchorage for visiting British ships, and King made contact with the principal native chief of the district, known to the British as Pomare, and in May 1801 HM Armed Brig *Porpoise* was despatched to the island. She returned four months later with 31 000 pounds of excellent salt pork, purchased 'at a trifling cost'.

In January 1801 the brig *Harbinger* had arrived in Sydney. She was a vessel of 56 tons burden, built in 1797 in Quebec of Canadian oak and in good condition. During the previous year the sloop *Norfolk*, in which Bass and Flinders had circumnavigated Van Diemen's Land, had been seized and wrecked by escaping convicts, and to replace her in carrying stores and despatches to Norfolk Island King bought the little *Harbinger* for £700 and renamed her *Norfolk*. On 8 November she sailed under William House for Tahiti for salt pork. It was in this commerce that Bass now saw a ready means of recouping his fortunes.

However, another matter was now of serious concern to Bass. Lieutenant Colonel William Paterson was at this time commanding officer of the New South Wales Corps, with Captain John Macarthur as second in command. Much of the bitter resentment felt by the military against John Hunter was now directed at Governor King. This became aggravated by a series of events that culminated in what was seen by some as the Governor's interference in the colony's judicial process. Inflamed by what he saw as insults to his honour, Macarthur, an aggressively egotistical man, attempted to isolate the Governor by urging his fellow officers not to visit Government House except on official business. When Paterson refused to comply, Macarthur turned his fierce and explosive antagonism against him. He publicised letters and private comments made by Paterson that were critical of some of King's actions. When this failed to shatter the association between the two, Macarthur made public a letter from Paterson's wife to his own, which exposed Elizabeth Paterson to criticism. For Paterson there was now no alternative but to challenge Macarthur to a duel.

Men of the time who were socially recognised as gentlemen lived — or were expected to live — by a particular code of honour that required an insulted person to confront his offender with a challenge to a duel. The question of who was right or wrong was not addressed, but the matter would be settled quickly and usually permanently, as the duel was felt to have satisfied honour on both sides and no further aggression was necessary. The British army's Articles of War forbade duelling between officers on pain of dismissal from the service, but so prevalent was the custom that to decline a challenge was a matter of serious disgrace. Macarthur's behaviour had been insupportably dishonourable, and if he were to preserve both the respect of others and his own self-respect, Paterson had no alternative. It is obvious that neither officer had any intention of avoiding the encounter.

Accordingly, Paterson's second, Captain Neil McKellar, delivered the challenge, to which Macarthur replied, 'Whenever he pleases.'[14] Wind and rain forced delays, but a location was finally determined at Parramatta and the appointed time set at one o'clock in the afternoon of Monday 14 September 1801. McKellar wrote:

> Capt. MacArthur loaded his own pistols . . . I loaded Col. Paterson's, and when done tossed up for the first fire, which was won by Capt. Piper [Macarthur's second] for Capt. McArthur; measured the distance (twelve paces) and desired Col. Paterson, who stood a little way off, to take his ground, which having done I gave him a pistol not cocked. Capt. McArthur fired, and his ball having hit the Colonel in the right shoulder he dropt his pistol . . . it was impossible he could return fire. I then told Capt. Piper that his principal might quit his ground, when Capt. McArthur sent me a message, as if exulting in victory, that he should be ready for Col. Paterson at any time.[15]

The wounded Paterson was attended by the New South Wales Corps surgeon, John Harris, the acting principal surgeon of the colony, James Thomson, and his friend, George Bass, despite being on leave. The consensus of opinion was not to attempt to remove the ball, and it remained in the shoulder, or from other descriptions in the upper arm. Paterson was not considered out of danger for over a week while, in effect, everyone waited.[16] Should he have died the *rencontre* would have been a much more serious transgression. In the interval King interviewed the two seconds and required their reports to determine that the duel had been carried out in accordance with the prescribed code of honour. Macarthur, Piper and McKellar were arrested, and as Paterson's condition improved, King requested his explanation of the event. In mid-November 1802 Macarthur left Sydney to be court-martialled in England. On 29 March 1803 Captain McKellar, carrying Macarthur's sword and Governor King's despatches on the duel, sailed in the 103-ton American schooner *Caroline*, which was headed for New Bedford, Massachusetts, from where McKellar would trans-ship for England. The *Caroline* disappeared at sea and McKellar was never heard from again. Paterson, meanwhile, recovered. A year later, however, further consultation by several doctors, including Bass, recommended that he withdraw from active service in the colony. Aside from the effects of the wound, he was probably suffering from the strain of deteriorating relations with King and very likely excessive drinking.

Bass, meanwhile, had pursued negotiations with Governor King for the importation of salt pork from the Pacific islands, and on 9 October a contract was signed between 'His Excellency Governor King, on the part of His Majesty, on the one part, and Mssrs. Bass and Bishop, merchants, on the other'.[17] The two merchants were to make their purchases at Matavai Bay on the island of Tahiti, known to the British as Otaheite, where the necessary diplomatic procedures were well known to the English, whereas on other islands a 'momentary error' in the sometimes elaborate courtesies involved could jeopardise the entire relationship. In addition, Bass and Bishop were authorised to carry as 'presents' for the chief Pomare or someone delegated by him, twelve muskets, 20 pounds of powder and 50 pounds of ball. King agreed to purchase the whole cargo of pork, if well cured, at sixpence per pound sterling, to be paid in a bill upon the Treasury. Casks to contain the pork would be provided by the government insofar as they could be spared. Additional casks would have to be provided by Bass and Bishop. The *Venus*'s merchandise from England was to be put in government stores free of charge until the expiration of the contract.

For Bass this was a depressing solution to the adversities of the voyage, a painful conclusion to the high hopes with which the adventure had been planned. It was, however, the best he could manage. A few days earlier he had received letters from Elizabeth and her father. Cheering as this was, his frustration and despondency were uncharacteristically evident in the letter he wrote in reply: 'I am in a gloomy mood Bess. I wish I had thee with me, but thou must wait at home till I fetch thee, w'ch shall be as soon as possible, for I long to have thy chatter. We will not part anymore.'[18]

The next day he wrote to Henry Waterhouse with a touch of bitter sarcasm: 'We go from hence amongst savages, we are tired of civilised life. Our brig is fitting with the necessary barricades and other securities, when they are completed we shall sail. In 8 or 10 months I think we shall return here and try our luck a second time.' Bass interrupted his writing: 'the colours are up at South Head for a large ship; this ship may be Flinders with fresh news of Tichborne Street'.[19] The incoming ship, however, was the *Porpoise* from Tahiti with salt pork.

Bass sent letters to Elizabeth by every opportunity, that is, by every ship leaving the colony. Whether these letters would reach her was always questionable, for most went to the Cape of Good Hope, to China or India, there hopefully to be sent on by some vessel bound for England. Bess, however, had 'claims upon me that admit not of my losing any opportunity however vague & uncertain it may be'. He wrote of his preparations for the pork-buying voyage, mustering casks and making every effort to speed the journey, 'But my love all this protracts, most cruelly protracts, our voyage. Necessity, however, leaves us without an appeal. it must be so!'[20]

Evidently Bass resumed his earlier friendships, and the personable young surgeon with recent news of affairs in England was welcome in the colonial homes. To Elizabeth he wrote, 'The ladies here make many inquiries after you (Mrs King & Patterson) and desire to be kindly remembered to you. They regret much you are not here.'[21] Thomas Jamison, William Kent and James Williamson had left for England in September 1800, Jamison taking with him Bass's books. Paterson, meanwhile, was 'recovering fast'. Macarthur, Bass asked Elizabeth to tell her brother Henry, was on his way to England, 'sent home to add or rather to restore peace to this country'.[22]

Thomas Palmer, James Ellis and John Boston had also left the colony. Palmer's sentence had expired and in January 1801 the three men and Boston's family had sailed for New Zealand, Fiji and finally Guam in the Marianas, where the Spanish seized the vessel as a prize and detained her company. In June 1802 Palmer died of dysentery, but his associates eventually reached Manila, where Boston and Ellis went into business.[23] Meanwhile, Governor King had ordered Acting Lieutenant John Murray to survey Bass Strait in HM Armed Survey Vessel *Lady Nelson*, a 53-foot craft uniquely built with three sliding keels. Murray consulted Bass on the dangers of the voyage. Of a reef off Albatross Island he wrote in his log, 'This Reef I named Lady Nelson Reef from our so narrowly escaping being on shore on it, for I have not the least doubt but it is what Mr Bass gave me a sketch of, the latitude and longitude so well correspond with his.'[24]

On 12 November Bass wrote a third letter to Elizabeth from Port Jackson, somewhat more optimistically. Without question the pork voyage would be profitable and probably would clear their debts in London. There were some very cheering rays of sunshine in the gloom, he said, and the promise of a 'burning day' to come. A peace with Spain would greatly improve matters, but even without it 'a few vigorous and wary exertions will make all go well'.[25] He did not explain further. More immediately, however, he intended that the *Venus* make a brief diversion from her intended course for Tahiti.

Six years earlier, in September 1795, the storeship *Endeavour*, Captain William Bampton, had sailed from Sydney for India by way of Norfolk Island and New Zealand. Off the southwest coast of New Zealand's South Island, the ship, leaking dangerously, was run into the shallows at Dusky Sound, a bight known to whalers. Over the succeeding two years her castaways had been gradually rescued, while the wreck of the ship remained aground. This, George Bass decided, would be his first stop. The forested shores would provide timber for making the pork chests he needed, and iron fittings salvaged from the wreck could be reworked on the *Venus*'s forge into trade goods or useful shipboard equipment.

Church of St Denis, Aswarby, Lincolnshire, parts of which date back to the twelfth century. The Bass family worshipped here and George Bass's father, also George Bass, was buried in its graveyard. (Photo by David Marsden, Grantham, Lincolnshire)

The City from Bankside, oil on canvas by Thomas Miles Richardson. The picture shows some of the activity on and along the Thames River that would have been familiar to George Bass. St Paul's Cathedral stands in the background. (Courtesy of the Museum of London)

Matthew Flinders (1774–1814), c. 1800, miniature portrait painted on ivory. Soon after arriving in Australia in 1795, Bass and Flinders explored sections of the southeast coast. In 1788-89 they traversed Bass Strait and circumnavigated Tasmania proving it to be an island. (ML Ref: MIN 52, Mitchell Library, State Library of New South Wales)

The Bass River, Western Port, Victoria. Following the Australian coast with a crew of six in a whaleboat, George Bass entered the inlet he named Western Port and rowed up the Bass River in search of fresh water. The group evidently camped on the river bank. (Photo by William F. Wilson, Melbourne and 'Bass River')

A modern replica of the sloop Norfolk in which George Bass and Matthew Flinders circumnavigated Tasmania. The voyage revealed a navigable strait connecting the Pacific and Indian oceans. (Photo by Michael Tierney, Stanley, Tasmania)

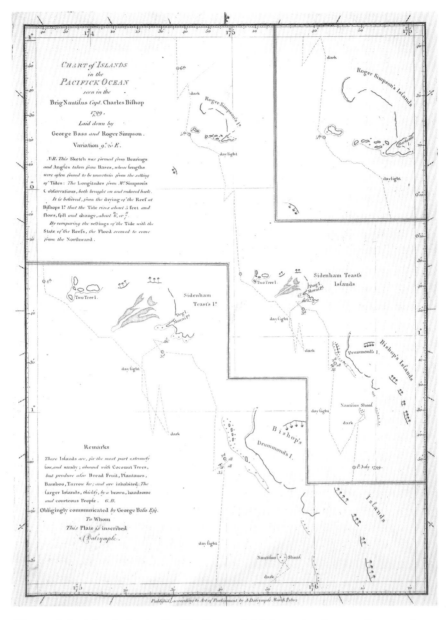

Chart of the islands in the Pacific Ocean laid down by George Bass and Roger Simpson, 1799. Sailing from New South Wales to Macau, Bass charted a number of islands now in the modern nations of Tuvalu, Kiribati and Marshall Islands. (© British Crown Copyright 2004. Published by permission of the Controller of Her Majesty's Stationery Office and the UK Hydrographic Office, www.ukho.gov.uk)

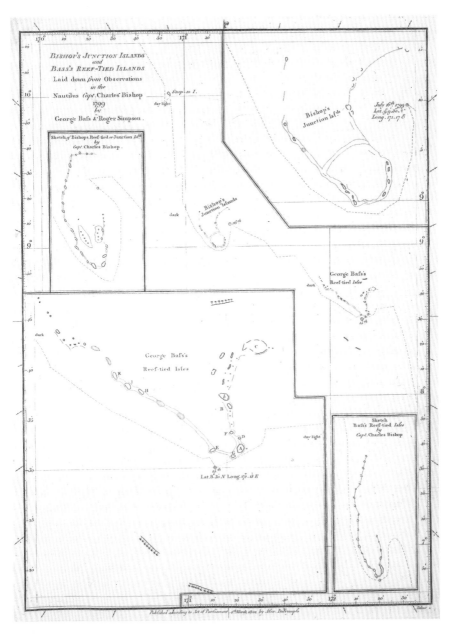

Bishop's Junction Islands and Bass's Reef-Tied Islands laid down from on board the Nautilus by George Bass and Roger Simpson, 1799. These islands are now part of Republic of the Marshall Islands. (© British Crown Copyright 2004. Published by permission of the Controller of Her Majesty's Stationery Office and the UK Hydrographic Office, www.ukho.gov.uk)

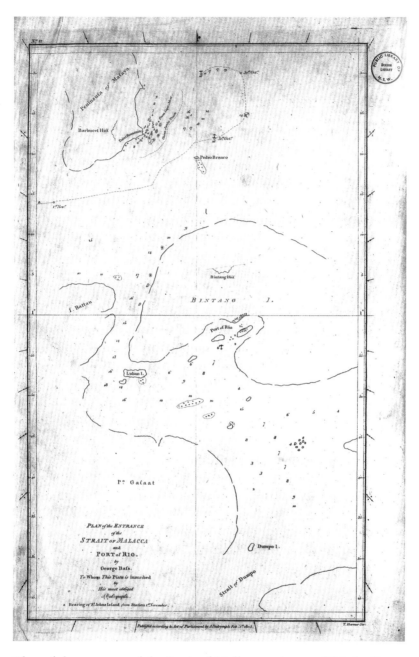

Plan of the entrance of the Strait of Mallaca and port of Rio by George Bass. Bass charted the low-lying area as he passed through the Singapore and Mallaca straits on his way to England. (Dixson Library, State Library of New South Wales)

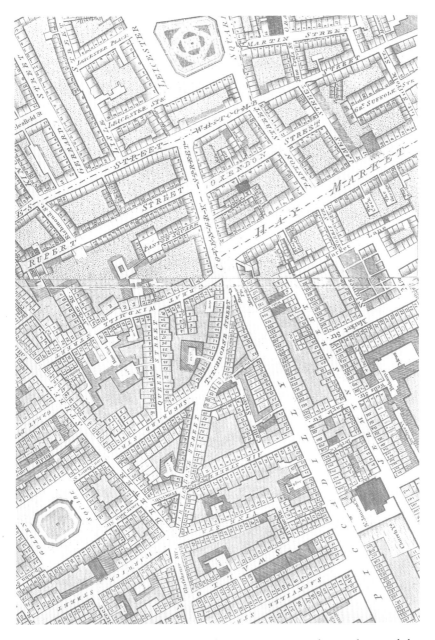

Piccadilly, detail from the Horwood Map, 1792–99. The residence of the Waterhouse family was at 29 Tichborne Street. It was here no doubt that Bass met Elizabeth, sister of his friend Henry Waterhouse. Two months later they married at nearby St James's Church. (Courtesy of the Museum of London)

In the presence of William Bass
Sarah Bass

No. 314 George Bass, of the parish of St Clement ...
in the County of Middlesex & Elizabeth Waterhouse
of this parish were married in this Church by Licence
from the Archbishop of Canterbury this Eighth day
of October in the Year 1800 —

J. Syone M. Maddy Curate
This marriage was solemnized between us
George Bass   Eliz Waterhouse
In the presence of H. Waterhouse, M. Waterhouse

*Marriage licence of
Elizabeth Waterhouse
and George Bass. Held
without the knowledge
of Elizabeth's parents,
the marriage was
witnessed by her
brother Henry and
sister Maria. (Courtesy
of William F. Wilson,
Melbourne and 'Bass
River')*

*Sydney, c. 1803, seen from the west side of the cove, watercolour, unsigned.
Beyond the open space in the foreground are the three long hospital buildings
where Bass evidently assisted after his arrival in 1795.
(ML Ref: XVI/1803/1. Mitchell Library, State Library of New South Wales)*

11

Into the Pacific

On 21 November 1801 the little *Venus* spread her sails, passed between Port Jackson's headlands and steered southeast through today's Tasman Sea for Dusky Sound.[1] Sixteen days later she let go her anchor in Facile Harbour, one of the Sound's many small inlets. At the head of the cove a sheer, almost overhanging precipice soared hundreds of feet up from the water's surface. The surrounding forest was dark and misty. Hauled into a narrow shallow-water recess in the shoreline lay the broken hulk of the East Indiaman *Endeavour*.

Bass and Bishop set up camp and for fourteen days the men of the *Venus* felled pine trees, cut planks to make pork chests, and 'rummaged' through the wreck, breaking out pieces of iron and salvaging any useful stores that had survived the years. Relatively sheltered, the ship's English oak and East Indian teak planking remained solid, as did her copper sheathing. Bass decided that two anchors and various iron fittings could await another trip.

On 21 December the *Venus* left Dusky Sound. Later Bass wrote to an unidentified correspondent, 'Sailing from thence and passing Cape West we discovered some inlets and large sounds which we have named the Inlets of Venus.'[2] Thus the *Venus* explored New Zealand's southernmost coast, and an interesting question is whether in rounding South Island Bass passed through the Foveaux Strait between Stewart Island and the mainland. If he did, Bass and Bishop would have been the first European navigators to do so. From Bass's later references, we know that he was aware of the small, rocky, uninhabited Snares Islands, discovered separately by George Vancouver and William Broughton in 1791, the desolate Antipodes Islands, then called the Penantipodes Isles and first seen from HMS *Reliance* in 1800, and the granite outcrops that are the windswept Bounty Islands, all within a few hundred miles east and southeast of New Zealand. Whether he saw them is not clear from his letters, and the brig's log no longer exists.

Now there lay before the *Venus* and her men the empty immensity of the Pacific, day after day of a level, featureless horizon, changing only with the gathering and dispersal of clouds, with the rise of the wind and its dying to stillness, an ocean mounting into windblown crests or subsiding into a sheet of polished metal. And the passage of dawn, the noonday calculation of the ship's position, sunset, and the darkness of a limitless sky above the swaying, inky etching of sails and spars.

Bass's letter to his unknown correspondent continued:

> in 23.50 S 211.45 E we fell in with a large island inhabited by people speaking the same language and apparently every way the same as the Otaheitians.[3] They were very shy at first, & very impudent afterwards. We called this Island after a friend of Bishops, Lord Boltons Island;[4] its name we think to be <u>Vavaitoo. The high land seen by the Chatham</u> lies some miles different in latitude.[5] Vavaitoo is I think one island only of an unknown group, of which Toobonai was the first discovered. The horizon was much pent up with rain clouds & squalls during the time we were near Vavaitoo. The which . . . prevented us from seeing to any great distance around us . . .[6]

In a letter to Governor King, Bass stated that on two different days he and Bishop 'communicated' with the people. Despite the recurring rain they evidently came ashore and very likely it was through the Sandwich Islander in his crew and his own limited vocabulary that Bass was able to speak with the Polynesian inhabitants.

The identity of Bass's Lord Bolton's Island is something of a mystery. Bass's reference to the 'high land seen by the Chatham', presumably today's Chatham Islands, suggests that Lord Bolton's Island, like the Chathams, was somewhere east of New Zealand. His given positioning of the island, however, puts it hundreds of miles to the northeast, virtually on the Tropic of Capricorn, at a spot where on today's charts there is no island. Nor does a Lord Bolton's Island or a Vavaitoo appear in such older sources as Findlay's *Directory of the South Pacific Ocean* (1884) or James Horsburgh's third edition. With rain and cloud Bass probably did not find his position accurately, but if his 'Toobonai' is taken to be Tubuai and Vavaitoo as perhaps Vavitu, also known as Raivavae, Bass would have been in the group now called the Tubuai or Austral Islands, some of which had been sighted by Cook. Roughly 400 miles to the southeast are the tiny, rocky Marotiri (or Morotiri) islets, recorded on some maps as Iles de Bass, but whether Bass reached these little outcrops is uncertain. The name may be based more on assumption than fact.

Now the *Venus* altered course to the north and for eleven days beat against a northeast wind. On 24 January 1802 they sighted Mehetia and with good winds covered the 60 miles to Tahiti's Matavai Bay the same day.

The island of Tahiti, some 17° south of the Equator and in the path of the easterly tradewinds, had been visited in 1767 by the British Captain Samuel Wallis, and subsequently by Antoine de Bougainville, James Cook and William Bligh. They found a Polynesian population with distinct political territories and a complex system of rank and authority closely tied to beliefs in the supernatural. In 1796 the London Missionary Society had established a station at the island's Matavai Bay. Their presence was deeply resented by the Tahitians and, faced with hostility amounting to violence, most of the English departed with the *Nautilus* when Bishop and Simpson called in 1798.

Thus when Bass and Bishop landed at Matavai Bay, they found the Reverend John Jefferson, only six of the first missionaries and nine recent arrivals. In Bass's view their position was virtually untenable. He wrote, 'The missionaries (poor creatures), our countrymen, are very civil and friendly in their little way', and without authority of any kind 'civility' was all they had to offer.[7] At Matavai Bass also found the colonial brig *Norfolk*, formerly the *Harbinger*, which had arrived five days earlier and now had its crew busily processing hogs into salt pork. The result was a degree of competition between the men of the two vessels which the natives used to their advantage in bartering pigs and foodstuffs—coconuts, breadfruit, taro and plantains. But, as Bass wrote to William Waterhouse:

> . . . we find the island yet so abundant in hogs we have determined to set up an establishment here which will aim at curing about two-fifths of our whole cargo, for which we have enough salt with us . . . The

Chief of the Island is our good friend, and will remain so as long as we shall want a friend here, because he knows we have much property of well assorted Indian trade [goods], which Gov'r King's stores will not afford until fresh supplies duly selected shall arrive from England.[8]

The muskets brought by Bass and Bishop were particularly coveted, and some were presented to the chief Pomare, his son, who was in fact the king, and members of his family, a move credited by some sources as the reason for Bass and Bishop securing more hogs than did William House of the *Norfolk*. Bass continued: 'Pomarre has given us one of his own houses on Pt. Venus, which was removed to the spot we fixed upon as most convenient for our work. We have in short everything we ask for that he can give.'

The exchange of gifts was in fact a method of trading. 'Our great present for example cost us about 6 guineas in England, but when he comes to square it in return, he will give 50, 60, or 80 large hogs . . .' Bass could not help comparing the abundance of food on the island for everyone with the 'starving condition' of impoverished English. On 31 January he wrote to Governor King, summarising the journey to that point and outlining his plans for a voyage to the Hawaiian islands. The letter would be carried to Sydney by the returning *Norfolk*.

Within days Bishop had been established in the transported house, now enclosed in she-oak palings. With six seamen from the *Venus* his task was to buy hogs, slaughter them and salt the meat, saw planks for pork chests and make up ironwork for barter. On 6 February 1802 Bass took command of the *Venus* and with the remaining crew headed for the Hawaiian Islands — the Sandwich Islands, as he knew them — stopping first at the islet of Eimeo for a supply of taro and possibly visiting others of the Society archipelago. A story tells of meeting an English castaway on Moina island, a man who in the course of several years had settled there, but no firm evidence for this seems to exist.

Hogs and salt were Bass's objectives in the Hawaiian Islands. With curing set up in two locations, their task would be completed that much more quickly. And salt, not available in sufficient quantity in Tahiti, had to be found. The shortage of salt in Tahiti was also noted a few years later by the Danish adventurer Jørgen Jørgensen, on the whaler *Alexander*, when the crew had to manufacture salt before processing the abundant fresh meat. The Tahitians had no need of preserving meat.

Bass wrote to his mother and to Elizabeth before sailing. The letter to Sarah Bass has evidently not survived, but to his Bess he lamented not having been able to take her on the voyage, 'which I fear must be very very long'. Yet by no means should she 'set out to attempt to join me at Port Jackson; no not even if thy father or thy brother Henry sh'd go there, for', with his voyaging, 'we shall certainly miss each other ... we may perhaps wander about after each other for years unsuccessfully'. He wanted her 'fixed' where he could surely find her. In Tahiti it could have been dangerous, he teased, 'for a married man to remain exposed for months to the temptations of 5000 handsome, naked females', but they only 'infinitely exalt thee in the opinion & esteem of thy husband'. The royal women, accompanying the king and his suite, often crowded into 'our little cabin' and 'have seen thy picture (<u>little Bess</u>); They much admire the <u>waheine of Brittance</u> and are much pleased when they hear that I will bring her by & by to visit them in person'.[9] Bass wrote neither descriptions nor comments of a scientific nature while in Tahiti. The naturalist had given way entirely to the adventurer with a mind firmly set on the financial success of his journey.

There would have been a special exhilaration in being in sole command of the *Venus* for the voyage to Hawaii. On the table in the little cabin he plotted her course with his dividers and scale ruler and the compass rose on charts with large empty spaces. From the deck he took the brig's latitudinal position, measuring with his sextant the angle between the sun or other celestial body and the horizon and following the necessary mathematical procedures, and with his chronometer worked out his position in degrees of longitude east of Greenwich. He watched the vessel's spread of canvas and scanned the ocean with his telescope, often from the masthead. By night too he would have walked the deck, watching the constellations cross the sky, checking the compass in the candle-lit binnacle, alert to any murmur of change in the wind in the shadowy curves of his sails.

There appears to be no record relating to Bass's handling of discipline. Probably he maintained much the same disciplinary standards and methods as he had observed in the navy; if fairly applied, experienced, realistic seamen of the time accepted this. Most likely his evident skill in handling the ship, even his love of her and of the sea, were qualities his men could respect.

Steering north, the *Venus* traversed some 3000 miles of ocean, an ocean empty except for a few minute and widely scattered coral atolls now mainly part of Kiribati's Line Islands. An uninhabited lagoon island came up on the horizon: 'Ran down along it's west side & round the north end, did not land because could not Anchor. No navigator on board in case of my being seperated from the Vessel by any accident. I think Captain Broughton saw the same Island . . .'[10]

Bass's inability to anchor was due to the depth of the sea around the island. His comment, however, on not having a navigator on board is curious, as Robert Scott was sailing with him. Scott had invested £260 in the venture, and the question arises whether he had received his position as first mate despite a lack of the necessary skills. Yet at a later date Bass appears to have been fully prepared to entrust the command of the *Venus* to Scott. The comment remains unexplained.

On 11 March Bass's efficient navigation brought the *Venus* into the mile-wide crescent of 'Karakakooa [Kealakekua] Bay' on the large island of Hawaii, where James Cook had died, and 'where having bought 200 Hogs of Tamaahmaah [Kamehameha] the King, I sailed for Woohoo to receive them'.[11]

Since their initial European discovery by James Cook in 1778, the Hawaiian islands had been visited intermittently by American and European vessels, stopping mainly for food and water. By the early 1800s the American whaling fleet had begun to spend its winters there. In the meantime, following a series of conquests, most of the islands had been united by 1796 into a single kingdom under one ruler, Kamehameha I.

Characteristically Bass threw himself into his task with determination. Shattering as had been the collapse of his original high hopes, and much as he clearly disliked the pork trade, 'habit and sturdy, unremitting industry, must not only teach us to bear it but also enable us to throw the burthen off from our shoulders'.[12] Local chiefs came on board at all hours to discuss, sometimes at great length, the purchases Bass desired. 'I have scarcely an instant of leisure time . . .'[13]

The exchange of European goods for hogs and provisions generally took place between the deck of the brig and the native canoes that came alongside, a laborious and often tricky process as both vessels surged up and down on the swell while screaming pigs were swayed up to the deck. Here pens had been erected, where the animals remained until unloaded where a curing station had been set up. Navigating in largely uncharted waters among unfamiliar reefs and islands, in unfamiliar winds and currents, was in itself extremely demanding for Bass and for his hard-working crew.

The *Venus*'s journeying among the islands is difficult to follow. No log or relevant charts survive, and the ship's track is suggested only by brief references in Bass's letters to a few places with Polynesian names, which he spelled as he thought he heard them and which do not always match well with modern versions. It is evident that on about 20 May, as the *Venus* lay off the jagged green cliffs of Molokai, which Bass wrote as Morokoi, he had found means of sending letters to England, possibly by meeting some home-bound ship. A letter to an unknown correspondent, of which there is an extant copy in the hand of William Waterhouse, describes some of his voyage.

> Three weeks we were in a little reef harbour and I then sailed for Attooi, leaving Scott & three hands to buy up all he c'd in my absence. Since that I have visited every island of the group & having done at Owhyhee [Hawaii] all that I can, am now running down again through the group to glean the field . . .[14]

Bass wrote no descriptions of the spectacular beauty of the islands, nor made any remark relating to natural history. He saw bold headlands thrust into silver-blue seas, green precipices threaded with slender waterfalls, pale yellow beaches in hot sunlight, but none of this reflects in his letters. Only one brief remark is made on something beyond the day's work: 'We labour hard, eat plenty of pork and tarro; and I have painted one Womans head a Sandwich islander.'[15] We have no other reference to any artistic endeavour before or afterwards by Bass. 'Oils' and 'brushes', without further description, were included in the list of trade goods taken on board in England, but beyond that fact one can only speculate. Yet he was aware of his surroundings. He wrote to Elizabeth, 'Eighteen months Bess thou gavest me for my voyage; alas, alas. I often

wish thee with me. My Bess w'd be delighted with this place . . .'
Nevertheless, the journey being what it was, it was best that she was not
there. 'Be assured that meet we will when we possibly can. It is far for
thee to come to me. it is nothing for me to sail thousands of miles to pick
thee up & carry thee away.' He had some 'feeble perceptions' of making
'such change with the warming glimpse of sunshine that living with thee
once more w'd occasion'. But 'being amongst the Islands trading with
canoes & taking care of the vessel takes up every instant of the day, and
often night. I can only find time to assure thee once again of firm un-
alterable love for my beloved wife'.[16]

In a letter apparently written to William Waterhouse, the tone was
more optimistic. Fortune, he said, 'barring accidents must soon look
chearily on us and our labours'. Their enterprise had suffered no actual
losses other than 'detention of sales, and loss of time and failure of
expected remittances to our friends in England'. He had 'slaughtered
and salted about 500 hogs since I have been here (Mar 10th) and our
vessel may be about 2 5ths filled. Bishop's purchases I expect will [be]
nearly 1 fifth more'. In addition he had on board about 60 tons of salt
'bo't here very cheap', most of which he intended to leave in Tahiti for
'a next voyage under contract sh'd that take place'. If not, he would
sell it to the colonial government as it lay on Tahiti in the care of the
missionaries. A second voyage would have several advantages, 'having
plenty of salt, a knowledge of the best islands for hogs, and an increasing facility in curing them'.[17] Curing pork in hot weather required
particular care.

A letter to his 'ever dear mother' outlined his immediate intentions
and his hopes:

> I shall proceed towards Otaheiti to pick up Bishop & his purchases
> from whence we shall jog down together through the Friendly, Society,
> Navigators, Feejees & Hebrides on the way to Port Jackson . . . this
> voyage I expect will clear off all our debts upon the cargo in London
> with what we remitted from Port Jackson. So once more we shall be
> clear of the world . . . God bless thee in these terrible times . . . Thy
> wants and inconveniences form no small part of the increased
> gnawings of this life. And I burn with anxiety to relieve them. Fortune
> must do better for us . . .

I must leave thee for a chief is come on board to trade. but I have nothing more to say than to assure you of my firm<u>est</u> affection & love which as time draws on increases more & more. Adieu adieu my dearest friend

Geo Bass[18]

Some five days earlier he had written to Thomas Jamison, certain that the voyage would be moderately profitable. 'It ought', he wrote, 'for the labour is no trifle'.[19]

Bass evidently intended to stop at 'the two pearl islands near the Marquesas' as he returned to Tahiti, but apparently did not do so.[20] On 1 August 1802 Bass steered the *Venus* back into Matavai Bay.

Some startling events had taken place in his absence. In late March the violent winds and torrential rain of a typhoon had struck the island, with heavy swells surging into Matavai Bay, where the colonial vessel *Norfolk* rode at anchor. The brig's small bower anchor cable parted. Plunging heavily and shipping water, with the sea repeatedly breaking over her, the *Norfolk* swung, rolled and pitched against her remaining cable. By the third day its strands were breaking. With no sign of the storm abating, and the possibility of her being driven onto rocks, her company decided to beach her. The fore staysail was set, the last strands of the cable were cut and 'in about 5 minutes' she had run onto the sand. William House wrote in his log:

And she soon beat herself high enough to Walk on Shore, between the Surfs, Captn. Bishop and Men the Missionaries and Natives were down upon the Beach and gave me all the Assistance in their Power to Save the things out of the Vessel . . . I had the Masts Cut away which seemed to greatly ease her.[21]

As the storm finally lessened, House, Bishop and their carpenters together with Jefferson inspected the hull. The *Norfolk* was pronounced irreparable unless materials and equipment could be speedily obtained from Port Jackson. No lives, however, had been lost and the cargo of salt pork was retrieved. The seventeen men of her company joined the missionaries and the *Venus*'s people already on shore, and the number of Europeans was suddenly increased with the arrival of the *Nautilus*, under the command of Roger Simpson.

Meanwhile quarrels between Pomare and his subjects and those of other chiefs had erupted into war. With killings and the burning of villages in areas coming gradually closer to Matavai, the British on the island had become increasingly anxious for their safety. Charles Bishop enthusiastically joined the conflict as an ally of Pomare. According to William House, he drilled Pomare's warriors in British army procedures for loading and firing muskets.[22] A sturdy stockade was built around the mission house, boards bristling with nails were sunk into the paths leading to it, and the verandah fortified with chests, bedding and other items. Four brass cannon retrieved from the *Norfolk* were mounted in the upper rooms. With a strong party of Englishmen, Bishop occupied a pass that blocked the way for the invaders. In early July, with the consent but without the participation of the missionaries, Bishop and 24 other Europeans, carrying guns, ammunition and a four-pound cannon, joined Pomare's warriors in forays against enemy strongholds. Their success was only partial, but resulted in at least a temporary cessation of hostilities, for which the missionaries were profoundly grateful to Bishop.

Bishop's role in this conflict has been described by some historians as verging on the neurotic. However his behaviour can be described, this military adventure seems to have been some kind of high point from which Bishop's mental and physical health rapidly deteriorated. On 8 July 1802 John Jefferson wrote a letter of thanks to him, but the navigator was too sick to receive it personally. A month later Jefferson wrote to Governor King that he would hear of events 'from Captn. Bishop should he live (for at present he is very ill) to see Sydney'.[23] Bishop's illness was not described.

On his arrival Bass examined the wreck of the *Norfolk*. The brig was deeply bedded in the sand and stripped of masts, rigging and sails which, however, had been brought under shelter. Timbers were sprung and separated from the planks of her bottom, and numerous planks throughout had started or were bulged and splintered. The oakum that had caulked her seams was a rotting mass. Her copper was coming off the starboard bilge. Nevertheless, many planks and timbers, her bottom planks included, remained perfectly sound. Here was a vessel that, in Bass's view, could yet be put to use.

Knowledge of the *Venus*'s 'jog' through the Pacific islands is slight.

Although Bass wrote to Henry Waterhouse that he had 'communi-cated' to Dalrymple some new geographical findings, no charts or journals appear to exist. Bass did not share his journal of the voyage, a deliberate act, as he wrote to Governor King, because of the 'unpara-lelled neglect' of his previous service to the British Government. Obviously, he referred to the lack of recognition of his earlier ex-plorations, although it was a resentment that had not been apparent at the time. Thus his findings on this voyage can be surmised only from the scant references made in letters—some islands he thought known to Broughton and Cook and one entry, almost cryptic, that reads 'ESE of Oparo the <u>Four Crowns</u> of Quiros, long expunged from the charts, not seen since 1606'.[24] He mentioned the Navigators' Islands, now Samoa, where he found the people 'excellent & very superior', deserv-ing of a better name for their island and to be better known. The French navigator Jacques Félix Emanuel Hamelin, whom Bass later met in Port Jackson, noted in his diary that Bass had called at the Society Islands, the Friendly Islands (today's Tonga), the Sandwich Islands and the Navigators' Islands. Bass himself mentioned later that he did not stop at Fiji.

On 15 November 1802 Governor King wrote to Robert Hobart, Baron Hobart and Earl of Buckinghamshire, who was Secretary of State for War and the Colonies:

> My Lord,
>   The French ships being detained until this date by contrary winds enables me further to inform your Lordship that Mr. Bass arrived here with the Venus the 14th inst., from Otaheite with 57 tons of salted pork.[25]

On the same day Bass wrote to Elizabeth: 'Two minutes must suffice to tell thee I love thee; and that I am yet alive as thou mayest perhaps surmise by my writing to thee. The Naturaliste bound for France sails in a few hours; we are just arrived . . .'[26] Briefly he then outlined the success of the pork voyage and the work that still lay before him.

Several ships were at anchor in Sydney Cove as the *Venus* moored. The French scientific exploration vessels, the *Géographe* and the *Naturaliste,* now preparing to sail, had been at Port Jackson since the previous May and June. HMS *Buffalo*, Captain William Kent, had arrived from London with stores, and the transports *Atlas* and *Alexander*, having delivered prisoners in October, remained at anchor. Thus Bass found to his pleasure that a number of naval friends were in Sydney. Regrettably, however, Matthew Flinders in his ship *Investigator* had arrived from England in May and sailed again in July, accompanied by the sloop *Lady Nelson*, on his voyage to circumnavigate the continent of Terra Australis. A letter from Flinders awaited Bass, describing his explorations so far on the *Investigator*, along with letters and parcels he had brought from England.

Bass immediately began disposing of his cargo. His contract with King allowed his sale of salt pork to private parties up to a certain date, the remainder then to be purchased by the government.[27] Thus the Commissary received 86 556 pounds of salt pork at six pence a pound, a considerable saving on pork brought from England. In addition Bass sold 30 034 pounds of high quality salt at one and a half pence per pound, which the Commissary would sell to the colonists at two and a half pence per pound, actually in exchange for wheat of that value. On 27 December 1802 George Bass received on behalf of Bass and Bishop bills of exchange on the Royal Treasury for £2351 12s 3d, and on 5 January 1803 he was able to write to James Sykes, his agent in London, that he had sent and was additionally sending bills for some £3700, which he hoped would 'stop a few holes' in his debts. Another matter had to be brought up with Sykes. This was to lodge an application with the Sick and Hurt Board for an extension of his sick leave. Obviously Bass had no intention of entirely leaving the navy. Perhaps he felt as did Elizabeth, who wrote that 'if all else fails, you have still a genteel profession'.[28] As it happened, in February 1802 Elizabeth and her father had visited Sykes's office in Arundel Street to remind him of the need to renew the leave application.

Bass, in the company of Governor King and Lieutenant William Kent, now boarded the *Naturaliste* to meet the French navigator Hamelin and presumably the expedition commander, Nicolas Thomas Baudin. Bass's reputation as the intrepid explorer who had sailed Bass Strait in a whaleboat, virtually proving the existence of a passage between Van Diemen's Land and New South Wales, had preceded him, as had the story of his attempt to cross the Blue Mountains. The French had been shown the whaleboat, preserved in the colony's arsenal, and

King presented Baudin with a fragment of wood from the boat's keel, set in silver engraved with the principal facts of the Bass Strait discovery.[29] Bass's scaling of the sheer rock faces of the 'terrifying mountains' west of Sydney and his descent on ropes down the face of a precipice profoundly impressed the naturalist François Péron, who wrote the main surviving description of the adventure. In his diary Hamelin referred to Bass as an 'enlightened' man. Nicolas Baudin also expressed admiration of the surgeon–navigator, apparently in Bass's view hyperbolising his achievements. Realistic about his early achievements and preoccupied with the adversities now facing him, Bass's private response was unappreciative. Adversity, he wrote to Elizabeth, could be a rough grindstone, but

> I am however now getting smoothened down with a drenching of P. Pinders Oil of fool administered by the hand of M Baudin the French Commodore who is collecting curiosities for the national Museum & has threatened me with a niche in the Glass Case.[30]

Obviously Bass enjoyed the witticisms of Peter Pindar, actually John Wolcot, a contemporary writer of satirical verse, and now wrote in a similar spirit. He knew, however, that Baudin's compliment would please Elizabeth and he himself could not be angry, he said, but if he were to be placed in a glass case, Bess would have to join him there. Bass presented the French commander with a number of Pacific island artefacts, while the French bought 10 000 pounds of salt pork from him.

The French were not alone in being impressed. George Caley, the botanist and explorer who, under the aegis of the government and Sir Joseph Banks, established a botanical garden at Parramatta, wrote of Bass as 'unrivalled' in terms of intelligence and ability.[31]

Charles Bishop was not recovering. Bass wrote to Elizabeth, 'Bishops ill health has thrown all cares & concerns upon my head both for ship & cargo and for some time they must remain those.'[32] On 1 January 1803 he wrote similarly to Henry Waterhouse:

> Bishop is still in ill health & likely to continue so. I have had no assistance from him from the time I left him at Otaheite in Jan last. He will I think be persuaded to stay behind until I make the next voyage, much to his advantage. Of course to no diminution of my labours and anxieties.[33]

Bass planned to dissolve their partnership on his return. Bishop subsequently showed some improvement, but remained in the colony when Bass again departed. His responsibility was to sell the merchandise that had been brought from England, and evidently he managed to do some of this. He was also entrusted with two letters to Matthew Flinders, which on his return to Sydney in June Flinders collected. He found Bishop 'wholly dispirited'.

In Sydney the anticipated departure of the French expedition had prompted a rush of letters written in time to be carried to Europe by the *Naturaliste*. Among them was Bass's letter to Elizabeth, when at eight o'clock in the morning of 18 November the French vessels sailed out of Sydney's great harbour.

On the other side of the world Elizabeth sat at her desk, a small fire keeping her room warm, as she wrote the many pages of her letters, carefully folded, addressed to 'Mr. George Bass, Brig Venus', and sealed with wax, for which she sought conveyance to Port Jackson or to China about once a month. From Portsmouth she had returned to the Waterhouse family home in Tichborne Street. The charts from Alexander Dalrymple, meant for Bass before he sailed, had finally been sent, but were probably never used, as they were maps of 'the Nutmegs', as Elizabeth wrote, presumably Indonesia, which Bass never reached.

About 23 April she received a visit from Matthew Flinders, who expected to leave shortly for Port Jackson in the *Investigator*. She wrote:

> Captain Flinders has been Married a Week they came to London on Thursday he called for my Letters offered to do anything in his power for me either at home or abroad sayd he was sorry their stay in London would be so short it was intirely out of his power to introduce Mrs. F. to [me] that he much wished it, with all my Heart I wish them happy, they have every prospect of being so as he has it in his power to take her out with him they can share each others Cares and pleasures, we can do neither. O George you have not been gone quite 4 Months I feel it as many Years.[34]

In fact, Flinders's plan to take his wife, Ann, with him on his voyage collapsed soon after, when the Lords of the Admiralty and his patron,

Joseph Banks, became aware of it. Invoking naval regulations, they made it clear that he would be superseded in his command of the expedition unless his wife remained in England. Ann left the ship. Flinders sailed on 17 July 1801. It would be nine and a half years before they saw each other again. Elizabeth's letter describing Flinders's visit, her sixth or seventh to her husband, was addressed in the care of 'Robert Berry, Esq. Merchant, Canton', and sent by way of the East India Company.

In August Elizabeth joined her father and a brother at the seaside resort of Margate, just south of the Thames River estuary. She had wanted to be away from the 'confined House in London', and avoiding Margate's tourist-oriented amusements spent time walking along the windy cliff top or on the sandy beach. The company of her father, her husband's firm friend and someone 'always kind to me', was a motivation as well, for William Waterhouse was clearly an important consolation and support to her. It was at Margate that Elizabeth received her first letter from Bass, written from San Salvador, seven months from the day of their parting. Her joy overflowed.

> O my love I felt more than I can describe, you was well, wrote in good spirits, and had not forgot your little Wife . . . sometimes I fancied you was laying in a French Prison, at other Ill, and worst of all an ever dear Husband friend and Protector lost to me for ever . . . I wish I could take little Besses place, if it was but for one Hour.[35]

Bass had asked her to write to him of her griefs and her joys, and she did so. Her grief was his absence and her joys his letters and his promise to return.

From the evidence George Bass and Elizabeth Waterhouse had known each other no more than two months, probably less, before their marriage. They were married three months before Bass's departure on the *Venus*. The parting was raw, deeply wounding, the fear and pain exacerbated by the time and distance that would lie between them and the dangers that were inevitably part of life at sea. Devotion to one another is palpable. Elizabeth wrote, 'I shall never find any one [else] I can Love so well.'[36] Bass wrote that he would be her 'loving husband <u>till death us do part</u>'.[37] And, 'ever look up to me as a man by whom thou never shalt be deceived. Be happy be happy', he concluded another letter.[38]

There were many differences in background and personality. Elizabeth, raised in London, thought it amusing that in his letters to her he employed the intimate second person singular, apparently a country usage. 'Are you all turned Quakers', she asked, 'for from the Thees and Thous in your letters to me it seems you are compleatly so'.[39] Yet Bass was educated well beyond most of his male peers and certainly far beyond Elizabeth, who had received the fairly basic training of a young woman of comfortable middle class status. His regard for Elizabeth clearly reflects the mind of a man who in Port Jackson had yearned for the intellectual world of Europe, who listened with interest to discussions of radical social and political ideas, and who apparently read the works of Mary Wollstonecraft, the dedicated feminist advocate of educational and social equality for women. He appreciated Elizabeth's 'good sense'. And aware that women could aspire to greater intellectual achievement than was customary, he urged her, in words probably reflecting something of his own sense of isolation, to improve herself. He had, he wrote, prepared a long letter which he had later destroyed in order to have the happiness of bringing her 'before me a second time', clearly an excuse, although fondly put. The letter he sent was short, but 'In the abstract I will tell thee what it [the original] contained':

> I earnestly and by every endearing tie besought thee to labour at the improvement of thy mind, that thou living in the midst of civilised society and in a country fruitful in new knowledge must make thyself able to instruct me upon my return from my wild uncivilised voyage, and by the new brilliance of thy mental endowments add strength to the powerful cement that lies, I trust, already between us. Make thyself my wisest and best counsellor, as well as my faithful, affectionate wife.[40]

This was a remarkable request for a man of the time. Enlightened, exceptionally gifted, Bass wanted a thoughtful, knowledgeable partner. But however lovingly phrased, the words inevitably stemmed from the same critical view that he held of his intellectual inferiors, which he had once almost ruthlessly expressed to Thomas Jamison and from which Matthew Flinders had at times suffered. Elizabeth reproached him for having destroyed any letter he had written to her, and continued:

you wish me to improve my Mind I will do my best, but I am ill able
to do anything now you are away, as to giving instructions, I must
always look to you for that, in French and Music I will try to improve
my self, but do not expect much of me, depend on it you will find me
ever an afectionate and faithful Wife and firmly yours.[41]

It was a thrust at his having left her. Bass was aware of this. Having urged
her to learn, he wrote that he could 'recommend several modes of
improvement to thee ... but leaving thee as I have done ... I ... must
leave thee to the guidance of thine own internal rectitude and distinction
between the probable and improbable means of preserving thy happiness
and my love'.[42] Sincerely as Bass loved his wife and did not want to
demand the 'improbable' from her, the element of her quality as a person,
intellectually and otherwise, was to some degree linked to his regard.

Bass's criticism could take what he undoubtedly saw as a humorous
turn. 'Dear wife, Do my love get into the habit of spelling a little better;
thou art a most notorious destroyer of good old english.'[43] Clever,
witty sarcasm amused and was returned by his male friends, and it is
possible that looking back to their short time together Bass remembered a quick-tongued Elizabeth who could be mischievously facetious;
he wrote of the 'waggery' and 'roguish' expression he saw in her
picture. But in letters to a young wife who saw herself as virtually
abandoned after three months of marriage, such badinage was
probably merely hurtful. William Waterhouse, an educated man as well
as a father concerned for his daughter's happiness, supported her
husband's suggestions:

> pray let me advise your proving how much you esteem his advice by
> your application; your affection and fidelity there is no doubt of, but
> you should make yourself the most agreeable companion, which will
> always last when other charms fail, and you know how he particularly
> wished you not to do any work, or what might hinder your application
> to improve your mind. therefore [sic] pray now determine to make up
> for lost time, and agreeably surprize him and me ...[44]

To Elizabeth's reply that she was too old to go to school, her father
answered that he was 'almost as old as you' and never thought it too
late to improve, 'which may be done by a little application & a little

assistance from a friend & books, that friend is never wanting while I exist'.[45] Waterhouse's comments also show that there had been some discussion on this subject before Bass's departure.

The moral and social values of the early 19th century also entered into the picture. 'Remember my Bess you have a husband who will not foresake you nor ever cease to love you as long as my Bess remains deserving of it.'[46] Her proper conduct during his absence was a theme he resorted to more than once and one Elizabeth generally accepted. He would never be ashamed of her behaviour, she assured him. Going out, she was always accompanied by her father. George and Elizabeth had, in fact, discussed her disadvantageous position as a young married woman without her husband. She wrote, 'If any one ofends me I tell them I have a Husband and am independent, all this my Love you desired.'[47]

The financial independence to which Elizabeth referred seems to have rested on her half of Bass's naval half pay, the other portion going to Sarah Bass. In November 1801 she received £20, which included her half of prize money Bass had acquired. On such an income, Bass wrote, she would know something about poverty. Nevertheless, at Margate she had promised to pay half the expenses. Protected by her family, she was comfortable enough. To provide for her future in the event of his death, the customary deduction of three pence per pound towards the Officers' Widows' Fund was made on Bass's naval income.

Many times too, Elizabeth asked George not to forget that he had a wife waiting for him in England. In a long separation after so short a time together there inevitably surfaced at times some concern for the fidelity of the other and, especially for the woman, socially irreproachable behaviour. Such feelings were naturally intensified when reassuring letters were lost and questions went unanswered. And letters were lost or long delayed. In February 1802 Elizabeth wrote:

> this will make the 23 [letter] since you left me, tho from not receiving any of them, my George has half accused his poor Bess of neglecting him. is it not so, my Love, well, I forgive you, if I had not been more fortunate perhaps I should have done the same.[48]

Bass kept his promise to send letters to Elizabeth by every possible opportunity, however uncertain and roundabout the route. 'I write to you my beloved Betsy, but great must be our luck if it ever reaches you.'[49] Most were short, hurried missives in a large, impatient hand, as if he were pressing his quill for greater and greater speed. They contained avowals of love for his 'beloved Betsy', hopes for their reunion, minimal references to his voyage, and little else. In contrast, Elizabeth's letters were long and heart-felt, several pages written in a small, neat script, and beyond her longing and her fears for him filled with news of family and friends. She was deeply disappointed in the brevity of her husband's letters:

> my George, I want longer Letters what success you meet with, a discription of the places you go too, what sort of Ladies you meet with (that I may be acquainted with the places & People I am to see) inshort everything that happens to you till our happy meeting.[50]

Bass did not comply. His letters remained short with little of what Elizabeth wanted to know. Despite having few spare moments either at sea or in port, he did manage to write informative letters of some length to Henry and William Waterhouse and to a few friends. Letters to Elizabeth, however, were despatched as often as the sailing of appropriate ships made possible. Letters to others were far less frequent. His treatment of Elizabeth is hard to explain. It is as if in spite of his truly profound regard for her and his desire for her self-improvement, writing to a young wife simply did not require the time and thought devoted to letters to his male friends. Did her lesser educational background make expressions of his devotion more or less sufficient? As it was accepted that letters to family members would be shared, she could learn more of his activities from her father and brother. Interestingly, Bass's letters to his mother, while fewer, were generally of greater length and tended to discuss more intimately his thoughts and intentions.

Towards the end of 1801 Elizabeth was confronted with another concern. Apparently in November Bass's friend Thomas Jamison visited the Waterhouses. During the course of the conversation he remarked that on his return to Port Jackson he would try to persuade Bass to remain in the colony for some years to carry on overseas trade. On seeing Elizabeth's shock at the comment, Jamison quickly reversed himself, saying he had himself suffered a separation and would do all he could to get Bass headed home as quickly as possible. Elizabeth's distress, however, was such that not only did she write of this to Bass— 'I am shure you have too much Love for me to be detained by any one longer than is absolutely necessary, come and fetch me and then it will be a matter of indifference where we go or stay'[51]—but her father wrote of it as well:

> Betsy is rather alarmed by Mr. Jemison having said he will use his influence with you to remain in that Country . . . we are too apt to presage unpleasant things to come, which I indeavour to diswade her from, and I hope with some effect, as she certainly would be very miserable to suppose it in Mr. Jemison's power to perswade you to remain there . . .[52]

Jamison had brought Bass's books to England, leaving them in Portsmouth with mutual friends. Elizabeth wanted the books with her but they would have to wait, she said, for George's return to be brought to London. There seems to be no further reference or knowledge regarding Bass's library. Only lists survive. One was apparently compiled by Thomas Fyshe Palmer and dated 23 September 1800, on which Palmer notes that he will 'send the London prizes [prices?] as far as I am able to make them out'.[53] One can only speculate as to the purpose of this. A second list, from the cashbook of the *Venus*, presumably records the books Bass bought for the voyage.

James Williamson also visited the Waterhouses and apparently made a point of telling William Waterhouse that he, Jamison and William Kent were fellow shareholders in Bass's company, mentioning the sums they had contributed. Waterhouse remarked upon this to Bass, but it seems unlikely that he did not already have this information. In late 1801 Captain William Kent, at Spithead with HMS *Buffalo*, also visited. Elizabeth wrote that Kent, who remained enthusiastic about the *Venus* investment, had acquired 'two Hundred of Mr. Williamsons share'. This was, in fact, part payment on a debt owed by Williamson to Kent. Elizabeth's great concern, however, was her belief that Williamson, like Jamison, hoped to detain Bass in New South Wales.

At some point during this time there was a curious incident involving Elizabeth Bass and Matthew Flinders. In February 1800, nine months after Bass had quitted Port Jackson for England, Flinders, then in Sydney, wrote his friend a letter discussing the publication of their charts and a book which Bass evidently intended to write on the colony, using some material from Flinders's journal and charts. Flinders went on to discuss what was clearly their shared interest in commercial speculations. 'Your promised information relative to our mercantile pursuits will be very acceptable', he wrote. He considered leaving the navy, adding, however, 'this is between ourselves'. In the somewhat effusive style of the time, he then wrote of his most valued friends, 'Franklin—Wiles—Smith—Bass, are names which will be ever dear to my heart . . .', and of the virtual hero-worship he had felt for Bass earlier in his life.

> I was so completely wrapped up in you, that no conversation but yours could give me a degree of pleasure; your footsteps upon the quarter-deck over my head, took me from my book, and brought me upon deck to walk with you; often, I fear, to your great annoyance . . .
>
> . . . your apparent coolness towards me, and the unpleasant manner you took to point out my failings, roused my pride and cooled my ardour . . . when pointed out by way of reproach,—there are few men whom it would not sting . . . There is one circumstance that will always keep you from me; your thirst after knowledge and information will not permit you to have the necessary consideration for one, who not only cannot afford you these; but has a far less stock than yourself.

Despite Bass's obvious impatience with ignorance and what was evidently his sometimes critical and probably sarcastic response to the younger, less well-informed Flinders, Matthew preserved his profound admiration for his charismatic friend, and went on to write of his

> knowledge and abilities . . . uprightness, integrity and humanity . . . how great is the service you have been of to me! My mind has often called you its Socrates. You have partly taught me to know my own good and bad qualities; from you I have learned to judge mankind more accurately.[54]

Sailing for England with the *Reliance* less than a month later, Flinders probably left the letter in Sydney for Bass to collect on his return to the colony. In pencil on the outside is written: 'To be directed for Mr. Bass [words illegible] where he is to be found—from Mr. Flinders.'[55] Someone then appears to have carried the letter to England and, as Bass had departed in the *Venus* possibly months before, delivered it to his wife. Astonishingly, it drew from Elizabeth a fierce expression of antipathy.

On the address wrapper of the letter, Elizabeth Bass wrote in ink:

> this George is written by a Man that bears a bad Character no one has seen this letter but I could tell you many things that makes me dislike him rest ashured he is no friend of yours or any ones farther than his own interest is concerned. Elizth Bass[56]

This extraordinary comment is difficult to explain. Elizabeth had written appreciatively of Flinders's visit in April 1801. She knew him to be her husband's close friend and quite possibly had met him previously through her brother Henry, under whom Flinders had served on HMS *Bellerophon* in 1794 and subsequently on HMS *Reliance*. What were the 'many things' that made her dislike him? What did she know of his 'bad Character'? Sharp-tongued as Elizabeth was known to be, none of her letters display any such anger against anyone else. It is possible that the letter was put into her hands by Thomas Jamison, who in expressing his hope that Bass would remain in New South Wales might have inferred that a similar attitude was taken by Flinders.

In writing his letter in February 1800, Flinders included a discussion of commercial prospects, which interested him at the time. By 1801, however, he had abandoned any thought of trade; he was totally committed to his voyage of exploration. Even a slight suggestion of such influence on Flinders's part would have struck the sensitive Elizabeth deeply and painfully. She might also have been profoundly, if quietly, jealous of the bond between the two men, who shared a world of seagoing experience and distant places, the very world that had taken her husband from her. She wrote 'no one has seen this letter'. One could ask whether 'no one' included Elizabeth. If not, was she alarmed by what appeared to be Flinders's wish to join Bass in business? Or by his expression of admiration and deep affection for Bass, and by her husband's place in the circle of male camaraderie cited by Flinders? Loyalties between men who shared for months and even years a hazardous life at sea and in places far from home could be very strong and possibly not easily understood by a young wife. As well, Elizabeth would have known by now of Flinders's departure on his voyage without his wife, which perhaps she saw as disloyalty on his part and a threatening influence on her own position. Had all of this combined to make Matthew Flinders a sinister shadow on her hopes for Bass's quick return to carry her away with him? The obvious depth of her feelings makes it seem at least a possibility. Or had she heard some fragment of unacceptable gossip that she felt was injurious to Bass? This possibility, however, raises the question of when Elizabeth received Flinders's letter, which we do not know. When in June 1803 Flinders returned to Sydney after his circumnavigation of Australia in the *Investigator*, he was met with allegations of misconduct through his role as the ship's purser as well as its commander. Specifically, the accusation was made that he had planned to profit financially by having the *Investigator* refitted at Rio de Janeiro, an allegation which he vigorously denied. This may have been the gossip, perhaps in an exaggerated form, that Elizabeth had heard, but necessarily in later 1803. Could she have seen a dishonest Flinders adding in some way to the difficulties Bass was already facing with a cargo of unsaleable goods? Whatever the reason—or perhaps combination of reasons—it appears that she was sufficiently alarmed to want to destroy her husband's regard for his friend.

There is no ready answer to this puzzle. If Elizabeth explained her feelings to Bass, she did so in a letter that has not survived. Equally unanswered is whether Flinders's letter ever reached Bass. If Bass did receive it, Elizabeth's comments seem to have had no effect on the friendship between the two men, who continued to correspond as usual whenever the opportunity presented. Flinders's last letter to Bass, written in June 1803, concluded with a promise to see 'your wife, in London, as well as her family'.[57] It was a letter Bass never received.

At the beginning of their marriage George and Elizabeth had hoped to conceive a child. As this did not eventuate and the lengthening separation grew more painful, their thoughts shifted to Elizabeth's joining Bass permanently in his life at sea. With some desperation she wrote, 'the next voyage I will go. your fate shall be mine. I shall be able to bare hardship and dangers with you and if we go to the bottom, of what consequence is it, we go together, and leave no helpless Children behind us'.[58]

In December 1802 Bass wrote:

We are preparing for another voyage to the S. Sea Islands for Pork, but it is not that alone which is the object of our voyage. If performed, I propose to turn homeward where I hope to meet thee well and ready to take a trip to this side of the globe for I wish never again [to] quit England without thee.[59]

What he planned aside from a cargo of pork he did not explain. For Elizabeth the important message was his return.

As the idea of his wife's joining him in his voyaging grew more definite, another concern occupied his thoughts. 'We shall not part anymore', he wrote. Bess would travel 'all over the world with me, but then thou must promise to make no third person for us'.[60] Childbirth in the early 19th century was invariably a serious threat to the lives of both mother and child, and the possibility of it occurring in a ship at sea was something Bass did not want to face.

12

The Last Voyage

By 1 January 1803 Bass had concluded most of his arrangements for the forthcoming months. Having been paid for his first Pacific cargo and taken steps to liquidate possibly most of his debts, he undoubtedly felt a freedom he had not experienced since his arrival in Port Jackson in August 1801. Ideas he had entertained for years and intriguing possibilities that had occurred to him on the recent voyage could be organised into a multiphased undertaking that would extricate him wholly from his financial problems and make possible a successful, even triumphant return to England. Without doubt the aspect of sheer adventure in his plans was a magnet as well.

On 4 December, just nineteen days after his return from Tahiti, he wrote to Governor King outlining the first of his schemes. He knew of an island in Australia's south coast Recherche Archipelago where Flinders, on his way from England to Sydney in 1802, had discovered a small lake with salt-saturated water and great quantities of fine crystallised salt on its margins. Bass now proposed to sail through Bass Strait, load the *Venus* with salt at Middle Island and head for the Dutch colonial settlement of Batavia, now Jakarta. With a document from King testifying to his being on a voyage of lawful commerce, he would sell the salt and take on board for Sydney rice, sugar, coffee, arrack and 'Java horses'. Aware of King's efforts to control the sale of spirits in the colony, he would leave the quantity and handling of the arrack to the Governor's discretion. The horses, a small, hardy breed which he thought suitable for the colonists, he would sell himself. The plan, however, went no further. Bass was working on better ideas.

On 1 January he wrote to Henry Waterhouse:

My dear friend

You must have heard from our beloved Bess that my pork hunting voyage No. 1 is accomplished and that No. 2 is about to commence. Small doings my friend, but great in comparison with the common run of adventures in this nether world. My fullest expectations were answered by it. Could I but say as much of those I had on leaving England!

The voyage before me is not altogether for pork. I mean to cross the South Pacific upon a venture; with the prospect that if a failure happens there, the original pork voyage to the Sandwich Isles are again before me. If this voyage ends anything near what I expect I shall then turn my head homewards as a Sealer; to recommence my commercial adventures with more ballast in my head and less sail upon it.

With this remark on his own need for a more realistic approach to his endeavours, Bass went on to describe a number of small islands he had seen, Bishop's ill-health, and the condition of the *Venus*, which

is heaving down to have some copper put on her gardboard str'k. she is a capital vessel & will I doubt not without accident remain so much longer than we shall want her. Believe me

Your sincere friend

Geo Bass'[1]

Two days later he wrote to Elizabeth.

My beloved Bess,

I have already written to thee twice since my arrival here from the Islands and shall now write again. I cannot therefore have much to tell thee than that I love thee . . . I am writing large to make my story look a long one . . . little Bess is well and still presides over the Timekeeper staring me in the face with her large eyes and reminds me of thee every morning as I am winding up that machine.

God bless thee my love . . . I wish a few happy years are yet in store for us. with my wife I could labour more chearfully . . . All I wish is to be able to give thee comfortable accomodation in a cabin large enough to take exercise and then we will sail all over the world together . . . I wish Bess I could just put out my arm across the globe and grapple thee. I'll warrant I'd bring thee over.

But I am called off; it is my dear to visit a lady, a lady too much of fashion & beauty, one whom I much esteem for love her I dare not, you know. Well then my dear not to teeze you any longer. I am called in the way of my profession; the lady has a *scabby bottom* which I mean to inspect most minutely for such a sight you know my dear is seldom to be seen.

Having examined the careened hull of the *Venus*, Bass returned to his letter.

Well, I have seen her bottom and have recommended the use of copper to be applied in large sheets . . . There's no end to writing to you, yes You and so no more from your loving husband <u>till death do us part</u>. Do you remember that Bess.

Geo. Bass[2]

Bass could not resist the clever, teasing remark, and the reference to a scabby bottom was one that Elizabeth's father found amusing as well.

Bass was not immune to the pressures of what he was trying to accomplish, the many threads of enterprise he was trying to bring together into one enormously important voyage, the knowledge of the dangers and exhaustion of the journey ahead, the profits he had failed to produce for his investors, his yearning for Elizabeth and the concerns of her being with him. At some point, probably in late January, when he had just returned to Sydney from taking leave of friends in Parramatta, he sat down and in an inebriated state wrote to Elizabeth. It was a confused and discordant letter in which all his hopes and anxieties concerning her came to the fore. Every 'beautiful prospect' he had seen from every pleasantly situated house had brought her to mind. She would 'one day or other admire them' with him, if she was good, or stay in England. There were enough of the bad sort in Sydney. He added, 'Thou shalt not breed & fill my cabin full of squallers, there's no room for such gentry.' He signed himself 'thy Affectionate fool' and added a scrawled postscript in which he referred to his drunkenness and to writing to her again within two months, presumably from some point in his voyage. 'Now Bess tell me what doest thou understand by all this letter', he asked.[3] The letter seems to have been a solitary aberration. Nevertheless it reached Elizabeth, leaving her confused and unhappy.

Crossing the Pacific was, however, only one project that he was organising. Commercial fishing was another. In January also he wrote to Governor King. He pointed out the savings to the government that his pork imports had made possible, in contrast to the expense of bringing salt pork from Britain. Then he wrote:

I have every proof short of actual experiment that fish may be caught in abundance near the South part of the Island of New Zealand, or at the neighbouring Islands and that a large quantity might be supplied Annually to the Public stores.

Government aiding me in the project, I will make the experiment—the Aid I ask of the Government is an exclusive privilege or Lease of the South part of New Zealand, of that South of Dusky Bay, drawing the line in the same parallel of Latitude across to the East side of the Island; as also of the Bounty Isles, Penantipodes Isle and the Snares, all being English discoveries together with Ten Leagues of Sea around their Coasts. The lease to continue for 7 years yet to come; renewable to 21 years, if the fishery within the first 7 years is judged likely to succeed.

Bass would supply the colony with a weekly ration of good salt fish at a price below the cost of a meat ration from England. No specific amount of fish could be promised until after the seven-year period, nor would the government be bound to take any specific quantity.

If your excellency thinks the above proposal worthy of your notice, I request of you at once to have the privilege, that I may begin to set matters in motion. If I can draw up food from the Sea, in places which are lying useless to the World, I surely am entitled, to make an exclusive property of the fruits of my ingenuity as much as the man who obtained Letters Patent for a Cork Screw or a Cake of Blacking.[4]

King's response was favourable insofar as the purchase of fish was concerned, since the government could accept only what it required. Of the leased area requested by Bass, the region south of a parallel a little north of modern Dunedin's latitude, he wrote to Lord Hobart: 'how far the lands described by him can or ought with propriety to be leased to Mr. Bass for so laudable an undertaking I must submit to your Lordship's wisdom'.[5] Meanwhile Bass, as he later wrote to his father-in-law, would wait to establish the fishery until after his return to 'old England', when he intended to seize his dear Bess and bring her out with him and make of her a '*poissarde*'.

In the meantime he had several plans for his current voyage. The hull of the brig *Norfolk* still lay on the beach at Matavai Bay, and Bass believed he could put it to use. Again he approached King. The result was an agreement that he would pay the colonial government £100 sterling for the hull if he could haul it up on dry land for repair or, having floated her, sail the damaged craft to another island, there to be drawn up on shore and restored. Should either of these efforts fail or the hull sink, no money need be paid. It was an eminently fair agreement, which both Bass and Bishop signed. Bass planned one stop on the way to Tahiti: a return to New Zealand's Dusky Sound, to further salvage useful metal, including two anchors, from the wreck of the East Indiaman *Endeavour*.

He also planned a sealing expedition before he returned to England. He had written to Henry Waterhouse of heading homeward 'as a Sealer', and the next day wrote similarly to William Waterhouse. Then, writing to his London agent on financial matters, he asked that he be sent as expeditiously as possible the London price of salted seal skins and 'seal & elephant [seal] oil'.

Obtaining pork, however, remained ostensibly the principal object of the voyage. In fact, it was not. Four years earlier, Bass had written to his mother, 'The Spanish settlements on the coast of Peru and Chile so long shut up from all the world are gradually attaining a profitable, though still contraband trade'.[6] The thought had never left him.

The approach he now had in mind was, at least overtly, entirely legal, as he now wrote to William Waterhouse on 5 January. Cattle were one objective, either animals he could 'salt down on the spot' or those he could transport live to New South Wales. If the *Venus* could not carry 'cattle of the Chili stature' he would, he said, be allowed to hire a ship large enough to do so. By what authority he would do this, he did not explain. Alternatively, he would purchase guanacos and alpacas, indigenous to South America, and

> very suitable animals for this country. The Governor wishes me to bring some of these animals. The Venus is perfectly equal to their size
> . . .

If from the strictness of their orders I can find no Spanish Governor who will allow me to purchase cattle, I shall then go to the Sandwich Isles, and set myself wholly upon a <u>real</u> pork voyage as before. That is the worst prospect.

Then he added:

Pendente el tiempo que yo serai en los puertos de Nova España yo no quedaré ocioso en respeto de commercio secreto para loqual yo voy <u>todavía preparado</u> y aprontado.

Translated, Bass had written:

During the time that I shall be in the ports of New Spain I shall not be idle with regard to secret commerce for which I go prepared and [promptly] ready.[7]

In this extraordinary sentence Bass made perfectly clear that if the opportunity presented, he would engage in contraband trade. It was an open admission to a planned and dangerous illegality, and is all the more remarkable in that he wrote in Spanish. Did William Waterhouse know Spanish? There is no evidence for this, but it must be assumed that he did or at least had a ready means of obtaining a translation. To Elizabeth her father remarked that the paragraph was 'much the same as we have heard before'.[8] It is not clear how explicit he was in explaining it to her. She was not, however, to mention it to Sarah Bass, to whom Elizabeth wrote regularly, presumably not to worry the older woman. But the reason for the Spanish remains a question. Was it merely an irresistible flourish of bravado?

Bass's letter to his father-in-law continues with cheerful optimism:

If our approaching voyage proves at all fortunate in its issue, I expect to make a handsome thing of it, and to be much expedited on my return to England. Sealskins and oil will most probably be the article imported by us there.

I have also some idea of selling the brig to the Spaniards, who cannot fail to admire so much beauty and strength . . . She is just the same vessel as when we left England—never complains nor cries, though we loaded her with pork most unmercifully; nor have we either split a sail or carried away a spar.[9]

The ship's performance, it should be noted, was a tribute too to her captain's good seamanship.

The repair, if possible, of the beached *Norfolk* at Matavai Bay was apparently last on his agenda for the voyage. If the *Norfolk*, to be renamed the *Resurrection*, could be saved, he would send the *Venus* and her cargo back to Port Jackson with one of the mates and in the restored vessel seek additional pork before heading back himself. Bishop was totally useless to him. 'I shall leave him here to recover . . . It is more than probable he will be in the grave before my return.' Bass continued:

> I have written to my beloved wife by the Naturaliste via France, and the Alexander via Bombay . . .
>
> With all my disappointments, my much beloved friend, I trust our voyage and affairs will turn to some good account. The want of a remittance must prove a great disappointment to you; it is a painful one to me. Be assured my labour will never be wanting to our success. Let but our next trip do well and all will do well. Be assured of the fidelity of
>> Yours &c.,
>> Geo. Bass[10]

He had planned an expansive, encompassing, remarkable and very ambitious voyage.

A last call upon his medical skills remained. On 25 January the New South Wales Corps surgeon, John Harris, asked the colony's other four surgeons, including Bass, to examine William Paterson, who had never recovered fully from the wound he had sustained in the duel with John Macarthur some fifteen months earlier. Together with Harris, the available 'Medical Gentlemen' made their examination. Their conclusion, as reported to Governor King, was that Paterson should not engage in public affairs for some time, and should be kept 'in as easy and tranquil a state as possible for the Reestablishment of his Health'.[11] Bass would have taken leave of his friend, no doubt with mutual promises of seeing each other again within some months.

By 1 February Bass had almost completed his preparations. The *Venus*, scraped, cleaned and re-coppered, lay at anchor in Sydney Cove as the final deliveries of water, provisions and firewood came alongside and were hoisted on board. Sails and rigging badly worn by months of working among islands had been repaired or replaced. The eight guns had been cleaned, the powder inspected, balls lined up in their racks, and the brig's barricades made secure. There is no mention of difficulties with the crew Bass and Bishop brought from England. Years before the young surgeon had readily secured volunteers for his whaleboat voyage into the then unknown waters of Bass Strait. Now apparently he easily brought his ship's company up to 25. Possibly his years of medical experience gave him an additional breadth of understanding in the handling of men, which combined well with his skilled seamanship, confidence and the absolute lack of fear Matthew Flinders had noted years before. The *Venus* was perhaps still the 'happy little vessel' Bass had claimed her to be.

On 2 February Bass wrote again to his father-in-law. Now he outlined his plans with no remarks on secret enterprise. He would be visiting the coast of Chile for

> provisions for the use of His Brit. Majesty's colony; and that they may not in that part of the world mistake me for a contrabandisto, I go provided with a very diplomatic looking certificate from the Governor here, stating the service upon which I am employed, requesting aid and protection in obtaining the food wanted.
>
> Bishop's state of health is improving, though very slowly. He being altogether unfit for strong undertakings stays behind till my return, or until one hears I am digging gold in So. America.

The dissolution of his and Bishop's partnership was 'a point fully fixed upon' to take place on Bass's return. He continued, 'Such part of our English cargo as suits this place are now for sale, and at last are doing tolerably. I trust no new arrivals will again glut the market . . . Pleasing prospects surround us, which time must give into our hands.' They had 'great plans in our heads; but like the basket of eggs, all depends on the success of the voyage I am now upon'. He added, 'Speak not of So. America to any one out of your family, for there is treason in the very name!'[12] Waterhouse received this letter probably in October, and would write back to Bass that his plans were scarcely secret. The family had heard of them from several acquaintances of Bishop, recently arrived in England. Bass's use of the term 'strong undertakings' has been debated. Was he indicating that the voyage would call for effort and daring beyond the usual? The reference to digging gold is also intriguing. Certainly it was not meant literally. Was it a clumsily phrased expression meaning to make a fortune? Did it suggest possible capture and enslavement in Peru's silver mines? One can only guess.

The following day Bass received from King the certificate addressed to 'all Governors and Commanders-in-Chief at any of the ports or places in His Catholic Majesty's territorys'. King certified that to his knowledge Bass's voyage was to procure food supplies and livestock for breeding in New South Wales, and requested protection and assistance for Bass should it be necessary for him to enter any harbour on the coast of His Catholic Majesty's American dominions. King later expressed to Lord Hobart his entire approval of the importation of guanacos and his belief that the certificate would create no political difficulties. Foreign whalers were allowed to operate along the South American west coast and could legally purchase provisions in coastal towns. It was, however, well known that foreign ships on the South American coast faced certain hazards. On the charge, true or otherwise, that they carried contraband, vessels had been seized by Spanish authorities in Valparaiso and other ports. Smuggling nevertheless remained a reality, as did piracy, by British crews among others. Obviously Bass was prepared to run the risks, risks that were compounded by the fact that the insurance taken out for the voyage at Lloyd's in London covered only losses incurred in New South Wales, New Holland, Van Diemen's Land 'or in the Islands adjacent'. 'Islands adjacent' could in no way include South America. Despite the protection of the certificate provided by Governor King, there might have been for Bass an underlying challenge in the possiblity of confrontation. In any case, he would have planned this new adventure with typical care and then embarked upon it with confidence and little concern for its hazards. The matter of insurance was apparently a potential problem he was prepared to overlook.

There is an argument to the effect that the *Venus*, which left Port Jackson in ballast, could not have carried a cargo of contraband goods.[13] Being in ballast did not, however, obviate Bass's taking with him a limited selection of the merchandise he thought most suitable for South American trade. The evidence points strongly to the fact that he did.

As he took his leave of the Governor and his wife, Mrs King told him that she would write to Elizabeth of Bass's good health and spirits as he departed, and that he had expressed his regret that he had not brought Elizabeth to New South Wales. A few months later Anna Josepha King wrote as promised, extending her affectionate good wishes and congratulations on George and Elizabeth's marriage and hoping, she said, to hear from Elizabeth. For Elizabeth it was glad reassurance that, at least on leaving Port Jackson, George was well.

On 5 February 1803, the brig *Venus* cleared outwards from the harbour of Port Jackson in ballast, her destination given as Otaheiti. Gauging the wind, calling out his orders, hearing the responding shouts and the squeal of the bosun's pipe, Bass watched the rigging come alive as the men swarmed upwards and masts and spars broke out in cascades of canvas that swiftly stiffened into great white billows. Nudged and then pushed by the wind, the *Venus* gathered way. Below her figurehead whorls of white water parted from her stem to slide along her sides into her wake. The harbour's great headlands moved past. Slowly *Venus* pressed forward into the infinity of the Pacific, until the pale blue outline of the continent sank and the vast, empty, unbroken ring of a limitless horizon encircled her. The *Venus* and her 25 men were never seen or heard from again.

13

The Fate of the Venus

In the first several months after Bass's departure, no concern was created by the silence emanating from the Pacific. No word was expected and other events occupied the attention of the colony. Plans for a settlement at Risdon Cove on Tasmania's Derwent River, explored by Bass and Flinders, were in progress. On 5 March 1803 there appeared the colony's first newspaper, the four pages of *The Sydney Gazette and New South Wales Advertiser*. On 9 June Matthew Flinders's exploration vessel, the *Investigator*, entered Port Jackson and came to anchor off Garden Island. Flinders had completed the first true circumnavigation of the Australian continent, proving that Terra Australis was a single land mass, with no seaway dividing it in two, but a heavy price had been paid. Men had died, others were dangerously ill, with many, including the commander, virtually crippled by scurvy. The ship itself was in a ruinous state.

Gradually uneasiness set in as to the welfare of Bass and the men of the *Venus*. On 26 February 1803, Secretary of State for war and Colonies, Lord Hobart, wrote to Governor King regarding a shipment of salt provisions being sent to New South Wales. Aware of King's salt pork contract with Bass, Hobart proposed that on Bass's return the contract be renewed to furnish breeding swine for the recently established settlement at Port Phillip, and eventually to bring sheep and cattle from the Cape of Good Hope or from India. The letter reached King on 1 March 1804. He replied the same day, discussing the expected provisions, and added, 'Respecting closing the contract with Mr. Bass . . . After a twelve-months' absence he is not yet returned, which makes me apprehensive for his safety.'[1] Just a month later, in a letter to Under Secretary J. Sullivan of the Colonial Office, King referred to the anticipated supply of salt pork from Bass. In the margin he wrote, 'No information has yet been received of Mr. Bass his safety is doubtful.'[2] Concern grew. A fortnight later, writing again to Hobart on the colony's ever-present problem of food, King added, 'I almost give up hopes of seeing Mr. Bass who I begin to conjecture has met with some accident which would deprive us of some Weeks salt Provisions.'[3] That Bass might have met with the fate of two American vessels and their crews, which on putting ashore on Pacific islands were slain by natives, was a possibility then raised by King in a letter to Joseph Banks. By December King concluded to Hobart 'there is no doubt some accident has occurred'.[4] Neither word nor evidence materialised in the months that followed.

What had happened to the *Venus*? To follow the course discussed by Bass in his final letters to William Waterhouse, one would steer first across the Tasman Sea to Dusky Sound on New Zealand's southwestern coast, a distance of some 1250 miles into the strong, cold westerlies sweeping the globe in the 40° south latitudes, frequently in very rough seas. As well, tropical cyclones developing farther north off the Australian east coast can on occasion transform into strong extra-tropical cyclones that affect the Tasman Sea. The Australian cyclone season runs from November to April. Bass sailed in its very midst. The *Venus* was a sturdy little ship and Bass was a competent seaman who had been in the region before. Yet it is necessary to ask, did he reach Dusky Sound?

In 1878, 75 years after Bass had embarked on his voyage, the New Zealand government steamer *Hinemoa*, Captain Fairchild, visited the wreck of the *Endeavour* in Dusky Sound. The East Indiaman was still grounded, but early whalers had chopped the vessel down to the water's edge for firewood. The upper decks were entirely gone. Copper bolts and sheathing remained, as did her ballast of greenstone, chalk and pieces of iron. The anchors sought by Bass were not mentioned in Fairchild's report. There was apparently no clue as to whether or not the *Venus* had been there.

Clearing Dusky Sound, Bass would have rounded South Island to sail eastward, as he had once before. Now his interest in this coast and its islands—windy, wooded Stewart Island, the barren, seal-inhabited Snares, Penantipodes and Bountys—would have been especially keen.

This was the territory he hoped to claim for his fishing enterprise. Here also he would perhaps complete his voyage with a cargo of seal skins. If Bass explored the area, very likely in wind-whipped seas, he may have discovered the Foveaux Strait if he had not done so on his previous journey. Or was he driven away from the coast in fierce, icy winds from the frigid Southern Ocean, caught in conditions that even the sturdy little *Venus* could not withstand? In 1810 the Australian sealer Frederick Hasselburg discovered Campbell Island and Macquarie Island, cold, windswept little scraps of land lying hundreds of miles south of New Zealand, and found ships' wreckage on their beaches. In 1810 a ship's mast was found at Stewart Island's South Cape. None of these remnants was ever identified.

Bass's agreement with Governor King on the possible repair and purchase of the *Norfolk*, beached at Tahiti's Matavai Bay, suggests that he might have headed next for Otaheiti, as he knew it. Leaving New Zealand waters, he faced the true immensity of the ocean that occupies a third of the planet's surface, months of sailing during which for weeks he might see no land, relying on his view from the masthead for indications of foul weather, guided day and night only by his capability with a sextant and a chronometer and his own seagoing experience. Riding winds and currents, the *Venus* would have sailed some 3500 miles first eastward and then to the north to reach the Society Islands and Tahiti.

No record exists of Bass's arrival at Matavai Bay. Local demands on government vessels in New South Wales were preventing King from communicating with Tahiti at the time. In late December 1804 he wrote to Lord Hobart:

> I very much regret that it has not been in my power to send any vessel belonging to the Crown from hence to Otaheiti . . . It is now two years since accounts from that island were received, but have been in constant expectation of hearing from thence by Mr. Bass, to whom there is no doubt some accident has occurred.[5]

In the same letter he referred to the killing by natives of an American landing party seeking sandalwood on the island of Tongataboo, that is, Tongatapu. Nor did later British contact with Tahiti bring news of Bass. The approach to Tahiti is scattered with small islands, at any of which Bass, confident and curious, might have decided to land.

The question then arises as to whether Bass decided to undertake salvaging the *Norfolk* later in his journey, as suggested in some of his letters, and headed first to South America. Assuming that he had sufficient salt provisions and other foodstuffs and had replenished wood and water in New Zealand, it would have been characteristic of him to be eager to embark on the South American venture. He would have had before him the fascination of the longest sea voyage of his life, his first crossing of the globe's greatest ocean, a thrill and a challenge without the repetitive labour of a pork voyage. It was a thought he had entertained for many years. There is no question but that Bass loved the sea. The man of science had always contended with the adventurer, a man intuitively a seaman. His medical career had been a means of going to sea. Even with a successful completion of his *Venus* venture and a reunion with his wife, he planned a seagoing existence for them both. '[I]t is nothing for me to sail thousands of miles', he wrote to Elizabeth.[6] Obviously he had been captivated by the lure of excitement and financial success in Peru or Chile. He was well prepared for this, even to the extent of some knowledge of Spanish. Before him then was the enormous, empty expanse of the southeastern Pacific Ocean which he would cross presumably between 40° south and 50° south, a windy yet relatively benign region in these summer months, although at times subject to the devastation of extra-tropical cyclones spilling south from the equatorial belt and to other storms.

In April 1803, three months after the *Venus*'s departure, there arrived in Port Jackson the 180-ton trading vessel *Harrington*, owned by the house of Chase, Chinnery and Co. at Madras and captained by the Scottish adventurer William Campbell. Campbell had brought a variety of cargoes into Sydney since 1797, and in October 1802 had sailed for South America with a quantity of goods apparently not saleable in Port Jackson. His story on his return in April the following year was dramatic. He had touched first at Más Afuera, the westernmost island of the Juan Fernández group, where he found English and American sealers at work. He then steered north along the Chilean coast, avoiding customs authorities and selling his English goods at unguarded ports, until at Coquimbo he turned south. Then, sighted by a Spanish armed vessel, the *Harrington* was pursued. She escaped, but her boat with thirteen men was seized.

Contraband goods did, in fact, make up a substantial part of the imports taken into South America, according to one source amounting to twice the value of legal imports during the years 1800 to 1810.[7] The pursuit of smugglers was therefore a serious affair. According to Campbell, the British whaler *Redbridge* had been caught with a quantity of specie on board received for contraband merchandise, and with five American vessels had been taken to Concepción and the men subsequently to Lima. Another American, also carrying profits from the sale of smuggled goods, had been captured. Campbell described the Spanish fleet guarding the South American west coast as consisting of two frigates, a 50-gun Peruvian-built vessel '(that sails very ill)', two armed whalers, a cutter-brig and a lugger. Clearly, as King wrote to Lord Hobart, hazards attended 'any commercial enterprize on that coast'.[8]

That April Bass had been away from Sydney not quite three months, and the later rumours that Campbell had said at the time that the *Venus* too had been taken by the Spanish were therefore entirely without substance. In the following January 1804 Campbell, now part-owner of the *Harrington*, returned to Port Jackson from Calcutta with a cargo of sugar, piece goods and arrack. In May he sailed once more for South America and on arrival there created an international incident. Campbell later declared that he had heard from American whalers that Britain and Spain were at war, and claiming that his commission in the East India Company as a captain of marines served as a letter of marque, he had captured at Coquimbo the Spanish merchant brig *San Francisco y San Paulo* and at Caldera the coastguard vessel *Estremina*, sailing them back to Australian waters as prizes. Governor King was placed in a position of acute embarrassment while it was determined whether the two nations were indeed at war at that particular time, and even more so when Spain was found not to have declared war on Britain until 12 December 1804, well after the event. It has been suggested that King was also concerned that Campbell's action could provoke retaliation on Bass, if indeed he was alive and a prisoner of the Spanish.[9] Despite the two nations having been at peace at the time, the convening of a special council, Campbell's detention and voluminous correspondence with London, in the end the Spanish vessels, both in very poor condition, were declared *à droit* of the

Admiralty and sold, and Campbell released. According to historian George William Rusden, proceeds from the sale of the ships were eventually handed over to the Spanish government.

These were sensational events for the colony. Yet there is no evidence that there emerged, in any of the extensive discussions, reports, letters or articles in the *Sydney Gazette*, any reference by Campbell to George Bass and the *Venus* having been seen on the South American coast. Governor King would certainly have added any such information to his letters to the Home Office. Bass's friends, among whom his planned South American venture was apparently well known, recorded no tales from Campbell or anyone else of any meeting between Bass and the Spanish.

Arriving in Sydney in June 1803 after his circumnavigation of Australia, Matthew Flinders picked up the letters from Bass that awaited him and wrote in reply. Flinders's letters contained no mention of the references to Bass supposedly made by Campbell back in April. Nor, writing years later of events in Sydney in June 1803, did Flinders comment on having heard of untoward circumstances befalling his friend. News of Campbell's adventures appeared in the *Sydney Gazette* and was certainly a popular topic of conversation. Yet there is no surviving comment from the time on Bass's being in South America.

The possibility that Bass had embarked on a privateering journey has also been raised. This is entirely without evidence. There is no suggestion of this in any of his letters, nor is there any record of his possessing letters of marque for such a voyage. Further, Governor King's discomfiture at the seizure of the two Spanish vessels by Campbell nullifies the idea that he might earlier have countenanced any such politically provocative plan. On the contrary, he had furnished Bass with an official document certifying his wish to engage in legal and peaceful commerce. Initially Bass had reduced the *Venus*'s armament from a possible twelve guns to eight, and there is no mention of increasing that number. Finally, with a ship's company of 25 the vessel would have been considerably undermanned for such aggressive action as piracy.[10] George Bass had been on naval vessels that stopped and boarded smugglers' crafts or perhaps French fishing boats, but it is amply evidenced that he was out to make a fortune through commerce, which he understood, not by warlike engagements for which he was ill prepared. Bass was daring and courageous, but he was neither combative nor foolhardy.

By 1805 speculation on Bass's demise was inevitable. In a letter to Joseph Banks dated 21 February, the naturalist Robert Brown summarised the conjectures circulating in the colony. 'Of Mr. Bass we begin to despair', he wrote:

> he has now been absent about two years, and it is to be fear'd has either fallen a sacrifice to the treachery of the South Sea Islanders, who are daily becoming more daring, or what is fully as probable, has expos'd himself to be captur'd on the coast of Peru.[11]

Towards the end of the year a letter from Charles Bishop's brother William expressed similar views, which he had certainly derived from correspondence with Sydney. Bass and his men had probably been cut down by islanders or had foundered at sea.

Storms and hostile islanders were not the only possible reasons for the disappearance of a ship. A freak accident, fire, sickness, an uncharted reef or failing winds—any of these could destroy a vessel. A Spanish galleon crossing the Pacific had burned in mid-ocean. Another ship, missing for more than a year, was found drifting with all on board dead of disease and starvation.

In 1805 a second British ship on its way to South America from Sydney disappeared into the Pacific. In June Governor King despatched Acting Lieutenant Charles Robbins to Chile under a flag of truce, with letters for Don Luis de Guzman, 'Captain General, Governor and President of the Royal Audience of the Kingdom of Chili', explaining William Campbell's seizure of the Spanish ships and the steps taken by King in response. They included an invitation to send to New South Wales appropriate persons to reclaim the vessels and to attend the trial of the commander and crew of the *Harrington*. Evidently Robbins was also instructed to make enquiries about Bass. Robbins sailed in late June 1805 in the 59-ton HM Armed '(but now disarmed)' Cutter *Integrity*. He was never seen or heard from again.

Charles Bishop remained at Port Jackson, where references to his deteriorating mental condition continue to appear. There is no detailed description of symptoms, but a letter he wrote in late 1804 reflects the disjointed and delusional thinking that suggests a manic-depressive (or bipolar) disorder.[12] He wrote of himself as 'His Majesty's Third Son', and later imagined that he was the governor. Although worsened, it was said, by grief over the disapperance of Bass, his condition was apparently episodic. In May 1803 he bought in the names of Bass and Bishop a farm at Prospect Hill, good agricultural land some 20 miles west of Sydney, where petty robberies 'particularly after Dark' forced him to take up residence, as was noted in the *Sydney Gazette* of 25 September 1803. Despite the efforts of Thomas Jamison to protect George Bass's interests, Bishop evidently was removing from their place of storage goods belonging to their company.

By 1804, however, Bishop seems to have been confined. A letter written in January 1805 to Bishop's brother in England, evidently by Elizabeth Paterson, brought no offer of assistance. Thus on 24 November 1805 the *Sydney Gazette* announced on its front page that the governor had summoned 'Twelve good and lawful men (being Freeholders) to come before him at Parramatta to form a Jury to make enquiry upon a view on examination of Charles Bishop, to say on their oaths whether the said Charles Bishop is a Lunatick'. He was declared 'incapable of governing himself, his chattels, lands, and tenements', and committed to the custody of John Macarthur and Samuel Marsden.[13] Jamison began organising the sale of the partners' property, advertising in the *Gazette* for those indebted to the concern of Bass and Bishop to discharge their obligations, 'a final settlement becoming absolutely necessary'.[14]

A complication arose in 1806 when the trader Simeon Lord sued Jamison for £400 for goods allegedly taken by Bass and for debts incurred by a Lieutenant William Cox in connection with *Venus* merchandise. The matter was eventually closed by Governor King in favour of the long-absent Bass. In March 1809 Lieutenant-Governor William Paterson informed the Navy that Bishop was insane and a pauper confined to gaol. Arrangements were made for his return to England. He sailed from New South Wales on 12 October 1809, whereupon the record of this kindly and well-meaning man comes to an end. The harshness of life at sea and the instabilities of commerce in the Pacific region had broken Charles Bishop.

The months that it took a letter to cross the oceans by sailing ship were simply part of early 19th century communication, and in England concern for Bass half a world away was not immediate. Gradually, however, as letters failed to arrive, Elizabeth's worries merged into anguish. What appears to have been her last letter from George was dated 3 January 1803. On 8 October 1803, their wedding anniversary, she drafted a letter which she seemed unable to finish and rewrote several days later.

Tichborne Street October 19th 1803

My ever dear George,

Little did I think this time three years [ago] we should have been so long and cruely seperated, indeed my Love it is a very hard task to be obliged to write again, I have been expecting you every Day these Six Months past to discribe my feelings the last Month is impossible, three ships arrived from Port Jackson, the Glatton, Greenwich & Venus [a whaler], all our friends received Letters, but none for me, my poor Father went to the Owners, to Deptford & inshort to every one that was likely to give him any information, I went to Mr. Norvils he showed me two Letters he had rec'd from Captain Bishop, they mentioned your having left P J on the 7th of February for the West ward, his being left at Sick quarters . . . [and] on your return perhaps you might settle your affairs and return to Old England only you might be out 6, 7, 10, 12, 14, or 15 Months only Guess my George one moment what I felt. the perhaps and the number of Months . . . I still believe I should have Letters, I never would think you could neglect me . . . I am ready to go all the World over with you, do not let them persuade you to stay any longer, surely by this time you have made enough to satisfy the parties concerned, and you are more to me than all the Riches in the World . . .

Rereading his brief letters, with no new word, unrelenting anxiety coiled through her mind. And with it a growing sense of injury. He had not specifically acknowledged her 'Eight and Twenty Letters . . . shurely some things in them where worth answering . . .'. In spirited vein, she continued:

if you do not I declare I will not get on the Chairs, you may hold your proud head as high as you please I will not Climb, or fill your Cabin with Squallers, you say you will Love me if I deserve it, have you any reason to doubt it, my love, I feel it a sting I do not deserve.

Bass had told her not to be concerned by his being surrounded by naked island women but, she now asked, had she no reason to fear the 'more Civilized Females of Port Jackson, it is a bad School for a Young, & a Married Man'. Elizabeth's relationship with George's mother remained close: 'we are both too fond of you to be happy in your absence', she wrote, and teased, 'indeed Sir you must behave very well to me or you will be scratched out of her Books'. But the brave stance crumbled. 'My George I have made you several jars of Pickles, must they spoil or will you come and eat them. Oh I wish you had them.'[15] She was cheered by Anna Josepha King's letter, which told her that on his departure for the Pacific islands in February, George was in good health and spirits. Yet the loss of many letters and the year and more between a letter sent and its answer's arrival bred grief and uncertainty. And now, unknowingly, she was writing into a void.

In May 1803 the Peace of Amiens collapsed. Concluded by England and France on 17 March 1802, it had lasted fourteen months. With Napoleon's economic measures and France's continued expansion on the continent, and England's refusal to surrender the island of Malta, war broke out once more. Its circumstances impinged upon the Waterhouse family. In mid-October William Waterhouse wrote to Bass:

> we are in hourly expectation of an Invasion by the French and tho their preparations are Perhaps greater than on any former occasions, still the preparations to receive them are equally great, which is likely to occasion much blood-shed. God send it soon over with success to this Country . . .[16]

He referred to the draft for payment received by Bass from Baudin's expedition for 10 000 pounds of salt pork. 'I am much affraid the drafts you sent Mr. Sykes for what you suply'd that ship with, will not be paid, at any rate at present, owing to the War being broke out again.'

Elizabeth wrote:

> we have nothing but Soldiers parading the Streets it is common to see a Thousand together, there is great talk of an Invasion . . . all our Males in London are Volunteers the Taxes are more than doubled, orders are sent to all the Inhabitants of the Sea Ports to leave at an

Hours notice to make room for troops. Oh my dear George if you are coming home I hope you will escape the French.[17]

Despite the war, Henry Waterhouse remained without a ship. His father wrote: 'My son Henry still remains unimploy'd, he has no parliamentary interest, and never served with Lord S. Vincent [First Lord of the Admiralty], and cannot brook servile attendance on great Men, nevertheless a little of that is necessary to get through life.'[18] Henry might have been succumbing to alcoholism. Matthew Flinders, writing to Bass in August, had commented on their friend, 'Accounts speak but indifferently of him; his sun seems to have passed the meridian, if they say true.'[19] All this was news which Bass would never receive.

In December William Waterhouse visited the office of Bass's agent, James Sykes, and learned of the remittances sent by Bass towards payment of his debts and a payment of £50 each to Elizabeth and to Sarah Bass. As well, there were the certificates necessary for an extension of Bass's leave of absence for an additional two years. Henry had received what was probably his last letter from Bass, and sent it to his father to be shared with Elizabeth. All this was cheering news. But the silence was descending.

In mid-December 1803 Matthew Flinders, on his way to England and unaware that war had resumed between Britain and France, landed at the island of Mauritius, a French colonial outpost in the Indian Ocean, seeking repairs for his vessel, the schooner *Cumberland*. The result was his detention on the island for six and a half years.

In October 1805 Captain William Kent brought Flinders's exploration ship, HMS *Investigator*, back to England, the sloop now a cut-down, brig-rigged and storm-battered hulk. Kent carried with him Governor King's lengthy despatches dated 30 April 1805, including those covering the Campbell–*Harrington* incident. The separate matter of the loss of George Bass was also reported. Kent had sailed from Port Jackson in late May 1805, two months after the arrival of William Campbell in the *Harrington* from Chile. Despite the undoubted opportunity, Kent had clearly heard nothing from Campbell of George Bass or the *Venus* having been seen in South America. In January 1806 Kent apparently certified for the Admiralty the disappearance at sea of his friend.[20] George Bass was thereafter recorded in Admiralty documents as having 'died soon after the Twentieth Day of February, One thousand Eight Hundred & three'.[21]

Elizabeth Bass, who did not possess 'a clear Annual Income to the value of Thirty Pounds', now became entitled to the benefits of the Charity For *Relief of Poor Widows of Commission and Warrant Officers of the Royal Navy*, to which her husband had made the required contribution throughout his naval career. [22] In 1806 Elizabeth made the necessary applications. Bass's half pay having terminated after 30 June 1803, his widow was granted £40 a year, dating from 1 July 1803.[23]

14
Aftermath

Few records survive from the next several years to throw light on the bereaved family in Tichborne Street. The childhood recollections of a woman who knew Sarah Bass described Elizabeth as steadfastly refusing to believe her husband would not return, turning down with indignation a later offer of marriage. She considered herself a married woman, waiting for her husband's return. The fact that she did not petition for a pension until January 1806, two and a half years after she apparently had become eligible with the cessation of George's half pay, tends to support this claim. Accepting that she was a widow was apparently a bitter experience, but perhaps a necessity, for there is evidence that William Waterhouse was in financial difficulties. In a letter dated 14 December 1803 he thanked Elizabeth for the offer of 'making use of your Money but that I never will do without I was reduced to the last extremity and hardly then . . .'. He was at the time house-hunting 'unsuccessfully', which seems to indicate that he was giving up the family home in Tichborne Street.[1]

Philip Gidley King, replaced as governor by William Bligh, came home to England a sick man, dying in 1808. Bass's friend William Paterson, also very ill, died aboard HMS *Dromedary* in 1810 en route to England. In the same year Matthew Flinders returned home from his long detention on the French island of Mauritius. He renewed contact with Henry Waterhouse, whom he found in poor health. Without doubt all of these returning friends of Bass and many others were queried by William and Henry Waterhouse for any word of George's disappearance. There was none.

In 1811 there suddenly surfaced a report, attributed to a Lieutenant William Fitzmaurice, which stated that on William Campbell's return to Port Jackson from South America 'in or about 1803', he claimed to have heard of the capture of George Bass, the *Venus* and her company by the Spanish in a Peruvian or Chilean port, and

> that Mr. G. Bass and Mr. Scott, mate, had, together with the crew, been sent either to the mines or further inland. A Spanish gentleman with whom Captain Campbell was trading told him that Mr. Bass was taken when landing in his boat, & that the vessel was seized afterwards— Captain Campbell had been to Quito, to Valparaiso, & to Valdivia; but it is uncertain at which of those places the affair happened.[2]

What brought about the emergence of this startling allegation eight years after no such event had even been suggested, either in 1803 or more creditably in 1805 after Campbell's second return from South America, is a puzzle indeed. The extensive documentation preserved from those two occasions contains no reference whatsoever to the fate of George Bass. There was, however, an event that took place during the intervening years that might have created a confused and garbled story. With the closure of the *Harrington* incident, Campbell continued with island trading in salt pork, sandalwood and pearl shell. On a voyage to Tahiti in 1809, Campbell had successfully recaptured a New South Wales schooner named *Venus* which had been seized by hostile natives, only to be shipwrecked in the same vessel on a subsequent journey. Perhaps this episode become entangled with speculation on Bass's disappearance.

There is yet another possibility. The popularity of the name *Venus* for vessels of all types no doubt contributed to rumour. In June 1806 a brig by that name was chartered by Governor King to carry provisions to the Tamar and Derwent River settlements in Van Diemen's Land. At Port Dalrymple the vessel was seized by a small group of convicts and mutineers, and according to *The Sydney Gazette* of 29 May 1808 'was last seen upon the coast of New Zealand, in a distressed condition, and has never since been heard of'.[3] Inevitably, however, there sprang up other versions of its fate. One account maintained that the vessel reached Chile, putting into the port of Talcahuano, where the ship was seized and sold at auction and the crew imprisoned.[4] Compounding the likelihood of diverse tales about the *Venus* were a whaler operating in Pacific waters, a small colonial coaster, and at least two other vessels known to have reached Tahiti and Antipodes Island, all of the same name.

Realistically, little credence can be given to the 1811 account of Bass's capture in South America. Together with this conjecture, however, there was a different piece of intelligence. On the back of this sheet, signed with the name William Fitzmaurice, was a statement that Fitzmaurice had been in Valparaiso and Santiago, Chile, and in Lima, Peru, in late 1808 and early 1809. It continued, 'The whole of the British Prisoners remaining in the vice-royalties of Peru & Chili and the Province of Conception, were released and Sent to Europe.' Fitzmaurice also thought he remembered having heard of someone named Bass being in Lima five or six years before he was there himself. The statement was dated 'London, May 30th, 1811'.[5]

When this report reached the Waterhouse family their hopes would have soared. Yet it was soon painfully obvious that if George Bass had been among the British who were alive, released and sent to Europe in 1808, he would have come home before 1811. If he had died, of the 24 other men aboard the *Venus* — if she had been captured by the Spanish — one at least should have survived to be liberated and repatriated to England to tell the story.[6] Unsubstantiated reports continued. In about 1813 one of Philip Gidley King's sons, Lieutenant Norfolk King, brought to London yet another story of Bass having been seen in South America by a naval officer and at the time fellow-prisoner, coincidentally named King. This man had supposedly returned to his home on the West Indian island of Barbados, and evidently did not respond to any enquiries by William Waterhouse or, reportedly, Joseph Banks.[7] As hope again failed, grief and resignation would have returned.

But yet another hope-inspiring report was to appear. This was a message sent to William Waterhouse by a Thomas Moore, evidently the New South Wales colony's former master boat- and shipbuilder, who would have known George Bass well. Moore had prospered, acquiring large grants of land and settling comfortably as a farmer and magistrate at Liverpool, west of Sydney. He became one of the founders of the Bank of New South Wales and was active in the affairs of the Church of England. On 15 December 1817 he wrote:

I have just heard that Mr. Bass is alive yet in South America. A captain of a vessel belonging to this port [Sydney], trading among the islands to the east, fell in with a whaler, and the captn. informed he had seen such a person, and described the person of Mr. Bass. The captn. of a vessel of this port knowing Mr. Bass well, he is of a belief, the description of the whaler gives him, it's certainly Mr. Bass—being a doctor too—which is still stronger reason.[8]

With this word from a respected citizen of the colony, William Waterhouse was galvanised into new efforts to find Bass. He turned to the highest authority and, probably in 1818, wrote at length to a Secretary of State, most likely Henry Addington, Viscount Sidmouth, Secretary of State for the Home Office (1812–22). Waterhouse summarised Bass's career in Australia and the Pacific and the several reports on his having been seen in South America. He provided a description of Bass: 'six feet high dark complexion wears glasses a very penetrating countenance, 50 years of age'. (Bass would actually have been 47 in 1818.) The letter concluded with an earnest and humble plea for the Secretary's assistance in liberating him, on behalf of Bass's 'afflicted wife and aged mother'.[9] No record seems to exist of any reply. Perhaps in the midst of Britain's industrial and political turmoil in the year 1818, the loss of George Bass seemed very minor indeed. And Thomas Moore's report, however well intended, contained, like all the other allegations, very little substance in terms of time or location, and was again based on hearsay.

Bass's disappearance continued to inspire imaginative narratives for several years more. In late 1800 or early 1801 there had arrived in Sydney a Danish adventurer, Jørgen Jørgensen, who variously called himself Jorgen Jorgenson or Jorgensen or John Johnson or Johnstone. An experienced seaman who had served on a variety of vessels, he was evidently aboard HMS *Lady Nelson* when from late 1801 to April 1804 the 60-ton brig took part in surveys and discoveries in Bass Strait and in establishing settlements in Van Diemen's Land. In company with Matthew Flinders's exploration ship, *Investigator*, the vessel also shared for three months in the surveying of the Australian east coast. At some point Jørgensen probably met George Bass; certainly he heard of him. With literary aspirations, Jørgensen wrote several books, recording colourfully much of his opportunistic and reckless life, which eventually brought him back to Van Diemen's Land as a convict. In 1835, fully pardoned, he began his autobiography, *A Shred of Auto-biography*, which like much of his writing was entertaining but not always factual. Here he claimed that Bass entered the Chilean port of Valparaiso with the *Venus*, demanding 'liberty to trade, under the alternative, if refused, of storming the place'. Receiving permission Bass and his men went ashore whereupon, according to Jørgensen, the Spanish seized the vessel and cargo, 'and taking Dr. Bass and his people prisoners, sent them to the Quicksilver mines, where they were never more heard of'.[10] This was, perhaps, the last of the tales surrounding the disappearance of George Bass. With Elizabeth and those of the Waterhouse family closest to him gone, it caused no more than a ripple in the myths surrounding the loss of Bass and the little brig *Venus*.

In about 1903 the historian and educationalist George William Rusden summarised the last known events leading to the disappearance of George Bass and Charles Robbins and passed these on to Don Pascual de Gayangos, a Spanish scholar, who undertook to make enquiries in Spain regarding the fates of the two navigators. In Rusden's words, 'Alas! he could ascertain nothing.'[11] In 2003 new research into Spanish naval records by Dr Jorge Ortiz-Sotelo of the Asociación de Historia Marítima y Naval Iberoamericana, Lima, Peru, failed to find any mention of the brig *Venus*.

On 10 October 2003 the National Archives of the Republic of Peru (Archivo General de la Nación) issued at the author's request an official statement on George Bass. This attested to a search having been made through commercial, military and naval archival documents for any reference to George Bass. None was found.[12] From the standpoint of Spanish authorities in the vice-royalty of Peru, which at the time included the captain-generalcy of Chile, George Bass never reached South America. This seems to close finally all conjectures that he did so. Somewhere in a stormy Tasman Sea or in the vastness of the Pacific Ocean the little *Venus* must have encountered conditions that she could not overcome, and like so many others of her time foundered and disappeared.

What did Sarah Bass, then in her eighties, know of these scraps of intelligence purporting to relate to her son? What we know of her after her son's disappearance derives mainly from several letters written some 75 years later by a Mrs A. M. Mapleston, who as a child apparently lived with her grandmother, Mrs Calder, in Lincoln. It was in rooms kept by Mrs Calder that Sarah Bass lived, probably from the time George joined the navy to the end of her life in 1828. Contacted by persons interested in George Bass's family background, Mrs Mapleston in 1878 recorded her childhood memories of Sarah and Elizabeth Bass in several letters, memories that she admitted were 'confused'. Apparently something of a favourite with the elderly woman, whom she described as stern-looking and imposing, the child spent time in her room, and later described the small mahogany table and books that had belonged to the boy George.

'It was her habit', Mapleston wrote of Sarah Bass, 'to fix her gaze lovingly on a picture that stood above a curious old looking-glass . . . and say "My poor, poor boy I shall never see him again". Then I used to climb up her knee and kiss "poor Bassey" as I used to call her'. Mapleston described the portrait of George Bass as having 'a dark olive-green shade, with the portrait of a young man in colours, of a healthy complexion. It seems to me it was only to his waist'.[13]

In existence today there is a portrait of Bass that is a photograph of a mysteriously vanished original. Was the original the picture on the wall in Sarah Bass's room? There appears to be no surviving record of George Bass having sat for his portrait but it is, of course, possible that he did so at some point before sailing finally for Australia. Nor is there any creditable word on what became of the picture on Sarah's death. Mapleston wrote that on her mother-in-law's death, Elizabeth probably took it along with other things she 'thought proper'. This must indeed be a confused memory, for Sarah Bass outlived her daughter-in-law by four years. Nevertheless, a portrait of Bass is known to have existed in London in the 1890s.

It is also possible that the original from which the photograph was taken was a miniature. George possessed a miniature portrait of Elizabeth, 'little Bess', which hung above his chronometer at the foot of his bed in his cabin on the *Venus*. Miniatures, pocket-sized portraits painted on thin ovals of ivory, were popular and readily obtained from professional miniature painters, the equivalent of a modern photographic portrait. Faced with separation, it is likely that the young wife had a miniature painted of herself to give her husband, or that she gave him one she already had. There is, however, no mention of a picture of Bass in any of Elizabeth's surviving letters, as might be expected. The idea of a miniature as the subject of the photograph does not, of course, reconcile with the portrait described by Mapleston as hanging on the wall in Sarah Bass's room. Oil paintings were not infrequently made from miniatures, and there is the possibility that Bass had a miniature made of himself which in turn was reproduced in a painting for his mother. However, the limited finances of both cast some doubt on this likelihood, and adds the question of what happened to the miniature—if there was one—to the mystery of the portrait. Recent efforts to trace the provenance of the surviving photograph of a picture of Bass have yielded no results.

Sarah Bass suffered financial reverses. Her investment in the voyage of the *Venus* was probably lost, and the failure of a bank in which she had placed her slender funds was an additional blow. It appears, however, that her treatment from the Calders was genuinely kind. Her hands crippled by gout, her letters were written for her by one of the young Calder women, and there was a certain amount of correspondence with naval men who had been friends of Bass. Through the friendship of a wealthy admirer of her youth she received small luxuries, as did the elder Mrs Calder in appreciation of her care of Sarah. Elizabeth Bass remained close, writing and possibly occasionally visiting her, as Mapleston professed to remember her. Whatever she was told of the efforts to discover George's fate, according to Mapleston, Sarah Bass entertained no hopes for her son's return. If he were alive, she said, 'neither bolts nor bars or even granite walls' would keep him from returning to her.[14]

Sarah Bass died on 19 November 1828. In her will she divided her small funds, evidently less than £300, among friends, a niece, and five members of Elizabeth's family, including Henry Waterhouse's daughter Maria, each receiving £23.[15] After Mrs Calder's death in 1854, Sarah's niece Mary Newman Morris examined the box in which George's mother had kept his letters. It was empty. Unfortunately, as Mrs Mapleston wrote, some at least had been burned by the Calders.

Mapleston's accounts are valuable additions to the scant information on Bass's family after his disappearance, but in some details they are notably incorrect. Perhaps impressed by the attention she received for her memories of the Bass family—she was eager to sell the few items she had from Sarah—Mapleston may have enriched her story. In any case, she wrote that a child was born to Elizabeth and George Bass after his departure, a boy who died at nine years of age. Elizabeth's own extant letters make it entirely clear that there was no child. She had hoped that there would be 'a little one on the Road that would be able to call you Father on your return, but in that I am disapointed'.[16] In another missive she commented on her being able to sail with George whatever the risks, there being no 'helpless Children' to be left behind.[17]

Little is known of Elizabeth in later years. At some point the family moved from Tichborne Street to Smith Square, Westminster, and perhaps it was at that time that Elizabeth took lodgings in nearby Marsham Street. Elizabeth's brother Henry died in 1812, aged 42, possibly from the effects of alcoholism, and was buried according to family tradition in St John's Cemetery, Westminster. Their mother, Susanna Waterhouse, died three years later. Perhaps the most painful loss to Elizabeth was the death in 1822 of her father, her unfailing friend and supporter in the difficult months and years following George's final departure from England. Elizabeth survived him by only two years and was buried at St John's. The existing correspondence of George and Elizabeth Bass and members of the Waterhouse family came in time to Elizabeth's younger sister Amelia and her husband, Henry Pownall, and remain the most revealing source of information on the personal life and character of George Bass.

George Bass's achievements in the exploration and charting of the Australian coast were significant, although not of the magnitude of the work of James Cook or Matthew Flinders. He pioneered the entry into Bass Strait, and shared with Flinders the voyage that proved it to be a seaway between oceans, showing the present Australian state of Tasmania to be an island. His earlier, lesser journeys, also shared with Flinders, contributed to the opening up of areas south of Sydney. He explored New Zealand's southernmost coastline, but left no known charts or detailed descriptions. In his later recording of islands now parts of the republics of Kiribati and the Marshall Islands, he had been preceded by other English captains. Possibly he discovered the tiny Iles de Bass in French Polynesia. His natural history investigations covered an extensive range of subjects, many of them well recorded—the composition of rocks and soil and theories as to how they were formed; the habits and anatomy of animals; plant life ranging from types of grass and shrubs to the varieties of trees he encountered. For this work he received the recognition of membership in London's Linnean Society. Particularly interesting from a modern standpoint are his speculations on the geological history of the rugged promontories of Tasmania's south coast and his questions on the environmental effect upon the Earth of the disposition of the southward reaches of the continents of Africa, South America and Australia, all three projecting towards the Antarctic.

George Bass stands out for the man he was, a striking, charismatic figure of exceptional intelligence and outstanding energy, who shared in the application of science and reason that was creating the intellectual and philosophical climate that nurtured the modern world. This was the Age of Enlightenment. Beyond the realm of geographical discovery, in itself so significant a part of the period, there was the ongoing study of navigation, hydrography, astronomy, people, natural worlds, landforms, the ocean itself. Scientific classification on the basis of likeness and the tracing of relationships was being applied to plants, animals, languages, minerals, and other areas. Humanity's problems, it was widely believed, could be solved through knowledge and rationality in social and political issues. Versatile and gifted, Bass was a natural part of this. He pursued his medical studies and, going beyond them, applied his scientific training to investigating the strange new world of Terra Australis. His anatomical studies of its animals and investigations of its plant life were among the first of their kind. He learned enough of Australian Aboriginal languages to compare those of different regions, and on Lord Bolton's Island recognised from the people's speech that they were related to Tahitians. Such information became part of the reservoir of knowledge, not always otherwise accessible to them, from which scholars and experts could draw.

Intellectual ambition combined in many men of this age with the desire to explore and an urge for adventure, endeavours from which they brought home knowledge that could often be applied to economic prosperity and the general improvement of society, among the aspirations of the time. Inevitably such ambition was often fuelled by political and economic goals, and individuals, like nations, engaged in wide-ranging enterprise for the betterment of their own lives. Denied recognition and reward for his early achievements, Bass turned to these objectives.

Intellectually and in the application of that intellect, Bass stood well above most men of his time. He learned languages as he came upon them. Encountering the open sea for the first time as an eighteen-year-old surgeon, he became a skilled seaman and navigator. He read classics and at the same time examined the more revolutionary philosophies of the day. He was impatient of ignorance and sharply critical of what he called 'insipidity', an attitude that shadowed even his closest personal relationships. Set apart by his own abilities, he yearned for the company of his intellectual equals, for the exchange of ideas that 'exalts the human intellect'. About himself and his achievements he was realistic, dismissing with irony what he saw as excessive praise. Inevitably there was an aloneness in being what he was, perhaps something he sought to fill with the restless activity of his life.

In an age when patronage and family connections were important in bettering one's social and economic position, Bass, a tenant farmer's son, knew that for him achievement rested on personal ability and effort, 'sturdy unremitting industry'—in other words, his own hard efforts—and risks when necessary, and in these he had absolute confidence and no sense of fear. The whaleboat voyage was an example of this, as was his plan to reach Spanish-held South America. Invariably he embarked on his ventures with an optimism and exuberance that seized the imagination of others—the governors of New South Wales who approved his plans, the friends and associates who invested in his company, the seamen who volunteered to sail with him. Yet his own emotional commitments were selective. He was devoted to his mother and in love with his wife. He formed his strongest ties of friendship with his wife's family, perhaps unconsciously compensating for having been an only child who lost his father at a young age.

The price paid by men like Bass for their goals could be heavy. Explorers perished in equatorial jungles and arctic snows and like Bass disappeared at sea. At home families waited for word that too often never came.

To Matthew Flinders, Bass's leadership was ardent, 'high spirited and able', and his accomplishments 'most conspicuous for the promotion of useful knowledge'.[18] The botanist and explorer George Caley wrote that he was 'one who stands unrivalled, and probably a long time may elapse before another gives as much intelligence or excels him'.[19] Fearless, clever, ambitious and inquisitive, George Bass exemplified to a very special degree the remarkable era in which he lived.

Appendix

INFORME No. 06 — 2003-DAC/TA

Certificate attesting to a search made for information on George Bass by the Archivo General de la Nación, Lima, Peru

ARCHIVO GENERAL DE LA NACION

Lima, 14 de octubre del 2003

OFICIO N° 1298-2003-AGN/J

Mrs.
MIRIAM ESTENSEN
Australia.-

ASUNTO: INFORMACION SOBRE PERSONAJE GEORGE BASS
REF : CARTA DEL 10-09-03

Tengo el agrado de dirigirme a usted, de acuerdo al documento de la referencia para remitirle adjunto al presente el Informe N° 06-2003-DAC/TA de la Dirección de Archivo Colonial de la Dirección Nacional de Archivo Histórico del Archivo General de la Nación, para su conocimiento y fines.

Sin otro particular, hago propicia la ocasión para expresarle las muestras de mi especial consideración.

Atentamente,

Teresa Carrasco Cavero
JEFA
Archivo General de la Nación

AGN/DNAH
DAC/smf.
Adj. Lo indicado

Jr. Manuel Cuadros s/n.- Palacio de Justicia
Telfs. 427-5930 - Fax: 428-2829
agnperu@terra.com.pe

Jefatura: 426-7222 DNDAAI: 426-3631
DNAH: 426-1837 ENA: 470-5206 OTA: 426-7221
Apartado 3124 - Lima - Perú

INFORME N° 06 - 2003-DAC/TA

Sr. ARMANDO DONAYRE MEDINA
Director del Archivo Colonial

DE : Sr. GREGORIO MORALES ORELLANA
    Técnico en Archivo IV

ASUNT : Información sobre documentos referente al personaje George Bass.

FECHA : Lima, 10 de octubre del 2003

    Por medio del presente es grato dirigirme a Ud. Para saludarlo y al mismo tiempo para informarle lo siguiente:

    Miriam Estense, con su carta de 10.09.03, ha solicitado al Archivo General de la Nación, la información sobre documentos que hacen referencia al personaje George Bass.

    Por lo que se ha verificado la documentación de **Real Tribunal del Consulado** (comercio, resguardo al comercio), **Real Hacienda** (Ejército y expediciones militares, Superintendencia General), **Guerra** (Guerra y Marina). No se ha podido localizar a los documentos solicitados.

    Es todo cuanto puedo informar a usted para los fines que estime pertinente.

    Atentamente.

    Gregorio Morales Orellana
    TA.4

NOTA.- Se adjunta al presente la carta de Miriam Estense, de fecha 10.09.03.

Lima, 10 de octubre de 2003
Visto el informe que antecede y que esta Dirección de Archivo Colonial hace suyo, elévese a Dirección Nacional de Archivo Histórico, para su conocimiento y fines pertinentes.

    Sr. ARMANDO DONAYRE MEDINA
    Director del Archivo Colonial

Chronology

1771	February 3 George Bass baptised at Aswarby, Lincolnshire
1777	Sarah Bass and her son George moved to Boston
1778	March 22 Bass apprenticed to surgeon/apothecary Patrick Francis
1789	April 2 Received diploma as surgeon
	June 4 Qualified as Naval Surgeon's Mate, any rate
	July to July 1790 Service on HMS *Flirt*, HMS *Gorgon*
1790	July 4 Qualified as Naval Surgeon, 2nd rate
	July to September 1793 Service on HMS *Fairy*, HMS *Pomona*, HMS *Vulcan*, HMS *Shark*
1793	November to April 1794 Service on HMS *Druid*
1794	March Reported for service on HMS *Reliance*
1795	February 15 Departure of HMS *Reliance* from England
	September 7 Arrival of HMS *Reliance* at Sydney, New South Wales
	October 26 to November 4 Exploration of Botany Bay and Georges River in the first *Tom Thumb*
	November Expedition to Cowpastures
1796	January to March *Reliance* to Norfolk Island and return
	March 24 to April 1 Voyage of the second *Tom Thumb*; discovery of Lake Illawarra
	June Attempt to cross the Blue Mountains
	September 29 *Reliance* and HMS *Supply* sailed for Cape of Good Hope for livestock
1797	June 26 Return of *Reliance* to Sydney
	August 5 to 13 Coal found at Coalscliff
	September Second expedition to Cowpastures
	December 3 Bass and whaleboat crew sailed from Sydney
1798	January 2 Wilsons Promontory sighted
	January 5 Discovery of Western Port
	February 25 Whaleboat returned to Sydney
	October 7 Departure of sloop *Norfolk* for Van Diemen's Land
	December 9 Existence of Bass Strait ascertained
	December 22 *Norfolk* entered Derwent River
1799	January 12 *Norfolk* returned to Sydney
	May 29 Departure of Bass from New South Wales

1800   August 4 Arrival of Bass in England
       September 18 Purchase of brig *Venus*
       October 8 Marriage of George Bass and Elizabeth Waterhouse
1801   January 8 Partnership formed between Bass and Charles Bishop
       January 9 *Venus* sailed from Portsmouth
       March to May 30 *Venus* on Brazilian coast
       June 3 Arrival at Cape of Good Hope
       August 29 Arrival at Port Jackson
       November 21 *Venus* sailed from Port Jackson on voyage to Dusky
          Bay, New Zealand, Matavai Bay, Tahiti, Hawaii and other Pacific
          islands
1802   November 14 *Venus* returned to Port Jackson
1803   February 5 *Venus* sailed on second voyage into the Pacific

Glossary

ALOFT—up above; up a mast or yard or high in the rigging

ANCHORS—bower, the biggest anchors; stream, the next largest anchors; kedge, smaller anchors for special purposes

ARRACK—any of various spirits distilled in the East from the fermented sap drawn from certain types of palms

AZIMUTH COMPASS—a compass that measures azimuth or bearing clockwise from due north

BARICA—a small barrel

BEAT—sailing as closely as possible to the wind by alternating tacks

BEND—to make fast, as a sail to a spar or a cable to an anchor; UNBEND to undo, remove sails from spars

BILGE—the curved part of the ship's hull next to the keel; BILGED when the bilge is broken

BOMB—a small, shallow-draught vessel built to carry mortars

BREAKER—a small water cask

BRIG—a two-masted square-rigged ship

CATLING—pointed, double-edged surgical instrument

CHAINS—the leadman's station under the bowsprit

CUTTER—a sloop-rigged boat with the mast farther aft than that of a sloop

DRAUGHT—the depth of water needed to float a boat or ship

FLAG RANK, FLAG OFFICER—an admiral's rank, an admiral

FLOG AROUND THE FLEET—to be whipped on board each of a series of ships

GARBOARD STRAKE—planks next to and on both sides of the keel

HEAVE—to haul in

HEAVE DOWN—to pull over a boat or ship to inspect or repair the bottom

HOGSHEAD — 52 gallons; cask or other container with 52-gallon capacity

HOLYSTONE — flat pieces of porous stone, usually sandstone, used for scrubbing decks

INDIAMAN — a large merchant ship in trade with India or the East or West Indies; hence, East Indiaman, West Indiaman

JOLLYBOAT — a ship's work boat, usually about 18 feet long

KNEES, RIDERS — parts of a ship's internal framing

LANCET — small two-edged, pointed surgical instrument

LEAD — a cone- or pyramid-shaped piece of lead with a line secured at the top and a small hole in the bottom for picking up samples of the sea floor formation; with a marked line it is used to take soundings

LEADSMAN — a sailor stationed in the chains under the bowsprit to heave the lead

LITTORAL — coast or shore

LUGGER — a boat rigged with a quadrilateral sail bent upon a yard that crosses the mast obliquely

LUGSAIL — sail of a lugger

OAKUM — strands of old rope used for caulking

PAY A SHIP'S SEAMS — to seal a ship's seams with pitch after they have been filled with oakum or cotton

PINTLE — a pin on which a boat's or ship's rudder pivots

POISSARDE — fishwife, implying sharp language

ROAD, ROADSTEAD — an anchorage that is some distance from shore

ROOM space, place; IN ROOM OF — in place or instead of

SCORBUTIC — pertaining to or affected by scurvy

SHIPS OF THE LINE — the largest naval warships; also called 'line of battle ships'

SHROUDS — ropes supporting the mast

SLOPS — clothing, bedding, etc., supplied to seamen or colonists from ships' or government stores

SNOW — a small sailing ship resembling a brig

STAND FOR — to sail towards

STAND OFF AND ON — to sail towards and then away in order to maintain position, usually at night or while waiting

SSTEM — the vertical timber at the bow of a ship, which supports the bow planks

TREAK, STRAKE — a ship's side plank

STRIKE—to lower, e.g. strike into the hold

SUPERCARGO—an officer on a merchant ship who is in charge of the cargo and commercial concerns of the trip

SUPERNUMERARY—an extra person; someone in excess of the usual prescribed number

SWEEP—a large oar

SWIVEL GUN—a gun mounted so that it can be swung from side to side

TAKING THE SIGHT—using the sextant to estimate the ship's latitude

TREND—to tend to take a particular direction

TURNSPIT DOG—a breed of dog with a long body and short legs, used to work a treadmill that turned a spit

WEIGH—to raise anchor

WHERRY—a light rowing boat commonly used to carry passengers and goods on rivers

WOODING—obtaining firewood

Abbreviations

ADM   Admiralty Records
HRA   *Historical Records of Australia*
HRNSW   *Historical Records of New South Wales*
LAO   Lincolnshire Archives Office
LTC   La Trobe Collections, State Library of Victoria
ML   Mitchell Library, State Library of New South Wales
NMM   National Maritime Museum, Greenwich
SLV   State Library of Victoria
TNA:PRO   The National Archives of the UK (TNA): Public Record Office
            (PRO)

Author's note: Spelling, punctuation and underlined words in all quotations
are as they were written at the time.

CHAPTER 1   THE YOUNG GEORGE BASS

1 A. M. Cook, *An Australian Boston: A Forgotten Chapter of Local History*, The Church House, Boston, 1943, p. 22
2 Will of George Bass Jnr, farmer and grazier of Aswarby, LAO Will 1777/11, LAO, Lincoln
3 A. M. Mapleton, letter to Brogden, 1 March 1878 (copy), Box 241–No. 2 (234) Shillinglaw Papers, SLV, Melbourne
4 A. M. Mapleton, letter to Brogden, 5 December 1880, Box 243–No. 4 (260) Shillinglaw Papers, SLV, Melbourne
5 Boston Corporation Minute Books, Folio 108, in K. M. Bowden, *George Bass—1771–1803*, Oxford University Press, Melbourne, p. 8
6 From tombstone inscription, churchyard at Gainsborough, Lincolnshire, quoted in A. M. Cook, *Lincolnshire Links with Australia*, The Subdeanery, Lincoln, 1951, p. 19

7 ibid.
8 *List of Those Examined and Approved Surgeons, July 1789*, from the private collection of William F. Wilson, Melbourne and 'Bass River', Victoria
9 ibid.
10 William James, *Naval History of Great Britain* in Nathan Miller, 'Appendix I: the Composition of the Royal Navy, 1793–1816' in *Broadsides: the Age of Fighting Sail, 1775–1815*, John Wiley & Sons, Inc., New York, 2000, p. 363

CHAPTER 2   THE ROYAL NAVY

1 Thomas Trotter to Admiral Lord Howe, 15 May 1795, *The Channel Fleet and the Blockade of Brest, 1793–1801*, ed. Roger Morris, Ashgate, Aldershot, 2001, p. 64
2 Michael Lewis, *A Social History of the Navy*, George Allen & Unwin, London, 1960, p. 406
3 ibid., p. 410
4 Uniforms as such were not made compulsory for seamen until 1857, but there was a certain standardisation in the clothing handed out by pursers from ships' stores
5 George Hamilton, *A Voyage Round the World in His Majesty's Frigate Pandora*, Hordern House, Sydney, 1998, p. 22
6 Brian Lavery, ed., *Shipboard Life and Organisation, 1731–1815*, Ashgate, Aldershot, p. 17
7 Brian Lavery, *Nelson's Navy: The Ships, Men and Organisation 1793–1815*, Conway Maritime Press, 1989, and the Naval Institute Press, Annapolis, 2000, p. 101
8 ibid., p. 254
9 Elizabeth Bass to George Bass, 8 February 1802, ZML MSS 6544 [ZSafe 1/187], ML, Sydney
10 George Bass to Sarah Bass, n.d. 1798, ZML MSS 6544 [ZSafe 1/187], ML, Sydney
11 Henry Waterhouse to William Waterhouse, 14 May 1796, ZML MSS 6544 [ZSafe 1/187], ML, Sydney
12 Brian Lavery, ed., 'Rules for the Cure of Sick and Hurt Seamen on Board their own Ships' in *Shipboard Life and Organisation, 1731–1815*, Ashgate, Aldershot, p. 17
13 Surgeons were expected to provide their own medications until after 1804. Brian Lavery, *Nelson's Navy*, op. cit., p. 213
14 This was the third lighthouse at Eddystone, signalling the approach to Plymouth. Completed in late 1759, it was built by John Smeaton using a revolutionary method of interlocking stone construction, and stood until replaced in 1882 by the present tower
15 George Bass to Sarah Bass, September 1798, ZML MSS 6544 [ZSafe 1/187], ML, Sydney

16 Log of HM Sloop *Shark*, 15 May to 20 May 1793, TNA: PRO, Kew, Richmond

17 Log of HM Sloop *Shark*, 28 May 1793, ADM 51/865, TNA: PRO, Kew, Richmond

18 Log of HM Sloop *Shark*, 26 July 1793, ADM 51/865, TNA: PRO, Kew, Richmond

19 Steve Pope, *Hornblower's Navy: Life at Sea in the Age of Nelson*, Orion Media, London, 1998, p. 35

CHAPTER 3 VOYAGE TO AUSTRALIA

1 George Bass to Joseph Banks, 27 May 1799, Banks Papers, Series 72.005, ML, Sydney

2 Sarah Bass to George Bass, 6 July 1797, ZML MSS 6544 [ZSafe 1/187], ML, Sydney

3 Matthew Flinders, *A Voyage to Terra Australis, Undertaken for the Purpose of Completing the Discovery of that Vast Country, and Prosecuted in the Years 1801, 1802, and 1803, in His Majesty's Ship the Investigator, and Subsequently in the armed Vessel Porpoise and Cumberland Schooner, with an Account of the Shipwreck of the Porpoise, Arrival of the Cumberland at Mauritius, and Imprisonment of the Commander during Six Years and a Half in that Island*, G. and W. Nicol, London, 1814, Australiana Facsimile Editions No. 37, Libraries Board of South Australia, Adelaide, 1966, vol. I, Introduction, p. xcvii

4 Frederik Henry as Chapman, *Architectura Navalis Mercatoria*, Coles, London, 1971. Selected parts of the 19th century translation by the Rev. James Inman of the (author's) *Tractat Om Skepps-Byggieret*, originally published as *Architectura Navalis Mercatoria*, Holmiae, 1768

5 John Hunter to Secretary Phillip Stephens, 9 August 1794, *HRNSW*, vol. II, 1893, p. 249

6 Phillip Stephens to John Hunter, 10 October 1794, *HRNSW*, vol. II, 1893, p. 257

7 Christopher Nevile to Joseph Banks, 27 May 1794, Series 72.125, ML, Sydney

8 John Hunter to the Navy Board, 19 March 1794, ADM 106/1353, TNA: PRO, Kew, Richmond

9 Henry Waterhouse to Arthur Phillip, 24 October 1795, Banks Papers, Series 37.28, ML, Sydney

10 Guns were regularly loaded in Long Reach, the Thames farther upstream being too shallow due to silting for the added weight to be placed on the big ships of the line

11 Captain's Log, HMS *Reliance*, 8 July 1794, ADM 1121, TNA: PRO, Kew, Richmond

12 C. C. Lloyd, 'Victualling of the Fleet in the Eighteenth and Nineteenth

Centuries' in *Starving Sailors*, J. Watt, E. J. Freeman and W. F. Bynum, eds, National Maritime Museum, Greenwich, 1981, p. 12

13 Matthew Flinders, *A Voyage to Terra Australis*, op. cit., vol. I, Introduction, p. xcvi

14 Matthew Flinders to George Bass, 15–21 February 1800, ZML MSS 7046, ML, Sydney

15 Matthew Flinders, *A Voyage to Terra Australis*, op. cit., vol. I, Introduction, p. xcvii

16 John Hunter to Under Secretary John King, 1 May 1794, *HRNSW*, vol. II, p. 214

17 Daniel Paine, *The Journal of Daniel Paine: 1794–1797, Together with Documents Illustrating the Beginning of Government Boat-Building and Timber-gathering in New South Wales, 1795–1804*, R. J. B. Knight and Alan Frost, eds, National Maritime Museum, Greenwich and Library of Australian History, Sydney, 1983, p. 1

18 *Watkin Tench, 1788*, Tim Flannery, ed., The Text Publishing Company, Melbourne, 1996, p. 118

19 John Hunter to Under Secretary John King, 25 January 1795, *HRNSW*, vol. II, p. 281

20 Daniel Paine, *The Journal of Daniel Paine: 1794–1797*, op. cit., p. 8

21 Log of HMS *Reliance*, 15 May 1795, ADM 1121, TNA: PRO, Kew, Richmond

22 Log of HMS *Reliance*, 8 September 1795, ADM 51/1121, TNA: PRO, Kew, Richmond

23 Governor Hunter's Commission, *HRA*, Series I, vol. I, pp. 513–14

24 John Hunter, 'State of the Settlements 25th October 1795', Enclosure No. 3 in a letter to the Duke of Portland, *HRNSW*, vol. II, Sydney, 1893, p. 334

25 Merval Hoare, *Norfolk Island—A Revised and Enlarged History 1774–1998*, Central Queensland University Press, Rockhampton, 1999

26 Michael Roe, 'Colonial Society in Embryo' in *Historical Studies: Australia and New Zealand*, vol. 7, November 1955–May 1957, University of Melbourne, Melbourne, p. 151

27 John Hunter to the Duke of Portland, 11 September 1795, *HRA*, Series I, vol. I, pp. 527–8

28 John Hunter to the Duke of Portland, 21 December 1795, *HRNSW*, vol. II, pp. 245–6

29 John Hunter to the Duke of Portland, 20 August 1796, *HRA*, Series I, vol. I, pp. 594–5

CHAPTER 4   THE FIRST EXPLORATIONS

1 Matthew Flinders, *A Voyage to Terra Australis, Undertaken for the Purpose of Completing the Discovery of that Vast Country, and Prosecuted in the Years 1801, 1802, and 1803, in His Majesty's Ship the Investigator, and Subsequently in the armed Vessel Porpoise and*

Cumberland Schooner, with an Account of the Shipwreck of the Porpoise, Arrival of the Cumberland at Mauritius, and Imprisonment of the Commander during Six Years and a Half in that Island, G. and W. Nicol, London, 1814, Australiana Facsimile Editions No. 37, Libraries Board of South Australia, Adelaide, 1966, vol. I, Introduction, p. xcvii

2 Matthew Flinders, *Matthew Flinders' Narrative of Tom Thumb's Cruize to Canoe Rivulet*, ed. Keith Bowden, South Eastern Historical Association, Brighton, Victoria, 1985, p. 2

3 'Condition of Norfolk Island', *HRNSW*, vol. III, p. 146

4 James Watt, 'The Colony's Health' in *Studies from Terra Australis to Australia*, eds John Hardy and Alan Frost, Highland Press and the Australian Academy of the Humanities, Canberra, 1989, p. 149

5 Daniel Paine, *The Journal of Daniel Paine: 1794–1797, Together with Documents Illustrating the Beginning of Government Boat-Building and Timber-gathering in New South Wales, 1795–1804*, eds R. J. B. Knight and Alan Frost, National Maritime Museum, Greenwich and Library of Australian History, Sydney, 1983, p. 22

6 ibid., p. 39

7 Matthew Flinders, *Matthew Flinders' Narrative of Tom Thumb's Cruise to Canoe Rivulet*, op. cit., p. 9

8 ibid., p. 10

9 Matthew Flinders, *A Voyage to Terra Australis*, op. cit., vol. I, Introduction, p. ci

10 ibid., vol. I, Introduction, p. ci

11 Matthew Flinders, *Matthew Flinders' Narrative of Tom Thumb's Cruise to Canoe Rivulet*, op. cit., p. 16

12 Matthew Flinders, *A Voyage to Terra Australis*, op. cit., vol. I, Introduction, p. cii

13 John Hunter to Secretary Evan Nepean, 31 August 1796, *HRA*, Series I, vol. I, p. 648

14 Keith M. Bowden, *George Bass 1771–1803, His Discoveries, Romantic Life and Tragic Disappearance*, Oxford University, Melbourne, 1852, p. 42

15 Matthew Flinders, *A Voyage to Terra Australis*, op. cit., vol. I, Introduction, p. cv, and Atlas, Plate VIII

16 Alan E. J. Andrews, 'Mount Hunter and Beyond: With Hunter, Bass, Tench, Wilson, Barrallier, Caley and Macquarie 1790 to 1815', *Journal of the Royal Australian Historical Society*, vol. 76, part 1, June 1990, History House, Sydney, p. 5

17 M. F. Péron, *Voyage de découvertes aux terres Australes, exécuté par ordre de Su Majesté l'Empereur et Roi, sur les corvettes le Géographe, le Naturaliste, et la goelette le Casuarina, pendant les anneés 1800, 1801, 1802, 1803 et 1804; publié par décret impérial, sous le ministére de M. de Champagny, et rédigé par M. F. Péron*, trans. Moreno Giovannoni, Tome premier, A Paris, De L'Impremerie impériale MDCCC, VII, 1807–1816, pp. 393–4

18 Philip Gidley King to Lord Hobart, 31 December 1802, *HRNSW*, vol. IV, p. 929

19 Matthew Flinders, *A Voyage to Terra Australis*, op. cit., vol. I, Introduction, p. cv
20 R. Else Mitchell, 'Bass's Land Explorations', *Royal Historical Society Journal and Proceedings*, vol. 17, part 4, Sydney, 1951, pp. 244–50

CHAPTER 5 MEDICAL PRACTICE AND POLITICAL VIEWS

1 William Balmain to Governor John Hunter, 16 October 1795, *HRNSW*, vol. II, p. 333
2 Patrick Campbell to the Commissioners of the Navy, 2 August 1794, *HRNSW*, vol. II, p. 857
3 ibid.
4 John Black to his father, 8 September 1798, *HRNSW*, vol. III, p. 730
5 John Hunter to the Duke of Portland, 30 April 1796, *HRNSW*, vol. III, p. 47
6 T. F. Palmer to Joyce, 5 May 1796, National Library of Australia MS 761, pp. 13–16 in James Watt, 'The Colony's Health' in *Studies from Terra Australis to Australia*, eds John Hardy and Alan Frost, Highland Press and the Australian Academy of the Humanities, Canberra, p. 149
7 David Collins, *An Account of the English Colony in New South Wales*, vol. I, ed. Brian H. Fletcher, A. H. & A. W. Reed and the Royal Australian Historical Society, Sydney, 1975, p. 381
8 Daniel Paine, *The Journal of Daniel Paine: 1794–1797, Together with Documents Illustrating the Beginning of Government Boat-Building and Timber-gathering in New South Wales, 1795–1804*, eds R. J. B. Knight and Alan Frost, National Maritime Museum, Greenwich and Library of Australian History, Sydney, 1983, p. 22
9 ibid., p. 29
10 W. G. McDonald, *The First-Footers: Bass and Flinders in Illawarra 1796–1797*, Illawarra Historical Society, Wollongong, 1975, p. 41
11 George Bass to Thomas Jamison, July 1797, in Michael Roe, 'New Light on George Bass, Entrepreneur and Intellectual', *Journal of the Royal Australian Historical Society*, vol. 72, 1987, p. 252
12 George Bass to Sarah Bass, September 1798, ZML MSS 6544 [ZSafe 1/187], ML, Sydney
13 George Bass to Elizabeth Bass, 15 November 1802, ZML MSS 6544 [ZSafe 1/187], ML, Sydney
14 Matthew Flinders to George Bass, 15–21 February 1800, ZML MSS 7046, ML, Sydney
15 George Sutter, *Memoirs of George Suttor, E.L.S., Banksian Collector (1774–1856)*, ed. George Mackaness, self published, Sydney, 1948, p. 42
16 Henry Waterhouse to William Waterhouse, March 1797, ZML MSS 6544 [ZSafe 1/187], ML, Sydney

17 Henry Waterhouse to William Waterhouse, 20 August 1797, ZML MSS 6544 [ZSafe 1/187], ML, Sydney
18 John Hunter to Secretary Evan Nepean, 31 August 1796, *HRA*, Series I, vol. I, p. 649
19 John Hunter to Under Secretary King, 15 September 1796, *HRA*, Series I, vol. I, p. 663
20 Henry Waterhouse, 26 June 1797, 'Importation of Live Stock on the Reliance from the Cape of Good Hope; Private Stock embarked on the Reliance, Cape of Good Hope', *HRNSW*, vol. III, p. 237
21 Henry Waterhouse to William Waterhouse, 20 August 1797, ZML MSS 6544 [ZSafe 1/187], ML, Sydney
22 George Bass to Sarah Bass, September 1798, ZML MSS 6544 [ZSafe 1/187], ML, Sydney
23 Henry Waterhouse to William Waterhouse, 20 August 1797, ZML MSS 6544 [ZSafe 1/187], ML, Sydney
24 John Hunter to the Duke of Portland, 25 June 1797, *HRA*, Series I, vol. II, p. 32
25 Survey of the *Supply*, 2 June 1797, *HRNSW*, vol. II, p. 280
26 Henry Waterhouse to William Waterhouse, March 1797, ZML MSS 6544 [ZSafe 1/187], ML, Sydney
27 Henry Waterhouse to William Waterhouse, 20 August 1797, ZML MSS 6544 [ZSafe 1/187], ML, Sydney
28 Survey of the *Reliance*, enclosed in letter of John Hunter to Secretary Evan Nepean, 19 November 1797, *HRA*, series I, vol. II, p. 113
29 John Hunter to the Duke of Portland, 6 July 1797, *HRA*, Series I, vol. II, p. 82
30 John Hunter to the Duke of Portland, 25 June 1797, *HRA*, Series I, vol. II, p. 33
31 George Bass to William Paterson, 20 August 1797, *HRNSW*, vol. III, pp. 289–90
32 ibid.
33 David Collins, *An Account of the English Colony in New South Wales*, op. cit., p.34

CHAPTER 6   THE WHALEBOAT

1 David Collins, *An Account of the English Colony in New South Wales*, vol. I, ed. Brian H. Fletcher, A. H. & A. W. Reed and the Royal Australian Historical Society, Sydney, 1975, pp. 67–8
2 George Bass to Thomas Jamison, July 1797, in Michael Roe, 'New Light on George Bass, Entrepreneur and Intellectual', *Journal of the Royal Australian Historical Society*, vol. 72, 1987, p. 252
3 Michael Lewis, *A Social History of the Navy 1793–1815*, George Allen & Unwin, London, 1960, p. 304
4 ibid., p. 244

5 Sarah Bass to George Bass, 6 July 1797, ZML MSS 6544 [ZSafe 1/187], ML, Sydney
6 George Bass to Sarah Bass, September 1798, ZML MSS 6544 [ZSafe 1/187, ML, Sydney
7 John Hunter to the Duke of Portland, 1 March 1798, *HRA*, Series I, vol. II, p. 132
8 John Hunter to Secretary Evan Nepean, 3 September 1798, *HRA*, Series I, vol. II, p. 220
9 Geoffrey C. Ingleton, *Matthew Flinders, Navigator and Chartmaker*, Genesis Publications in association with Hedley Australia, 1986, p. 29; Keith Bowden, *George Bass: 1771–1803*, Oxford University Press, Melbourne, 1952, p. 59, gives the length as 28 feet and 7 inches
10 George Bass, *Journal*, 3 December 1797, *HRNSW*, vol. III, p. 312–13
11 ibid., 6 December 1797, vol. III, p. 313
12 ibid.
13 ibid p.314
14 ibid., 7 December 1797, vol. III, p. 315
15 ibid., 17 December 1797, vol. III, p. 316
16 Lawrence FitzGerald, 'Bass's "Barmouth Creek"', p. 4; from a talk given by Lawrence FitzGerald on 3 June 1976 to the Tathra Historical Society, Tathra, New South Wales
17 George Bass, *Journal*, op. cit., 18 December 1797, vol. III, p. 318
18 Lawrence FitzGerald, 'Bass's "Barmouth Creek"', op. cit, p. 8
19 George Bass, *Journal*, 31 December 1797, op. cit., vol. III, p. 320
20 Matthew Flinders, *A Voyage to Terra Australis, Undertaken for the Purpose of Completing the Discovery of that Vast Country, and Prosecuted in the Years 1801, 1802, and 1803, in His Majesty's Ship the Investigator, and Subsequently in the armed Vessel Porpoise and Cumberland Schooner, with an Account of the Shipwreck of the Porpoise, Arrival of the Cumberland at Mauritius, and Imprisonment of the Commander during Six Years and a Half in that Island*, G. and W. Nicol, London, 1814, Australiana Facsimile Editions No. 37, Libraries Board of South Australia, Adelaide, 1966, vol. I, Introduction, note, p. cxv
21 George Bass, *Journal*, 3 to 5 January 1798, *HRNSW*, vol. III, p. 322
22 Matthew Flinders, *A Voyage to Terra Australis*, op. cit., vol. I, Introduction, p. cxii
23 John Hunter to the Duke of Portland, 1 March 1798, *HRA*, Series I, vol. II, p. 133
24 George Bass, *Journal*, op. cit., 5 January 1798, vol. III, p. 323
25 ibid.
26 ibid.
27 ibid.
28 John Hunter to the Duke of Portland, 3 September 1798, *HRA*, Series I, vol. II, p. 221
29 Matthew Flinders, *A Voyage to Terra Australis*, op. cit., Atlas, Sheet V, South Coast
30 George Bass, *Journal*, op. cit., 5 January 1798, vol. III, p. 323

31 ibid., vol. III, p. 324
32 ibid.
33 Matthew Flinders, *A Voyage to Terra Australis*, op. cit., vol. I, Introduction, p. cxix
34 ibid., vol. I, Introduction, note, p. cxvii
35 The seven escapees who took the boat headed north, plundering small craft and settlements until they were wrecked and gave themselves up. The two ringleaders were hanged, the others reprieved
36 George Bass, *Journal*, op. cit., 15 January 1798, vol. III, p. 330
37 ibid.
38 John Hunter to the Duke of Portland, 1 March 1798, *HRNSW*, vol. III, p. 363
39 Matthew Flinders, *A Voyage to Terra Australis*, op. cit., vol. I, Introduction, p. cxix
40 ibid., vol. I, Introduction, pp. cxix–cxx
41 George Bass to Thomas Jamison, 7 September 1798, in Michael Roe, op. cit., p. 254
42 David Collins, *An Account of the English Colony in New South Wales*, vol. II, ed. Brian H. Fletcher, A. H. & A. W. Reed, Sydney, 1975, p. 95
43 Thomas Jamison to George Bass, 1 November 1797, in Michael Roe, op. cit., p. 254
44 George Bass to Sarah Bass, September 1798, ZML MSS 6544 [ZSafe 1/187], ML, Sydney
45 ibid.

CHAPTER 7 'AND SHOULD A STRAIT BE FOUND . . .'

1 John Hunter to Secretary Evan Nepean, 3 September 1798, *HRNSW*, vol. III, p. 475
2 Matthew Flinders, *A Voyage to Terra Australis, Undertaken for the Purpose of Completing the Discovery of that Vast Country, and Prosecuted in the Years 1801, 1802, and 1803, in His Majesty's Ship the Investigator, and Subsequently in the armed Vessel Porpoise and Cumberland Schooner, with an Account of the Shipwreck of the Porpoise, Arrival of the Cumberland at Mauritius, and Imprisonment of the Commander during Six Years and a Half in that Island*, G. and W. Nicol, London, 1814, Australiana Facsimile Editions No. 37, Libraries Board of South Australia, Adelaide, 1966, vol. I, Introduction, p. cxxxviii
3 ibid., vol. I, Introduction, p. cxxxviii
4 George Bass, *Journal describing Two-Fold Bay in New South Wales Furneaux's Islands in Bass's Strait and the Coast and Harbours of Van Dieman's Land from Notes made on board the Colonial Sloop Norfolk in 1798 and 1799*, ML C228, ML, Sydney, p. 2
5 ibid., p. 3

6 ibid., p. 4

7 ibid., p. 3

8 ibid., p. 6

9 David Collins, *An Account of the English Colony in New South Wales*, vol. II, ed. Brian H. Fletcher, A. H. & A. W. Reed, Sydney, 1975, p. 107. The paragraph containing this observation does not occur in the surviving copy of Bass's manuscript. Collins may have used a version that has been lost

10 George Bass, *Journal describing Two-Fold Bay in New South Wales*, op. cit., pp. 8–9

11 David Collins, *An Account of the English Colony in New South Wales*, op. cit., vol. II, pp. 111–13

12 George Bass, *Journal describing Two-Fold Bay in New South Wales*, op. cit., p. 45

13 Matthew Flinders, 'Narrative of an Expedition in the Colonial sloop Norfolk, from Port Jackson, through the Strait which separates Van Diemen's Land from New Holland, and from thence round the South Cape back to Port Jackson, completing the circumnavigation of the former Island, with some remarks on the coasts and harbours, by Matthew Flinders, 2nd l't, H.M.S. Reliance', *HRNSW*, vol. III, Appendix B, p. 776

14 David Collins, *An Account of the English Colony in New South Wales*, op. cit., vol. II, p. 116

15 ibid., vol. II, p. 117

16 Matthew Flinders, *A Voyage to Terra Australis*, op. cit., vol. I, Introduction, p. cliii

17 George Bass, *Journal describing Two-Fold Bay in New South Wales*, op. cit., p. 18

18 ibid., p. 20

19 ibid.

20 Matthew Flinders, *A Voyage to Terra Australis*, op. cit., vol. I, Introduction, p. clv

21 George Bass, *Journal describing Two-Fold Bay in New South Wales*, op. cit., p. 20

22 ibid., p. 22

23 Matthew Flinders, 'Narrative of an Expedition in the Colonial sloop Norfolk', op. cit., *HRA*, Series I, vol. III, Appendix B, p. 786

24 ibid., p. 787

25 ibid., p. 796

26 Matthew Flinders, *A Voyage to Terra Australis*, op. cit., vol. I, Introduction, p. clxx

27 ibid., vol. I, Introduction, p. clxx

28 George Bass, *Journal describing Two-Fold Bay in New South Wales*, op. cit., pp. 25–6

29 Matthew Flinders, 'Narrative of an Expedition in the Colonial sloop Norfolk', op. cit., Series I, vol. III, Appendix B, p. 801

30 Matthew Flinders, *A Voyage to Terra Australis*, op. cit., vol. I, Introduction, p. clxxvi

31 Matthew Flinders, 'Narrative of an Expedition in the Colonial sloop Norfolk', op cit., Series I, vol. III, Appendix B, p. 802
32 ibid., p. 804
33 George Bass, *Journal describing Two-Fold Bay in New South Wales,* op. cit., pp. 31–2
34 Matthew Flinders, 'Narrative of an Expedition in the Colonial sloop Norfolk', op. cit., Series I, vol. III, Appendix B, p. 812
35 David Collins, *An Account of the English Colony in New South Wales,* op. cit., vol. II, note 22, p. 269

CHAPTER 8   A CHANGE OF COURSE

1 John Hunter to Secretary Evan Nepean, 15 August 1799, *HRA,* Series I, vol. II, p. 381
2 Philip Gidley King to the Duke of Portland, 1 March 1802, *HRA,* Series I, vol. III, p. 437
3 John Hunter to Secretary Evan Nepean, 15 August 1799, *HRA,* Series I, vol. II, p. 380
4 Joseph Banks to John Hunter, 1 February 1799, *HRNSW,* vol. III, p. 532
5 Letter by 'Oceanus', *The Naval Chronicle for 1813 Containing a General and Biographical History of The Royal Navy of the United Kingdom; with a Variety of Original Papers on Nautical Subjects,* vol. XXX, Joyce Gold, London, 1813, p. 201
6 George Bass to Thomas Jamison, 17 February 1799, in Michael Roe, 'New Light on George Bass, Entrepreneur and Intellectual', *Journal of the Royal Australian Historical Society,* vol. 72, part 5, 1987, p. 256
7 ibid.
8 ibid., p. 259
9 George Bass to Thomas Jamison, 3 April 1799, in Michael Roe, op. cit., p. 258
10 David Collins, *An Account of the English Colony in New South Wales,* op. cit., vol. II, p. 100
11 George Bass to William Paterson, 20 August 1797, *HRNSW,* vol. III, pp. 289–90
12 George Bass to Thomas Jamison, 26 May 1799, in Michael Roe, op. cit., p. 258
13 ibid., pp. 258–9
14 Charles Bishop to John Hunter, request for Letter of Marques Commission, 6 May 1799, *The Journal and Letters of Captain Charles Bishop on the North-West Coast of America, in the Pacific and in New South Wales 1794–1799,* The Hakluyt Society, Cambridge University Press, London, 1966, pp. 314
15 *Chart of Islands in the Pacifick Islands, seen in the brig Nautilus Capt. Charles Bishop in 1799; laid down by George Bass and Roger Simpson,* The United Kingdom Hydrographic Office, Taunton, UK. In the Gilberts,

THE LIFE OF GEORGE BASS

Bishop's Island is in fact Tabiteuea; Dog Island, Nonouti; Harbottle Island, Abemama. In the Marshalls, George Bass's Reef-tied Isles is Maloelap and Steep-to I, Jemo

16 Houng, Hong or Cohong was the corporation of licensed Chinese merchants at Guangzhou (Canton) who before 1842 had the monopoly of trade with Europeans

17 George Bass to Thomas Jamison, 22 May 1800, in Michael Roe, op. cit., p. 260

18 Robert Shepherdson to George Bass, 30 October 1801, Waterhouse Family Papers ZML MSS 6544 [ZSafe 1/187], ML, Sydney

19 George Bass to Thomas Jamison, 22 May 1800, in Michael Roe, op. cit., p. 260

20 *The Times*, Monday, 4 August 1800; from the private collection of William F. Wilson, Melbourne and 'Bass River', Victoria

CHAPTER 9   THE *VENUS* VENTURE

1 T. Howson to Brogden, 1 March 1878 (copy), Box 241, No. 2 (234) Shillinglaw Papers, SLV, Melbourne

2 Sarah Bass to George Bass, 6 July 1797, ZML MSS 6544 [ZSafe 1/187], ML, Sydney

3 Printed prospectus offering for sale the brig *Venus*, 18 September 1800, ZML MSS 6544 [ZSafe 1/187], ML, Sydney

4 *HRNSW*, vol. IV, n.d., p. 587

5 Governor Hunter's Commission, *HRA*, Series I, vol. I, pp. 513–14

6 Articles of Agreement, 8 January 1801, ZML MSS 6544 [ZSafe 1/187], ML, Sydney

7 Henry Waterhouse to William Waterhouse, 20 August 1797, ZML MSS 6544 [ZSafe 1/187], ML, Sydney

8 St James's Church, Piccadilly, was evidently designed by and its construction closely associated with Sir Christopher Wren. It was consecrated in 1684. William Blake, born in 1757, was baptised here. A memorial tablet notes the death of the eminent physician, William Hunter, in 1783

9 George Bass to William Waterhouse, 8 October 1800, ZML MSS 6544 [ZSafe 1/187], ML, Sydney

10 Henry Waterhouse to William Waterhouse, 8 October 1800, ZML MSS 6544 [ZSafe 1/187], ML, Sydney

11 Michael Roe, 'New Light on George Bass, Entrepreneur and Intellectual', *Journal of the Royal Australian Historical Society*, vol. 72, part 5, 1987, p. 261

12 George Bass to Sarah Bass, 8 January 1801, ZML MSS 6544 [ZSafe 1/187], ML, Sydney

13 Elizabeth Bass to George Bass, 15 December 1801, ZML MSS 6544 [ZSafe 1/187], ML, Sydney

14 Elizabeth Bass to Sarah Bass, 14 January 1801, ZML MSS 6544 [ZSafe 1/187], ML, Sydney

15 George Bass to Henry Waterhouse, 9 January 1801, ZML MSS 6544 [ZSafe 1/187], ML, Sydney

16 Elizabeth Bass to Sarah Bass, 14 January 1801, ZML MSS 6544 [ZSafe 1/187], ML, Sydney

17 George Bass to Elizabeth Bass, 9 January 1801, ZML MSS 6544 [ZSafe 1/187], ML, Sydney

18 Elizabeth Bass to George Bass, 15 December 1801, ZML MSS 6544 [ZSafe 1/187], ML, Sydney

19 George Bass to Elizabeth Bass, 9 January 1801, ZML MSS 6544 [ZSafe 1/187], ML, Sydney

20 Elizabeth Bass to George Bass, 28 January 1801, ZML MSS 6544 [ZSafe 1/187], ML, Sydney

21 George Bass to Elizabeth Bass, 8 March 1801, ZML MSS 6544 [ZSafe 1/187], ML, Sydney

CHAPTER 10   ADVERSITY AND SOLUTIONS

1 George Bass to Elizabeth Bass, 8 March 1801, ZML MSS 6544 [ZSafe 1/187], ML, Sydney

2 George Bass to Elizabeth Bass, 27 April 1801, ZML MSS 6544 [ZSafe 1/187], ML, Sydney

3 George Bass to Elizabeth Bass, 27 April 1801, ZML MSS 6544 [ZSafe 1/187], ML, Sydney

4 George Bass, list of trade goods, in Michael Roe, 'New Light on George Bass, Entrepreneur and Intellectual', *Journal of the Royal Australian Historical Society*, vol. 72, 1987, p. 261

5 Michael Roe, 'New Light on George Bass, Entrepreneur and Intellectual', ibid., p. 263

6 George Bass to William Waterhouse, 30 June 1801, ZML MSS 6544 [ZSafe 1/187], ML, Sydney; also in *HRNSW*, vol. IV, pp. 420–1

7 ibid.

8 George Bass to Elizabeth Bass, 30 June 1801, ZML MSS 6544 [ZSafe 1/187], ML, Sydney

9 George Bass to Henry Waterhouse, 4 October 1801, ZML MSS 6544 [ZSafe 1/187], ML, Sydney

10 George Bass to Thomas Jamison, 15 May 1802, in Michael Roe, op. cit., p. 264

11 George Bass to Henry Waterhouse, 4 October 1801, ZML MSS 6544 [ZSafe 1/187], ML, Sydney

12 Thomas Rowley to Henry Waterhouse, 14 May 1802, *HRNSW*, vol. IV, p. 753

13 Account of Bills drawn by Commissary Palmer, 1800–1803, *HRA*, Series I, vol. III, p. 473

14 Michael Duffy, *Man of Honour, John Macarthur, Duellist, Rebel, Founding Father*, Macmillan Australia, Sydney, 2003, p. 196
15 Captain McKellar's Account, Enclosure No. 5 in Philip Gidley King to Secretary Evan Nepean, 31 October 1801, *HRA*, Series I, vol. III, p. 297
16 Paterson's wound has been described as in the arm, presumably in the upper arm, as well as in the shoulder. Bass, however, one of the attending doctors, says shoulder. Governor King in a general order of 21 September 1801 states that 'the surgeons have this day reported that Lieut.-Col. Paterson is not out of danger from the wound he received on the 14th inst'. Government and General Order, 21 September 1801, *HRNSW*, vol. IV, p. 566
17 Contract with Bass and Bishop for the Importation of Pork, 9 October 1801, *HRA*, Series I, vol. III, p. 337
18 George Bass to Elizabeth Bass, 3 October 1801, ZML MSS 6544 [ZSafe 1/187], ML, Sydney
19 George Bass to Henry Waterhouse, 4 October 1801, ZML MSS 6544 [ZSafe 1/187], ML, Sydney
20 George Bass to Elizabeth Bass, 20 October 1801, ZML MSS 6544 [ZSafe 1/187], ML, Sydney
21 George Bass to Elizabeth Bass, 3 October 1801, ZML MSS 6544 [ZSafe 1/187], ML, Sydney
22 George Bass to Elizabeth Bass, 20 October 1801, ZML MSS 6544 [ZSafe 1/187], ML, Sydney
23 In 1804 Boston returned to Sydney and in September sailed on a commercial voyage. Putting ashore in a boat at Nukualofa in Tongatapu, he and seven other men were killed as they landed
24 Ida Lee, 'H.M.S. Surveying Vessel Lady Nelson on Discovery. Lieutenant-Commander John Murray' in *The Logbooks of the 'Lady Nelson' with a Journal of her First Commander, Lieutenant James Grant, R.N.*, Grafton & Co., London, 1915, p. 124
25 George Bass to Elizabeth Bass, 12 November 1801, in K. M. Bowden, 'George Bass, 1771–1803, Surgeon and Sailor', *Bulletin of the Post Graduate Committee in Medicine, University of Sydney*, vol. 17, May 1861, Sydney, pp. 49–50

CHAPTER 11 INTO THE PACIFIC

1 This is the date given by Bass in his letter to Henry Waterhouse, 30 January 1802. Shipping Returns for 1 July 1801 to 31 December 1801 puts the *Venus*'s clearance date at 23 November
2 George Bass to an unknown correspondent, 20 May 1802. Extant copy in the hand of William Waterhouse, ZML MSS 6544 [ZSafe 1/187], ML, Sydney
3 The meridian of the transit instrument at the Royal Observatory, Greenwich, was adopted as the prime or zero meridian by an interna-

tional conference at Washington, D.C. in October 1884. A theoretical date line at 180° from Greenwich was recognised, but its course was never defined by any international treaty or agreement. Mapmakers today tend to follow recommendations issued by the hydrographic departments of the British or American navies. But sailing east in 1802, Bass recorded his longitude continuously from Greenwich

4 This was Thomas Orde-Powlett, first Lord Bolton (1746–1807), formerly a Secretary of State and at the time Lord Lieutenant of Hampshire

5 The Chatham Islands, a group of ten islands about 500 miles (800 kilometres) east of New Zealand's South Island, were discovered by William R. Broughton of the ship *Chatham,* when en route to Tahiti in 1791

6 George Bass to an unknown correspondent, 20 May 1802 op. cit.

7 George Bass to William Waterhouse, 30 January 1802, ZML MSS 6544 [ZSafe 1/187], ML, Sydney; also *HRNSW,* vol. IV, p. 690

8 George Bass to William Waterhouse, 30 January 1802, ZML MSS 6544 [ZSafe 1/187], ML, Sydney; also *HRNSW,* vol. IV, pp. 689–90

9 George Bass to Elizabeth Bass, 30 January 1802, ZML MSS 6544 [ZSafe 1/187], ML, Sydney

10 George Bass to an unknown correspondent, 20 May 1802, op. cit.

11 ibid.; in another letter Bass gives the date of arrival as 10 March

12 George Bass to Thomas Jamison, 15 May 1802, in Michael Roe, 'New Light on George Bass, Entrepreneur and Intellectual', *Journal of the Royal Australian Historical Society,* vol. 72, Sydney, 1987, p. 264

13 George Bass to William Waterhouse, 20 May 1802, ZML MSS 6544 [ZSafe 1/187], ML, Sydney

14 George Bass to an unknown correspondent, 20 May 1802, op. cit.

15 ibid.

16 George Bass to Elizabeth Bass, 20 May 1802, ZML MSS 6544 [ZSafe 1/187], ML, Sydney

17 George Bass to William Waterhouse, 20 May 1802, ZML MSS 6544 [ZSafe 1/187], ML, Sydney

18 George Bass to Sarah Bass, 20 May 1802, ZML MSS 6544 [ZSafe 1/187], ML, Sydney

19 George Bass to Thomas Jamison, 15 May 1802, in Michael Roe, op. cit., p. 264

20 George Bass to an unknown correspondent, 20 May 1802, op. cit.

21 'Extracts from the Log book of the *Norfolk* Armed colonial Brig respecting the Wreck of that Vessel in Matavai Bay, Otaheite', in *HRA,* Series I, vol. III, p. 729

22 Michael Roe, ed., *The Journal and Letters of Captain Charles Bishop on the North-West Coast of America, in the Pacific and in New South Wales 1794–1799,* The Hakluyt Society, Cambridge, 1967, Introduction, p. xlviii

23 John Jefferson to Philip Gidley King, 9 August 1802, *HRA,* Series I, vol. III, p. 726

24 George Bass to Henry Waterhouse, 1 January 1803, ZML MSS 6544 [ZSafe 1/187], ML, Sydney

25 Philip Gidley King to Lord Hobart, 15 November 1802, *HRA*, Series I, vol. III, p. 724
26 George Bass to Elizabeth Bass, 15 November 1802, ZML MSS 6544 [ZSafe 1/187], ML, Sydney
27 Philip Gidley King to Lord Hobart, 7 August 1803, Enclosure No. 7, 'Government and General Orders', 15 November 1802, *HRA*, Series I, vol. IV, p. 327
28 Elizabeth Bass to George Bass, 5 February 1802, ZML MSS 6544 [ZSafe 1/187], ML, Sydney
29 Frank Horner, *The French Renaissance: Baudin in Australia 1801–1803*, Melbourne University Press, Melbourne, 1987, p. 250
30 Peter Pindar or John Wolcot (1738–1819) wrote satirical verse on society, politics and individuals. His verse caricatures included George III, James Boswell and the painter Benjamin West. Paul Brunton, Senior Curator, Mitchell Library, Sydney, suggests that *Oil of Fool* may have been one of his books; George Bass to Elizabeth Bass, 15 November 1802, ZML MSS 6544 [ZSafe 1/187], ML, Sydney
31 George Caley to Joseph Banks, 1 November 1802, in R. Else Mitchell, 'George Caley: His Life and Work', *Royal Australian Historical Society Journal and Proceediungs*, vol. XXV, part VI, 1939, Sydney
32 George Bass to Elizabeth Bass, 15 November 1802, ZML MSS 6544 [ZSafe 1/187], ML, Sydney
33 George Bass to Henry Waterhouse, 1 January 1803, ZML MSS 6544 [ZSafe 1/187], ML, Sydney
34 Elizabeth Bass to George Bass, 25 April 1801, ZML MSS 6544 [ZSafe 1/187], ML, Sydney
35 Elizabeth Bass to George Bass, August 1801, ZML MSS 6544 [ZSafe 1/187], ML, Sydney
36 Elizabeth Bass to George Bass, 9 November 1801, ZML MSS 6544 [ZSafe 1/187], ML, Sydney
37 George Bass to Elizabeth Bass, 3 January 1803, ZML MSS 6544 [ZSafe 1/187], ML, Sydney
38 George Bass to Elizabeth Bass, 18 March 1801, ZML MSS 6544 [ZSafe 1/187], ML, Sydney
39 Elizabeth Bass to George Bass, 9 November 1801, ZML MSS 6544 [ZSafe 1/187], ML, Sydney
40 George Bass to Elizabeth Bass, 30 June 1801, ZML MSS 6544 [ZSafe 1/187], ML, Sydney
41 Elizabeth Bass to George Bass, 9 November 1801, ZML MSS 6544 [ZSafe 1/187], ML, Sydney
42 George Bass to Elizabeth Bass, 30 June 1801, ZML MSS 6544 [ZSafe 1/187], ML, Sydney
43 George Bass to Elizabeth Bass, 5 January 1803, ZML MSS 6544 [ZSafe 1/187], ML, Sydney
44 William Waterhouse to Elizabeth Bass, 9 December 1803, ZML MSS 6544 [ZSafe 1/187], ML, Sydney

45 William Waterhouse to Elizabeth Bass, 14 December 1803, ZML MSS 6544 [ZSafe 1/187], ML, Sydney

46 George Bass to Elizabeth Bass, 30 June 1801, ZML MSS 6544 [ZSafe 1/187], ML, Sydney

47 Elizabeth Bass to George Bass, August 1801, ZML MSS 6544 [ZSafe 1/187], ML, Sydney

48 Elizabeth Bass to George Bass, 8(?) February 1802, ZML MSS 6544 [ZSafe 1/187], ML, Sydney

49 George Bass to Elizabeth Bass, 27 April 1800, ZML MSS 6544 [ZSafe 1/187], ML, Sydney. The date 1800 is a mistake; it would have had to be 1801

50 Elizabeth Bass to George Bass, 9 November 1801, ZML MSS 6544 [ZSafe 1/187], ML, Sydney

51 Elizabeth Bass to George Bass, August 1801, ZML MSS 6544 [ZSafe 1/187], ML, Sydney

52 William Waterhouse to George Bass, 19 August 1801, ZML MSS 6544 [ZSafe 1/187], ML, Sydney

53 Thomas Fyshe Palmer, 23 September 1800, 'Inventory of Mr. Bass's Books', Bonwick Transcripts, Biography ZML A2000/1–4: CY Reel 679, ML, Sydney

54 Matthew Flinders to George Bass, 15–21 February 1800, ZML MSS 7046, ML, Sydney

55 ibid.

56 Elizabeth Bass, note on letter from Matthew Flinders to George Bass, ZML MSS 7046, ML, Sydney

57 Matthew Flinders to George Bass, 8 August 1803, ZML MSS [Zsafe 1/187], ML, Sydney

58 Elizabeth Bass to George Bass, August 1801, ZML MSS 6544 [ZSafe 1/187], ML, Sydney

59 George Bass to Elizabeth Bass, 21 December 1802, ZML MSS 6544 [ZSafe 1/187], ML, Sydney

60 George Bass to Elizabeth Bass, 3 October 1801, ZML MSS 6544 [ZSafe 1/187], ML, Sydney

CHAPTER 12 THE LAST VOYAGE

1 George Bass to Henry Waterhouse, 1 January 1803, ZML MSS 6544 [ZSafe 1/187], ML, Sydney

2 George Bass to Elizabeth Bass, 3 January 1803, ZML MSS 6544 [ZSafe 1/187], ML, Sydney

3 George Bass to Elizabeth Bass, n.d., 1803, ZML MSS 6544 [ZSafe 1/187], ML, Sydney

4 George Bass to Philip Gidley King, January 1803, HRA, Series I, vol. IV, pp. 156–7

5 Philip Gidley King to Lord Hobart, 9 May 1803, HRA, Series I, vol. IV, p. 147

6 George Bass to Sarah Bass, September 1798, ZML MSS 6544 [ZSafe 1/187], ML, Sydney
7 George Bass to William Waterhouse, 5 January 1803, ZML MSS 6544 [ZSafe 1/187], ML, Sydney
8 William Waterhouse to Elizabeth Bass, 8 December 1803, ZML MSS 6544 [ZSafe 1/187], ML, Sydney
9 George Bass to William Waterhouse, 5 January 1803, *HRNSW*, vol. V, pp. 1–3
10 ibid.
11 John Harris to Philip Gidley King, 25 January 1803, *HRA,* Series I, vol. IV, p. 218
12 George Bass to William Waterhouse, 2 February 1803, *HRNSW*, vol. V, p. 15
13 Frederick Watson, ed., *HRA,* Series I, vol. IV, note 68, pp. 669–70

CHAPTER 13   THE FATE OF THE *VENUS*

1 Philip Gidley King to Robert, Lord Hobart, Secretary of State for War and Colonies, 1 March 1804, *HRA*, Series I, vol. IV, pp. 523–4
2 Philip Gidley King to Under Secretary J. Sullivan, Colonial Office, 1 April 1804, *HRA*, Series I, vol. IV, p. 607
3 Philip Gidley King to Lord Hobart, 16 April 1804, *HRA*, Series I, vol. IV, p. 628
4 Philip Gidley King to Lord Hobart, 20 December 1804, *HRA*, Series I, vol. IV, p. 172
5 Philip Gidley King to Lord Hobart, 20 December 1804, *HRNSW*, vol. V, p. 518
6 George Bass to Elizabeth Bass, 20 May 1802, ZML MSS 6544 [ZSafe 1/187], ML, Sydney
7 Francisco Quiroz Chueca, *De la Colonia a la República Independiente*, Callao, 1956, p. 707
8 Philip Gidley King to Lord Hobart, 9 May 1803, *HRA*, Series I, vol. IV, p. 148
9 Robert Brown, *Nature's Investigator: The Diary of Robert Brown In Australia, 1801–1805*, eds T. G. Vallance, D. T. Moore and E. W. Groves, Australian Biological Resources Study (Flora), Canberra, 2001, p. 581
10 Frederick Watson, ed., *HRA*, Series I, vol. IV, note 68, pp. 669–70
11 Robert Brown to Joseph Banks, 21 February 1805, *HRNSW*, vol. V, p. 560
12 Charles Bishop to Rowland Hassall, a Sydney retailer, 21 November 1804, Rowland Hassall Papers, ML, Sydney
13 *The Sydney Gazette and New South Wales Advertiser,* 24 November 1805, p. 1, in *The Sydney Gazette and New South Wales Advertiser*, A Facsimile Reproduction of Volume Three, 3 March 1805 to 9 March 1806, The Trustees of the Public Library of New South Wales in Association with Angus & Robertson, Sydney, 1966

14 *The Sydney Gazette and New South Wales Advertiser*, 2 February 1806, in *The Sydney Gazette and New South Wales Advertiser*, ibid.

15 Elizabeth Bass to George Bass, 19 October 1803, ZML MSS 6544 [ZSafe 1/187], ML, Sydney

16 William Waterhouse to George Bass, 17 October 1803, ZML MSS 6544 [ZSafe 1/187], ML, Sydney

17 Elizabeth Bass to George Bass, 19 October 1803, ZML MSS 6544 [ZSafe 1/187], ML, Sydney

18 William Waterhouse to George Bass, 17 October 1803, ZML MSS 6544 [ZSafe 1/187], ML, Sydney

19 Matthew Flinders to George Bass, 8 August 1803, ZML MSS 6544 [ZSafe 1/187], ML, Sydney

20 K. M. Bowden, in his biography *George Bass, 1771–1803, His Discoveries, Romantic Life and Tragic Disappearance*, Oxford University Press, Melbourne, 1952, quotes Admiralty documents to this effect. These documents have not been found in a recent search of Admiralty and Royal Naval Museum records

21 Records of the Court of Assistants for managing the Charity For *Relief of Poor Widows of Commission and Warrant Officers of the Royal Navy*, TNA: PRO, ADM 6/343, 25 January 1806

22 ibid.

23 Register of Minutes of Meetings of Court of Assistants managing the Charity For *Relief of Poor Widows of Commission and Warrant Officers of the Royal Navy*, Meeting held on Tuesday, 15 July 1806, ADM 6/333, pp. 18–19

CHAPTER 14   AFTERMATH

1 William Waterhouse to Elizabeth Bass, 14 December 1803, ZML MSS 6544 [ZSafe 1/187], ML, Sydney

2 William Fitzmaurice, 30 May 1811, ML A2000/1, pp. 216–19, ML, Sydney; also quoted by Frederick Watson, ed., *HRA*, Series I, vol. IV, note 68, p. 670

3 *Sydney Gazette and New South Wales Advertiser*, 29 May 1808, p. 2, in *Sydney Gazette and New South Wales Advertiser*, A Facsimile Reproduction, vols 6 and 7, 15 May 1808 to 31 December 1809, The Trustees of the Public Library of New South Wales in Association with Angus & Robertson, Sydney, 1969

4 K. M. Bowden, in 'George Bass, 1771–1803, Surgeon and Sailor', *Bulletin of the Post-Graduate Committee in Medicine, University of Sydney*, vol. 17, May 1961; also in K. M. Bowden, *George Bass, 1771–1803: His Discoveries, Romantic Life and Tragic Disappearance*, Oxford University Press, Melbourne, 1952, p. 139

5 William Fitzmaurice, quoted by Frederick Watson, ed., *HRA*, Series I, vol. IV, note 68, p. 670; also in Bonwick Transcripts, Biography [ZML A2000/1-4: CY Reel 679], ML, Sydney

6 Lieutenant William Fitzmaurice appears to have been the same officer who from Valparaiso in October 1808 conveyed to British authorities the information that Captain Mayhew Folger of the American ship *Topaz* had landed at Pitcairn's Island and found there the last of the HMS *Bounty* mutineers. Extracted by Fitzmaurice from the log of the *Topaz*, this was the first news of the fate of the *Bounty* to reach the outside world

7 K. M. Bowden, *George Bass, 1771–1803: His Discoveries, Romantic Life and Tragic Disappearance*, Oxford University Press, Melbourne, 1952, p. 130

8 ibid., p. 131

9 William Waterhouse to (probably) Henry Addington, Viscount Sidmouth, Secretary of State for the Home Office, n.d., c.1818, ML A2000/1(4), ML, Sydney, pp. 216–19

10 Jorgen Jorgenson, *A Shred of Autobiography*, Sullivan's Cove, Adelaide, 1981, p. 22

11 George William Rusden, notes from Rusden Manuscript, Rusden Collection, 1903, Trinity College Library, University of Melbourne, Melbourne

12 This official document, Informe No. 06–2003-DAC/TA, was issued at Lima, Peru, on 10 October 2003, following a request by the author for a search of relative archival records. It is now in the author's possession

13 A. M. Mapleston to Brogden, 5 March 1878 (copy), Shillinglaw Collection, Box 241, No. 2, LTC, Melbourne

14 ibid.

15 The Will of Sarah Bass of the Parish of St Swithin in the City of Lincoln, Lincolnshire. Courtesy of Canon David Pink, Swarby, Lincolnshire. Among the recipients was Elizabeth's sister Amelia, married to Henry Pownall, a London barrister. Letters and other items pertaining to George and Elizabeth Bass were preserved by the Pownalls; some are now in Australia. Elizabeth's siblings Ann Gimmingham, Maria Waterhouse and John Waterhouse were the other beneficiaries.

16 Elizabeth Bass to George Bass, 25 April 1801, ZML MSS 6544 [ZSafe 1/187], ML, Sydney

17 Elizabeth Bass to George Bass, August 1801, ZML MSS 6544 [ZSafe 1/187], ML, Sydney

18 Matthew Flinders, *A Voyage to Terra Australis, Undertaken for the Purpose of Completing the Discovery of that Vast Country, and Prosecuted in the Years 1801, 1802, and 1803, in His Majesty's Ship the Investigator, and Subsequently in the armed Vessel Porpoise and Cumberland Schooner, with an Account of the Shipwreck of the Porpoise, Arrival of the Cumberland at Mauritius, and Imprisonment of the Commander during Six Years and a Half in that Island*, G. and W. Nicol, London, 1814, Australiana Facsimile Editions No. 37, Libraries Board of South Australia, Adelaide, 1966, vol. I, Introduction, p. cxx

19 George Caley to Joseph Banks, 1 November 1802, in R. Else Mitchell, 'George Caley: His Life and Work', *Royal Australian Historical Society Journal and Proceedings*, vol XXV, part VI, 1939, Sydney; also R. Else Mitchell, 'Bass's Land Explorations', *Royal Australian Historical Society Journal and Proceedings*, vol. XXXVII, part IV, 1951, Sydney

Bibliography

PRIMARY SOURCES

Bass, George, 'Bass's Journal of the Whaleboat Voyage' in *Matthew Flinders's Narrative of His Voyage in the Schooner Francis, 1798, Preceded and Followed by Notes on Flinders, Bass, the Wreck of the Sydney Cove, &c by Geoffrey Rawson*, ed. Geoffrey Rawson, Golden Cockerel Press, Great Britain, 1946

Baudin, Nicolas, *The Journal of Post Captain Nicolas Baudin, Commander-in-Chief of the Corvettes Géographe and Naturaliste*, trans. Christine Cornell, Libraries Board of South Australia, Adelaide 1974

Bishop, Charles, *The Journal and Letters of Captain Charles Bishop on the North-West Coast of America, in the Pacific and in New South Wales 1794–1799*, ed. Michael Roe, The Hakluyt Society, London, 1967

Brown, Robert, *Nature's Investigator: The Diary of Robert Brown In Australia, 1801–1805*, eds T. G. Vallance, D. T. Moore and E. W. Groves, Australian Biological Resorces Study (Flora), Canberra, 2001

Caley, George, *Reflections on the Colony of New South Wales*, ed. J. E. B. Currey, Resources Study, Canberra, 1866

Collins, David, *An Account of the English Colony in New South Wales, with Remarks on the Dispositions, Customs, Manners, etc., of the Native Inhabitants of that country*, vols I and II, ed. Brian H. Fletcher, A. H. & A. W. Reed, Sydney, 1975

Cook, James, *The Journal of Captain James Cook, edited from his original manuscripts by J. C. Beaglehole*, The Hakluyt Society, Cambridge University Press, Cambridge, 1955–1974

—— *Captain Cook's Journal during His First Voyage Round the World made in H.M. Bark 'Endeavour' 1768–1771*, ed. W. J. L. Wharton, Eliot Stock, London 1893; Australiana Facsimile Editions no. 188, Libraries Board of South Australia, Adelaide, 1968

—— *Captain Cook in New Zealand: Extracts from the journals of Captain James Cook giving a full account in his own words of his adventures and discoveries in New Zealand*, 2nd edn, eds A. H. and A. W. Reed, A. H. & A. W. Reed, Wellington, 1969

Cullen, Peter, 'Memoirs of Peter Cullen' in *Five Naval Journals 1789–1817*, ed. H. G. Thursfield, Navy Records Society, London, 1951

Flinders, Matthew, *Charts of Terra Australis or Australia, showing the Parts Explored between 1798–1803 by M. Flinders, Commander of H. M. S. Investigator*, G. & W. Nicols, London, 1814

—— *Matthew Flinders' Narrative of His Voyage in the Schooner Francis, 1798, Preceded and Followed by Notes on Flinders, Bass, the Wreck of the Sydney Cove, &c by Geoffrey Rawson*, ed. Geoffrey Rawson, Golden Cockerel Press, Great Britain, 1946

—— *Observations on the Coasts of Van Diemen's Land, on Bass's Strait and its Islands, and on part of the coasts of New South Wales; intended to accompany the charts of the late discoveries in those countries*, John Nicols, London, 1801. Australiana Facsimile Editions no. 66, Libraries Board of South Australia, Adelaide, 1965

—— *A Voyage to Terra Australis; undertaken for the Purpose of Completing the Discovery of that Vast Country, and Prosecuted in the Years 1801, 1802, and 1803, in His Majesty's Ship the Investigator, and Subsequently in the Armed Vessel Porpoise and Cumberland Schooner, with an Account of the Shipwreck of the Porpoise, Arrival of the Cumberland at Mauritius, and Imprisonment of the Commander during Six Years and a Half on that Island*, vol. 1, G. and W. Nicol, London, 1814; Australiana Facsimile Editions no. 37, Libraries Board of South Australia, Adelaide, 1966

—— *Matthew Flinders' Narrative of Tom Thumb's Cruise to Canoe Rivulet*, ed. Keith M. Bowden, Southern Historical Association, Brighton, Victoria, 1985

Hamilton, George, *A Voyage Round the World in His Majesty's Frigate Pandora*, Hordern House, Sydney, 1998

Hawkesworth, John, *An Account of a Voyage round the World with a Full Account of the Voyage of the Endeavour: in the Year MDCCLXX along the East Coast of Australia by Lieutenant James Cook, Commander of His Majesty's Bark Endeavour, compiled by D. Warrington Evans; Illustrated with a Variety of Cuts and Charts Relative to the Country Discovered*, W. R. Smith & Paterson, Brisbane, 1969

Historical Records of Australia, Governors' Despatches to and from England, Series I, vols I, II, III, IV, V, ed. Frederick Watson, the Library Committee of the Commonwealth Parliament, Sydney, 1914–1915

Historical Records of New South Wales, vols I, II, III, IV, ed. F. M. Bladen, Charles Potter Government Printer, Sydney, and vol. V, ed. F. M. Bladen, William Applegate Gullick, Government Printer, Sydney, 1892, 1893, 1895, 1896, 1897

Historical Records of New Zealand, vol. 1, ed. Robert McNab, Government Printer, Wellington, 1908–1914

Jorgenson, Jorgen, *A Shred of Autobiography*, Sullivan's Cove, Adelaide, 1981

King, Philip Gidley, *The Journal of Philip Gidley King: Lieutenant, R.N., 1787–1790*, eds Paul G. Fidlon and R. J. Ryan, Australian Documents Library, Sydney, 1980

Lee, Ida, *The Logbooks of the 'Lady Nelson' with the Journal of Her First Commander Lieutenant James Grant, R. N.*, Grafton & Co., London, 1915

Noah, William, *Voyage to Sydney in the Ship Hillsborough 1798–1799 and a Description of the Colony*, Library of Australian History, Sydney, 1978

Paine, Daniel, *The Journal of Daniel Paine: 1794–1797, Together with Documents Illustrating the Beginning of Government Boat-Building and Timber-gathering in New South Wales, 1795–1804*, eds R. J. B. Knight and Alan Frost, National Maritime Museum, Greenwich and Library of Australian History, Sydney, 1983

Péron, M. F., *Voyage de découvertes aux terres Australes, exécuté par ordre de Su Majesté l'Empereur et Roi, sur les corvettes le Géographe, le Naturaliste, et la goelette le Casuarina, pendant les anneés 1800, 1801, 1802, 1803 et 1804; publié par décret impérial, sous le ministére de M. de Champagny, et rédigé par M. F. Péron*, trans. Moreno Giovannoni, Tome premier, A Paris, De L'Impremerie impériale MDCCC, VII, 1807–1816, pp. 393–4

Péron, François M., *A Voyage of Discovery to the Southern Hemisphere, Performed by the Order of the Emperor Napoleon, during the Years 1801, 1802, 1803, and 1804*, translated from the French, Marsh Walsh, North Melbourne, 1975

Suttor, George, *Memoirs of George Suttor, F. L. S., Banksian Collector (1774–1859)*, ed. George Mackaness, D. S. Ford, Sydney, 1948

SECONDARY SOURCES

Aplin, Graeme, ed., *A Difficult Infant: Sydney before Macquarie*, New South Wales University Press, Kensington, 1988

Atkinson, Alan, *The Europeans in Australia: A History*, vol. 1, Oxford University Press, Melbourne, Victoria, 1997

Australian Dictionary of Biography, vol. 1, 1788–1850, eds A. G. L. Shaw and C. M. H. Clark, Melbourne University Press, London, 1966

Australian Encyclopaedia, The, editor-in-chief Alec H. Chisholm, Grolier Society, Sydney, 1965

Badger, Geoffrey, *The Explorers of the Pacific*, 2nd edn, Kangaroo Press, Kenthurst, New South Wales, 1988, 1996

Barclay, Glen, *A History of the Pacific from the Stone Age to the Present Day*, Sidgwick & Jackson, London, 1978

Barker, Anthony, *When Was That? Chronology of Australia*, John Ferguson, Surry Hills, New South Wales, 1988

Bassett, Marnie, *The Governor's Lady: Mrs. Philip Gidley King*, Melbourne University Press, Melbourne, 1961

Beaglehole, J. C., *The Exploration of the Pacific*, Stanford University Press, Stanford, California, 1966

—— *The Life of Captain James Cook*, Adam and Charles Black, London, 1974

Beasley, A. W., *Fellowship of Three—The Lives and Association of John Hunter (1728–1793), the Surgeon; James Cook (1728–1779), the*

Navigator; and Joseph Banks (1743–1820), the Naturalist, Kangaroo Press, Kenthurst, New South Wales, 1993

Becke, Louis, and Jeffrey, Walter, *The Naval Pioneers of Australia*, John Murray, London, 1899

Begg, A. Charles, and Begg, Neil C., *Dusky Bay*, Whitcombe & Tombs, Christchurch, New Zealand, 1966; rev. edn 1968

Bernier, Oliver, *The World in 1800*, John Wiley & Sons, New York, 2000

Black, Jeremy, *Visions of the World: A History of Maps*, Mitchell Beazley, London, 2003

Blainey, Geoffrey, *The Tyranny of Distance: How Distance Shaped Australia's History*, rev. edn, Sun, Sydney, 1983

Bowden, Keith M., *George Bass: 1771–1803, His Discoveries, Romantic Life and Tragic Disappearance*, Oxford University Press, Melbourne, 1952

Brissenden, Alan, and Higham, Charles, *They Came to Australia*, F. W. Cheshire, Melbourne, 1961

Brodsky, Isadore, *Bennelong Profile: Dreamtime Reveries of a Native of Sydney Cove*, University Co-operative Bookshop, Sydney, 1973

Brown, Anthony, *Ill-Starred Captains: Flinders and Baudin*, Crawford House, Adelaide, 2000

Bryant, Joseph, *Captain Matthew Flinders, R.N., his voyages, discoveries and fortunes*, The Epworth Press, London, 1928

Butlin, S. J., *Foundations of the Australian Monetary System 1788–1851*, Sydney University Press, Sydney, 1968

Cameron, Hector Charles, *Sir Joseph Banks*, Angus & Robertson, Sydney, 1952

Campbell, I. C., *Worlds Apart: A History of the Pacific Islands*, Canterbury University Press, Christchurch, New Zealand, 2003

Campbell, Leon G., *The Military and Society in Colonial Peru, 1750–1810*, American Philosophical Society, Philadelphia, 1978

Carter, Harold B., *Sir Joseph Banks 1743–1820*, British Museum (Natural History), London, 1988

Chancellor, E. Beresford, *The XVIIIth Century in London: An Account of Its Social Life and Arts*, B. T. Batsford, London, 1920

Charles, Daniel, *Lighthouses of the Atlantic*, Cassell, London, 2001

Churchill, Winston S., *A History of the English-Speaking Peoples*, vol. III, 'The Age of Revolution', Cassell, London, 1950, 1982

Clancy, Robert, *The Mapping of Terra Australis*, Universal Press, Macquarie Park, New South Wales, 1995

Clark, C. M. H., *A History of Australia: From the Earliest Times to the Age of Macquarie*, Melbourne University Press, Melbourne, 1962

Clowes, William Laird, *The Royal Navy: A History From the Earliest Times to the Present*, vol. IV, Sampson Low, Marston, London, 1900

Clune, Frank, and Stephensen, P. R., *The Viking of Van Diemen's Land: The Stormy Life of Jorgen Jorgensen*, Angus & Robertson, Sydney, 1954

Cobley, John, *Sydney Cove 1793–1795: The Spread of Settlement*, Angus & Robertson, Sydney, 1983

—— *Sydney Cove 1795–1800: The Second Governor*, Angus & Robertson, North Ryde, New South Wales, 1986

Cole, Harry, and Cole, Valda, *Mr. Bass's Western Port: The Whaleboat Voyage*, Hastings–Western Port Historical Society in conjunction with the South Eastern Historical Association, Hastings, Victoria, 1997

Colledge, J. J., *Ships of the Royal Navy: An Historical Index*, vol. 1, David & Charles, Newton Abbot, England, 1969

Cook, A. M., *An Australian Boston: A Forgotten Chapter of Local History*, The Church House, Boston, England, 1943

—— *Lincolnshire Links with Australia*, Keyworth & Sons, Lincoln, 1951

Cridland, Frank, *The Story of Port Hacking, Cronulla and Sutherland Shire*, Angus & Robertson, Sydney, 1924

Cumpston, J. H. L., *The Inland Sea and the Great River: The Story of Australian Exploration*, Angus & Robertson, Sydney, 1964

Cumpston, J. S., *Shipping Arrivals and Departures Sydney, 1788–1825*, Roebuck Society, Canberra, 1977

Dalrymple, Alexander, *An Historical Collection of the Several Voyages and Discoveries in the South Pacific Ocean*, Nourse, London, 1770

Daniel, Hawthorne, *Islands of the Pacific*, G. P. Putnam's Sons, New York, 1843

Dening, Greg, *Readings/Writings*, Melbourne University Press, Carlton South, Victoria, 1998

Duffy, Michael, *Man of Honour, John Macarthur: Duellist, Rebel, Founding Father*, Macmillan, Sydney, 2003

Dugard, Martin, *Farther Than Any Man: The Rise and Fall of Captain James Cook*, Allen & Unwin, Sydney, 2003

Ehrman, John, *The Younger Pitt: The Reluctant Transition*, Constable, London, 1983

Eisler, William, and Smith, Bernard, *Terra Australis, the Furthest Shore*, Internation Cultural Corporation of Australia, Sydney, 1988

Ellis, M. H., *John Macarthur*, Angus & Robertson, Sydney, 1978

Ellis, William, *Polynesian Researches, during a Residency of Nearly Six Years in the South Sea Islands; including descriptions of the natural history and scenery of the islands, with remarks on the history, mythology, traditions, government, arts, manners and customs of the inhabitants*, vol. 1, Dowsons of Pall Mall, London, 1967

Evans, Susanna, *Historic Sydney as Seen by its Early Artists*, Doubleday, Lane Cove, New South Wales, 1983

Fernández-Shaw, Carlos M., *España y Australia. Cinco Siglos de Historia Spain and Australia. Five Centuries of History*, edición Alonso Ibarrola y Mercedes Palau, Dirección General de Relacióones Culturales y Científicas, Ministerio de Asuntus Exteriores de España, Spain

Findlay, Alexander George, *A Directory for the Navigation of the South Pacific Ocean; with descriptions of its Coasts, Islands, etc.; from the Strait of Magalhaens to Panama, and those of New Zealand, Australia, etc.; Its winds, currents and passages*, 5th edn, Richard Holmes, Laurie, London, 1884

Fisher, J. R., *Government and Society in Colonial Peru: The intendant system 1784–1814*, University of London, Athlone P. 1970

Fisher, Robin, and Johnston, Hugh, *Captain James Cook and His Times*, Australian National University Press, Canberra, 1979

Fleming, Fergus, *Barrow's Boys*, Granta Books, London, 1998

Flynn, Michael, *The Second Fleet: Britain's Grim Convict Armada of 1790*, Library of Australian History, Sydney, 1993

Fraser, Don, ed., *Sydney—from Settlement to City: An Engineering History of Sydney*, Engineers Australia Pty Ltd, Sydney, 1999

Fregosi, Paul, *Dreams of Empire: Napoleon and the First World War 1792–1815*, Hutchinson, Sydney, 1989

Frost, Alan, 'A Place of Exile—Norfolk Island' in *Journeys into History*, ed. Graeme Davidson, Weldon Russell, Willoughby, New South Wales, 1990

—— *Botany Bay Mirages: Illusions of Australia's Convict Beginnings*, Melbourne University Press, Melbourne, 1995

—— *The Voyage of the Endeavour: Captain Cook and the Discovery of the Great South Land*, Allen & Unwin, Sydney, 1998

Frost, Alan, and Samson, Jane, eds, *Pacific Empires: Essays in Honour of Glyndwr Williams*, Melbourne University Press, Carlton South, Victoria, 1999

Garran, Andrew, ed., *Picturesque Atlas of Australia*, vols 1, 2, Picturesque Atlas Publishing, Melbourne, 1886

Gascoigne, John, *Joseph Banks and the English Enlightenment: useful knowledge and polite culture*, Cambridge University Press, Cambridge, 1994

—— *The Enlightenment and the European Origins of Australia*, Cambridge University Press, Port Melbourne, Victoria, 2002

Gershoy, Leo, *The French Revolution and Napoleon*, Appleton-Century-Crofts, New York, 1933

Gibbons, Tony, gen. ed., *The Encyclopedia of Ships*, Silverdale, Enderby, Leicester, England, 2001

Hainsworth, D. R., *The Sydney Traders: Simeon Lord and His Contemporaries 1788–1821*, Melbourne University Press, Melbourne, 1981

Harben, Henry, *A Dictionary of London, being notes topographical and historical relating to the streets and principal buildings in the city of London*, Herbert Jenkins, London, 1918

Hardy, John, and Frost, Alan, eds, *European Voyaging towards Australia*, Australian Academy of the Humanities, Canberra, 1990

Hazard, Paul, *The European Mind (1680–1715)*, Meridian, Cleveland, Ohio, 1963, 1964

Hill-Reid, W. S., *John Grant's Journey: A Convict's Story—1803–1811*, Heinemann, Melbourne, London, 1957

Hoare, Merval, *Norfolk Island: A Revised and Enlarged History 1774–1998*, 5th edn, Central Queensland University Press, Rockhampton, Queensland, 1999

Holmes, (Mrs) Basil, *The London Burial Grounds—Notes on their history from the earliest times to the present day*, T. Fisher Unwin, London, 1846

Horner, Frank, *The French Renaissance: Baudin in Australia 1801–1803*, Melbourne University Press, Melbourne, 1987

Hough, Richard, *Captain James Cook*, Hodder & Stoughton, London, 1944

Howgego, Raymond John, *Encyclopaedia of Exploration to 1800*, Hordern House Rare Books, Potts Point, New South Wales, 2003

Hunter, Susan, and Carter, Paul, *Terre Napoléon: Australia through French Eyes 1800–1804*, Historic Houses Trust of New South Wales, in association with Hordern House, Sydney, 1999

Ingleton, Geoffrey C., *Matthew Flinders: Navigator and Chartmaker*, Genesis Publications, Guildford, Surrey, in association with Hedley Australia, Alphington, Victoria, 1986

Ingram, C. W. N., *New Zealand Shipwrecks 1795–1970*, rev. edn, A. H. & A. W. Reed, Auckland, 1972

James, William, *The Naval History of Great Britain from the Declaration of War by France in 1793 to the Accession of George IV*, vol. 1, Macmillan, New York, 1902

Jardine, Lisa, *Ingenious Pursuits: Building the Scientific Revolution*, Little, Brown & Co., London, 1999

Johnson, Paul, *The Offshore Islanders: A History of the English People*, rev. edn, Phoenix, London, 1992

Jones, Eric, and Raby, Geoffrey, 'The Fatal Shortage: Establishing a European Economy in New South Wales, 1788–1805' in *Studies from Terra Australis to Australia*, eds John Hardy and Alan Frost, Australian Academy of the Humanities, Canberra, 1989

Jones, Francis Avery, and Greenhill, Basil, eds, *Starving Sailors*, Trustees of the National Maritime Museum, Greenwich, 1981

Jorgensen, Jorgen, *The Convict King, being the Life and Adventures of Jorgen Jorgensen, Monarch of Iceland . . . etc.*, retold by James Francis Hogan, J. Walch & Sons, Hobart, 1891(?)

Kelly's Directory of Lincolnshire 1905, Kelly's Directories Ltd, London, 1905

Kenny, John, *Before the First Fleet: The European Discovery of Australia 1606–1777*, Kangaroo Press, Kenthurst, New South Wales, 1995

King, Jonathan and King, John, *Philip Gidley King: A Biography of the Third Governor of New South Wales*, Methuen Australia, North Ryde, New South Wales, 1981

King, Michael, *New Zealand in Colour*, A. H. & A. W. Reed, Auckland, 1983

King, Robert J., *The Secret History of the Convict Colony: Alexandro Malaspina's Report on the British Settlement of New South Wales*, Allen & Unwin, Sydney, 1990

Kiple, Kenneth, *Plague, Pox and Pestilence, Diseases in History*, Phoenix, London, 1999

Kippis, Andrew, *Captain Cook's Voyages*, Alfred A. Knopf, New York, 1925

Lavery, Brian, *Nelson's Navy: The Ships, Men and Organisation 1793–1815*, Conway Maritime Press, London, 1989

—— *Shipboard Life and Organisation 1731–1815*, Ashgate Publishing, Aldershot, 1998

Lee, Stephen J., *Aspects of European History 1494–1789*, 2nd edn, Routledge, London, 1978, 1984

Lewis, Michael, *The Navy of Great Britain: A Historical Portrait*, George Allen & Unwin, London, 1948
—— *The History of the British Navy*, Penguin, Harmondsworth, Middlesex, 1957
—— *A Social History of the Navy*, George Allen & Unwin, London, 1960
Lloyd, Christopher, and Coulter, Jack L. S., *Medicine and the Navy: 1200–1900*, vol. IV, 1815–1900, E. & S. Livingston, Edinburgh and London, 1963
Lyte, Charles, *Sir Joseph Banks: 18th Century Explorer, Botanist and Entrepreneur*, A. H. & A. W. Reed, Sydney, 1980
Mackaness, George, *Sir Joseph Banks: His Relations with Australia*, Angus & Robertson, Sydney, 1936
MacDonald, Barrie, *Cinderellas of the Empire: Towards a History of Kiribati and Tuvalu*, Australian National University Press, Canberra, 1982
McDonald, W. G., *The First-Footers: Bass and Flinders in Illawarra— 1796–1797*, Illawarra Historical Society, Wollongong, New South Wales, 1975
Mackesy, Piers, *War without Victory: The Downfall of Pitt 1799–1802*, Clarendon Press, Oxford, 1984
McNab, Robert, *Murihiku: A History of the South Island of New Zealand and the Islands Adjacent and Lying to the South from 1642 to 1835*, Whitcomb & Tombs, Wellington, 1909
Maiden, J. H., *Sir Joseph Banks: The 'Father of Australia'*, William Applegate Gullick, Sydney, 1909
Marcus, G. J., *A Naval History of England: The Age of Nelson*, George Allen & Unwin, London, 1948
Markham, Felix, *Napoleon*, Mentor, New York, 1963
Masefield, John, *Sea Life in Nelson's Time*, 3rd edn, Conway Maritime Press, London, 1971
Maurois, André, *A History of England*, The Bodley Head, London, 1956
Mee, Arthur, ed., *The King's England: Lincolnshire, A County of Infinite Charm*, Hodder & Stoughton, London, 1949
Miller, David Philip, and Reill, Peters Hanns, eds, *Visions of Empire: Voyages, Botany and Representations of Nature*, Cambridge University Press, Cambridge, 1996
Miller, Nathan, *Broadsides: The Age of Fighting Sail, 1775–1815*, John Wiley & Sons, New York, 2000
Morris, Kenneth, *George Bass in Western Port, Incorporating George Bass and the Convicts*, Bass Valley Historical Society, Bass Valley, 1997
Morris, Roger, ed., *The Channel Fleet and the Blockade of Brest 1793–1801*, Ashgate for the Navy Records Society, Aldershot, 2000
Mourot, Suzanne, *This Was Sydney: A Pictorial History from 1788 to the Present*, Ure Smith, Sydney, 1969
Mulvaney, D. J., and White, Peter, eds, *Australians to 1788*, Fairfax Syme & Weldon, Broadway, New South Wales, 1987
Naval Chronicle, The, for 1813: Containing a General and Biographical History of the Royal Navy of the United Kingdom; with a variety of

original papers on nautical subjects, vol. XXX, Correspondence: letter from 'Oceanus', pp. 200–2, Joyce Gold, London, 1813

Nicholson, Ian, *Log of Logs: A catalogue of logs, journals, shipboard diaries, letters, and all forms of voyage narratives, 1788–1988, for Australia and New Zealand, and surrounding oceans*, Roebuck Society No. 41, published by the author jointly with the Australian Association for Maritime History, Nambour, Queensland, n.d.

O'Brian, Patrick, *Joseph Banks: A Life*, Collins Narvill, London, 1987

Parkin, Ray, *H. M. Bark Endeavour: Her Place in Australian History, with an Account of her Construction, Crew and Equipment and a Narrative of her Voyage on the East Coast of New Holland in the Year 1770*, 2nd edn, Miegunyah Press, Melbourne, 2003

Perry, T. M., *The Discovery of Australia: The Charts and Maps of the Navigators and Explorers*, Nelson, Melbourne, 1982

Peters, Merle, *The Bankstown Story: A Comprehensive History of the District*, published by the author, Yagoona, 1969

Plomley, N. J. B., *Jorgen Jorgenson and the Aborigines of Van Diemen's Land*, Blubber Head Press, Hobart, 1991

Pope, Steve, *Hornblower's Navy: Life at Sea in the Age of Nelson*, Orion, London, 1998

Proudfoot, Helen, Bickford, Anne, Egloff, Brian, and Stocks, Robyn, *Australia's First Government House*, Allen & Unwin, Sydney, 1991

Quiroz Chueca, Francisco, *De la Colonia a la República Independiente*, Callao, Peru, 1956

Radok, Rainer, *Capes and Captains: A Comprehensive Study of the Australian Coast*, Surrey Beaty & Sons, Chipping Norton, New South Wales, 1990

Readers's Digest Guide to the Australian Coast, Reader's Digest Services, Surry Hills, New South Wales, 1983

Reed, A. W., ed., *Captain Cook in Australia: Extracts from the Journals of Captain James Cook, giving a full account in his own words of his adventures and discoveries in Australia*, A. H. & A. W. Reed, Sydney, 1969

Roberts, J. M., *The Penguin History of the World*, Penguin Books, Harmondsworth, Middlesex, 1997

Ross, John, editor-in-chief, *Chronicle of Australia*, Viking, Penguin Books Australia, Ringwood, Victoria, 2000

Rusden, G. W., *A History of New Zealand*, vol. 1, Melville, Mullen & Slade, Melbourne, 1885

—— *Curiosities of Colonization*, (no publisher), London, 1874

—— *History of Australia*, vol. 1, Melville, Mullen & Slade, Melbourne, 1897

Sailing Directions (Enroute) for the Pacific Islands, Defence Mapping Agency and Hydrographic/Topographic Center, Washington, D. C., 1982

Schom, Alan, *Napoleon Bonaparte*, HarperCollins, New York, 1997

Schurz, William Lytle, *The Spanish Galleons*, E. P. Dutton, New York, 1959

Scott, Ernest, *The Life of Captain Matthew Flinders, R.N.*, Angus & Robertson, Sydney, 1914

Shaw, A. G. L., and Clark, C. M. H., eds, *Australian Dictionary of Biography, 1788–1850*, vols 1, 2, Melbourne University Press, Melbourne, 1966

Sidney, Samuel, *The Land of the Kangaroo and the Boomerang: Also giving a true history of the discovery, settlement and wonderful growth of the Australian colonies*, Hurst & Co., New York, 1880

Skelton, R. A., *Explorers' Maps: Chapters in the Cartographic Record of Geographical Discovery*, Routledge & Kegan Paul, London, 1958

Smith, Bernard, *Imagining the Pacific: In the Wake of the Cook Voyages*, Miegunyah Press, Carlton South, Victoria, 1992

Soper, Tony, *The National Trust Guide to the Coast*, Webb & Bower, Exeter, Devon, 1984

Sprod, Dan, *The Usurper: Jorgen Jorgenson and his Turbulent Life in Iceland and Van Diemen's Land, 1780–1841*, Blubber Head Press, Hobart, 2001

Stephensen, P. R. and Kennedy, Brian, *The History and Description of Sydney Harbour*, A. H. & A. W. Reed, Sydney, 1980

Storey, Edward, *Spirit of the Fens: A View of Fenland Life Past and Present*, Robert Hale, London, 1985

Summerson, John, *Georgian London*, Borne & Jenkins, London, 1988

Taylor, Peter, *Australia: The First Twelve Years*, George Allen & Unwin, Sydney, 1982

Tench, Watkin, *1788*, ed. Tim Flannery, Text Publishing Company, Melbourne, 1996

Thompson, Pishey, *The History and Antiquities of Boston, and the Villages of Skirbeck, Fishtoft, Frelston, Butterwick, Benington, Leverton, Leake, and Wrangle; Comprising the Hundred of Skirbeck in the County of Lincoln*, John Noble, Jun., Boston, England, 1856

Tooley, Ronald Vere, *Maps and Map-Makers*, Batsford, London, 1952

—— *Tooley's Dictionary of Mapmakers*, Map Collector Publications, Tring, Hersfordshire, England, 1979

Villiers, Alan, *Captain Cook, the Seaman's Seaman*, Penguin, Harmondsworth, Middlesex, 2001

Wace, Nigel, and Lovett, Bessie, *Yankee Maritime Activities and the Early History of Australia*, Australian National University, Canberra, 1973

Walsh, Michael, and Yallop, Colin, eds, *Language and Culture in Aboriginal Australia*, Aboriginal Studies Press, Canberra, 1993

Ward, Russel, *Concise History of Australia*, rev. edn, University of Queensland Press, St Lucia, Queensland, 1992

Watt, James, 'The Colony's Health' in *Studies from Terra Australis to Australia*, eds John Hardy and Alan Frost, Australian Academy of the Humanities, Canberra, 1989

—— 'The Health of Sailors' in *European Voyaging towards Australia*, eds John Hardy and Alan Frost, Australian Academy of the Humanities, Canberra, 1990

Watt, J., Freeman, E. J., and Bynum, W. F., eds, *Starving Sailors: The Influence of Nutrition upon Naval and Maritime History*, National Maritime Museum, Greenwich, 1981

Way, Thomas R., and Bell, Walter G., *The Thames from Chelsea to the Nore*, John Lane, The Bodley Head, London, 1907

Weinreb, Ben, and Hibbert, Christopher, eds, *The London Encyclopaedia*, Macmillan, London, 1983
Williams, Glyndwr, and Frost, Alan, eds, *Terra Australis to Australia*, Oxford University Press, Melbourne, 1988
Wills, Geoffrey, *The English Life Series: c. 1760–1820, George III*, vol. IV, Wheaton, Exeter, 1968

ARTICLES

Andrews, Alan E. J., 'Mount Hunter and Beyond: with Hunter, Bass, Tench, Wilson, Barrallier, Caley, King, and Macquarie, 1790–1815', *Journal of the Royal Australian Historical Society*, vol. 76, no. 1, pp. 3–15
Bowden, K. M., 'George Bass, 1771–1803, Surgeon and Sailor', *Bulletin of the Post-Graduate Committee in Medicine, University of Sydney*, vol. 17, May 1961, University of Sydney, Sydney, pp. 33–55
Coleman, Edith, 'George Bass, Victoria's First Explorer and Naturalist', *Victorian Naturalist*, vol. 67, The Field Naturalist Club of Victoria, Melbourne, 1950, pp. 3–9
Cook, A. M., 'Men of Lincoln Who Sailed with Cook', *Royal Australian Historical Society Journal and Proceedings*, vol. 35, part 2, Sydney, 1949, pp. 116–30
Else-Mitchell, R., 'Bass's Land Explorations', *Royal Historical Society*, vol. xxxvii, part IV, January 1952, Sydney, 1951, pp. 244–50
Graves, Kathleen E., 'The Distant Climate and Savage Shore—Being the Life of George Bass', *Walkabout—Australian Geographical Magazine*, 1 August 1957, pp. 10–14
Morris, Kenneth, *George Bass and the Convicts*, Bass Valley Historical Society, Bass Valley, 1994
—— *George Bass in Western Port*, Bass Valley Historical Society, Bass Valley, 1997
Norrie, H., 'Australia's Debt to Her Early Medicos', *Sydney University Medical Journal*, July 1933, vol. XXVII, part I, pp. 136–43
Parsons, T. G., 'Was John Boston's Pig a Political Radical? The Reaction to Popular Radicalism in New South Wales', *Journal of the Royal Australian Historical Society*, vol. 71, part 5, 1986, pp. 163–77
Roe, Michael, 'Colonial Society in Embryo', *Historical Studies: Australia and New Zealand*, vol. 7, November 1955–May 1957, University of Melbourne, Melbourne, pp. 149–59
—— 'Australia's Place in the "Swing to the East" 1788–1810', *Historical Studies: Australia and New Zealand*, vol. 8, November 1957–May 1959, University of Melbourne, Melbourne, pp. 202–13
—— 'New Light on George Bass, Entrepreneur and Intellectual', *Journal of the Royal Australian Historical Society*, vol. 72, part 5, 1987, pp. 251–73
Scott, Ernest, 'The Early History of Western Port, Part I', *The Victorian Historical Magazine*, vol. 6, no. 1, September 1917, pp. 1–4

MANUSCRIPTS

Bonwick Transcripts, Mitchell and Dixson Libraries, State Library of New South Wales

George Bass, *Journal describing Two-Fold Bay in New South Wales, Furneaux's Islands in Bass's Strait and the coasts and harbours of Van Dieman's Land. From notes made on board the colonial sloop Norfolk in 1798 and 1799* [ms. copy], Mitchell Library, State Library of New South Wales, Sydney

Logs of HMS *Flirt, Gorgon, Fairy, Pomona, Vulcan, Shark, Druid, Reliance*, The National Archives: Public Record Office, Kew, Richmond

Rusden Collection, Trinity College, University of Melbourne, Melbourne

Shillinglaw Papers, Australian Manuscript Collection, State Library of Victoria, Melbourne

Waterhouse Family Papers, 1782–1819, Mitchell and Dixson Libraries, State Library of New South Wales, Sydney

MISCELLANEOUS

Fitzgerald, Lawrence, Bass's 'Barmouth Creek', address given at Tathra, New South Wales, 3 June 1976 to the Tathra Historical Society

Hobart Town Almanack and Van Diemen's Land Annual, The, James Ross, Hobart Town, 1831 and 1835

Hocken, T. M., 'The Early History of New Zealand—Being a Series of Lectures Delivered before the Otago Institute; also a Lecturette on the Maoris of South Island', John Mackay, Government Printer, Wellington, 1914

Informe No. 06—2003–DAC/TA, Archivo General de la Nación, Lima, Peru

'List of Those Examined and Approved Surgeons', The Corporation of Surgeons of London, Private Collection of William F. Wilson, Melbourne and 'Bass River'

The Sydney Gazette and New South Wales Advertiser, Facsimile Reproductions, vols 1, 2, 3, 6 and 7, The Trustees of the Public Library of New South Wales in Association with Angus & Robertson, Sydney, 1964, 1966, 1969

Index

In this index 'GB' refers to George Bass.

Aborigines
  GB's care of Bennelong, 37, 40
  GB's encounters with, 51–53,
    55, 82, 100, 106, 112–113
Aked, Sally, 31, 76, 129
albatrosses, 109
alpacas, 177

Babel Isles, 113
Balmain, William, 59, 63, 93
Bampton, William Wright, 43
Banks, Sir Joseph
  local fame in Lincolnshire, 6
  correspondence with William
    Paterson, 17
  requests plant cabin for
    Reliance, 20
  GB and, 30, 33, 128
  sent coal specimens, 73
  urges Governor Hunter to
    persevere, 117
  Flinders proposes expedition
    of discovery, 128
Banks Town, 91–92
Barallier, Francis, 73
Barmouth Creek, 82

Barnes (Baines), Elizabeth, 76
Bass, Elizabeth (*née* Waterhouse;
  GB's wife)
  character and appearance,
    132–133
  marries GB, 133
  with GB in Portsmouth,
    135–137
  fails to become pregnant,
    137–138
  distress at GB's absence, 138,
    163, 167–168, 171–172,
    191–192
  visited by Matthew Flinders,
    162
  correspondence with GB,
    163–166, 168, 191
  urged by GB to improve her
    mind, 164–167
  income and finances, 166,
    193–194, 195
  antipathy towards Matthew
    Flinders, 168–171
  GB plans seagoing future for,
    171–172, 186
  closeness to GB's mother, 192